DATE DUE

DELINQUENT BEHAVIOR

DELINQUENT BEHAVIOR

Don C. Gibbons
Portland State University

PRENTICE-HALL, INC.
Englewood Cliffs, New Jersey

PRENTICE-HALL SOCIOLOGY SERIES
HERBERT BLUMER, Editor

© 1970 by Prentice-Hall, Inc., Englewood Cliffs, New Jersey

13-197897-7   ←——   SBN

Library of Congress Catalog Card Number 70-89817
Printed in the United States of America

Current Printing (last digit):
12   11   10   9   8   7   6   5   4   3

PRENTICE-HALL INTERNATIONAL, INC., *London*
PRENTICE-HALL OF AUSTRALIA, PTY. LTD., *Sidney*
PRENTICE-HALL OF CANADA, LTD., *Toronto*
PRENTICE-HALL OF INDIA PRIVATE LIMITED, *New Delhi*
PRENTICE-HALL OF JAPAN, INC., *Tokyo*

PREFACE

This is a small book with a large cast of characters. Apprehended juvenile offenders in the United States number at least a million each year, while from another perspective, nearly all youngsters are juvenile delinquents. Then too, the index of this book lists over three hundred behavioral and social scientists who have contributed to the serious study of youthful misconduct. Juvenile delinquency is a complex phenomenon, and the reader will therefore be confronted with a large number of theories and pieces of research in the pages to follow.

This is a delinquency textbook which endeavors to take stock of the knowledge accumulated to date. I have tried to avoid assembling an eclectic collection of bits and pieces of material on delinquency. Rather, the chapters of the book contain a number of generalizations or propositions drawn out of the existing data, and these claims are collected in Chapter Eleven in the form of a propositional inventory. In short, this book tries to provide a succinct, coherent picture of the major facets of youthful lawbreaking.

This is a sociological work; social factors and influences in delinquent conduct are given heavy stress. At the same time, there is considerable evidence that the behavior of some juvenile offenders is a response to psychological pressures and atypical life experiences. I have endeavored to identify some of the ways in which psychological factors mesh with sociological ones to produce delinquency, and have attempted to indicate those kinds of youthful deviance in which psychological tensions loom large.

Delinquent Behavior is the final part of criminological trilogy. The first work, *Changing the Lawbreaker,* put forth claims about offender types or role-careers, and it discussed the correctional treatment of offenders in detail. The second book, *Society, Crime, and Criminal Careers,* brought together the existing evidence on offender types among adult criminals. *Delinquent Behavior* collects the available evidence on delinquent types or behavior patterns.

This book is purposely brief and compact. In my view, a text is needed which deals mainly with delinquency causation. Correctional patterns and processes are discussed here as they have to do with offender role-careers. Thus the commentary on training schools in this book centers about the part these institutions play in the continuation of misconduct by some offenders. No attempt has been made to provide a full exposition of correctional programs, treatment tactics, or other matters of that kind.

I have received a good deal of support and encouragement from a variety of persons in the writing of this book. However, my good friend Jim Clark, formerly of Prentice-Hall, Inc., ought to be singled out for special mention. He played a major part in all three of the books I have written. In addition, Peter Garabedian was extremely helpful, particularly in prodding me to do more work on the book than I might otherwise have done. I am sure that he will recognize his contributions in many sections of the book. Of course, the defects of the book are solely my own responsibility.

DON C. GIBBONS

Portland, Oregon

CONTENTS

chapter one

INTRODUCTION

THE STUDY OF DELINQUENCY

Who is best qualified to speak about juvenile delinquency, to explain it, or to provide directions for its amelioration? Perhaps not sociologists, if we are to believe the unflattering characterizations of them that often appear in the mass media. Some journalists are fond of describing them as individuals with modest intellectual talents, at best, whose major stock in trade is the obfuscation of problems through esoteric jargon and tortured reasoning. In this view, behavioral scientists are persons who deliberately make matters more confusing than they are in fact. We, however, hold that such a description is in error, that social scientists address themselves to extremely complicated phenomena, and that the formulations they make about these behaviors cannot be simple if they are to be valid.

The subject of delinquency is one in which most members of the general public are interested. We need not search far for indications that they have a number of firm opinions about delinquency, including beliefs about its causes and views about its eradication. Most of these popular attitudes and beliefs are straightforward instances of folk wisdom. They imply that the causes of delinquency are easily discernible to any reasonable man and that delinquency can be curbed by one panacea or another. Like a good deal of folk wisdom these opinions about delinquency are, in most instances, wide of the mark.

1

Juvenile delinquency represents a topic for study of heroic proportions, so that few bold and unequivocal claims can be advanced which
have the full force of facts behind them. Many factors play a part in
delinquency, and they intertwine in complex ways with other variables to produce juvenile misconduct.

The following paragraphs introduce a broad sketch of the major
dimensions of delinquency. Some of the major fallacies about juvenile
lawbreaking contained in folk wisdom are noted, as are some of the
major facets of delinquency which are overlooked by the general public. The section to follow also hints at the outlines of a sociological
perspective on delinquency.

AN OVERVIEW ON DELINQUENCY

The prevailing public conception of juvenile delinquency is that
delinquency is the undesirable opposite of some unnamed state of
affairs characteristic of the majority of youths. Delinquency is seen as
juvenile crime. Those youngsters who are involved in delinquency
steal cars or other kinds of property; they commit serious acts of
vandalism; they are sexually promiscuous; they behave in other ways
which violate the law. Juvenile delinquents, engaging in wicked and
antisocial acts, stand outside the mainstream of youth and adolescent
activity. A person rarely supposes that any delinquents live on his
street or even in his neighborhood; instead, they inhabit some other
part of the community. The delinquents' dissimilarity from "normal
youngsters" provides the warrant for public agitation about them.
Juvenile delinquents constitute a social problem about which something must be done; these children must be converted into normal,
nondelinquent individuals by some rehabilitative tactic or another.

But in point of fact, juvenile delinquency is not a relatively homogeneous form of behavior, made up of a few similar acts which are
prohibited in the criminal law. The body of criminal statutes to which
adults are subject in modern societies prohibits a wide range of dis-
similar actions. Criminal codes enjoin persons from myriad kinds of
sexual behavior, forbid a vast number of acts against private property,
regulate the conduct of business affairs, prohibit many kinds of interpersonal behavior, and endeavor to suppress many other types of conduct. Accordingly, if we regard delinquency as juvenile crime, we will
therefore have to pay attention to a heterogeneous mixture of youthful
transgressions.

But the problem is not only that the criminal laws which juveniles
violate are disparate in form. Juvenile delinquency statutes in the

United States also include an omnibus clause which gives the juvenile court control over youngsters who are identified as "immoral," "ungovernable," "wayward," or "incorrigible." The specific language of these laws varies from state to state, but they all have the effect of allowing the court to take control over youths who have not violated a provision of the criminal code but who are believed to fall within one of these broader and more ambiguous categories, to extend its jurisdiction to nearly every kind of youthful peccadillo, no matter how trivial. The statutes declare, in effect, that all misbehavior of juveniles, however slight, is juvenile delinquency which falls within the purview of the courts.

Since the laws are so broad, it is apparent that large numbers of youths engage in acts which technically qualify as delinquency. From this perspective, delinquency is not confined to a minority of the juvenile population; instead, it is in some degree characteristic of most youngsters. So the public defends its view of delinquency by claiming to be interested only in "real delinquency." The person contends that he is concerned with "serious stuff" by juveniles, not with pranks, petty vandalism, and the like. He argues that "real delinquency" is characteristic of only a small segment of the youth population.

The statistical data from official sources initially seem to confirm this opinion. In any single year, less than five percent of the youth population appears in a juvenile court. Most of the cases which these young people have been involved in concern relatively petty acts of deviance. The police and other agencies which serve as referral sources to the courts process a good many petty cases, too, which they normally do not send on to the the juvenile courts. Thus not all of those youngsters who turn up in official records or statistics have been involved in major violations of law. A goodly share of "official delinquency" is of a serious nature, but these cases add up to only a minority of the youth group; the records therefore show that serious lawbreaking is relatively uncommon.

However, the total number of delinquents in the nation is far greater than is revealed in court statistics and police records. There is an abundance of evidence from studies of "hidden" misbehavior in which youths admit behavior ranging over the entire gamut of delinquent acts. Most of the juveniles who confess these actions indicate that they have had no dealings with the police or the courts. Even in areas with high rates of official delinquency, the true extent of juvenile misconduct is far greater than reflected in police or court records.

What is the role of the police in curbing delinquency? Are they passive agents who behave uniformly toward all instances of lawbreaking which they observe? Do they merely sift the serious cases of

lawbreaking which are to be sent on to courts from other inconsequential acts which are to be disposed of informally? Or are police
actions heavily influenced by such things as the racial or socioeconomic backgrounds of violators?

The police are actively involved in differential responses to youths
reported to them. Some cases are disposed of informally, others are
sent on to juvenile courts. These decisions are not solely a matter of
the seriousness of the behavior reported, although this consideration
does weigh heavily in police actions. The likelihood that a misbehaving juvenile will become legally tagged as a "juvenile delinquent"
depends in part upon the nature of the offending conduct, but it also
rests upon his racial background and his attitudes toward the policeman. Police departments show varied patterns of responding to juvenile offenders; behavior which would be handled informally in one
police department is the basis for court referral in another. Thus rates
of official delinquency are a measure of police behavior as well as of
juvenile misconduct.

What are the causes of delinquency, official or otherwise? If the
man on the street is asked a question about nuclear physics he is not
likely to have a ready answer, but if he is queried on the causes of
juvenile misconduct, he shows little hesitation in providing a response.
The particular factor or factors that are singled out as being responsible for juvenile misconduct vary from person to person, but most fall
within what Albert Cohen has called the "evil causes evil" fallacy.[1]
In other words, laymen usually attribute the evil of juvenile misconduct to a few bad influences; forces from which the public-respondent
is immune. These are events or circumstances that are alien to "good,
upstanding citizens." The catalogue of these factors includes broken
or otherwise defective homes, families which have forsaken Chris-
tianity, the lack of recreational facilities, and bad companions who
lead youths astray.

There are gross defects in this "evil causes evil" line of thinking;
the causes of delinquent conduct are infinitely more numerous and
complex than reflected in public understandings. Juvenile delinquency is not all of one kind, so that the etiological processes which
operate in one kind of youthful deviance are not the same as those
which are implicated in another form of lawbreaking. Nor is delinquent behavior some kind of foreign virus afflicting a generally
healthy social body. Instead, at least a goodly share of juvenile law-

---

[1] Albert K. Cohen, *Juvenile Delinquency and the Social Structure* (unpublished
Ph.D. dissertation, Harvard University, 1951), pp. 5–13; see also Edwin H. Suth-
erland and Donald R. Cressey, *Principles of Criminology*, 7th ed. (Philadelphia:
J. B. Lippincott Co., 1966), pp. 63–65.

breaking is as normal a product of social organization as is nondeviant conduct; the causes of juvenile misconduct are to be found in aspects of social structure, rather than in a few "bad" factors. Succeeding chapters will focus upon the part played in delinquency by such societal features as social class value patterns, differentials in the availability of routes to success and in the upward mobility of social class groups, variations in family life styles between social strata, and subcultural differences in norms and beliefs. In short, the causes of delinquency are neither evil in character nor few in number.

Another erroneous perspective on delinquency held by some groups is that most juvenile offenders are psychologically maladjusted, and are believed to be the products of disordered families. These maladjusted families are regarded as atypical of American life, for most families are healthy ones which, of course, turn out normal, law-abiding juveniles. The evidence fails to support this picture of psychologically maladjusted delinquents. Existing data indicate that there are many juvenile deviants whose mental health is no different from that of nonoffenders. In short, there are about as many "normal" delinquents as there are normal nondelinquents.

The first order of business in the study of delinquency is that of definition. We cannot make much sense out of juvenile lawbreaking until we first agree on what we mean by "delinquency" and understand the nature of delinquency laws.

JUVENILE MISCONDUCT AND DELINQUENCY LAWS

The penal codes of Western societies prohibit a wide spectrum of conduct ranging from seemingly harmless acts to exceedingly heinous forms of behavior, so that it cannot be said that dangerous and socially harmful activities solely concern the statutes. At the same time, there are kinds of devious and harmful behavior which are not forbidden by the criminal codes. Then, too, it is obvious that criminal law in any nation has changed over time, so that it does not represent a body of stable behavioral norms. Similarly, in any one country, such as the United States, variations are found from one jurisdiction to another in both the content and language of criminal statutes. In short, that which is crime in one area may not have been crime in another place or at a prior time.

This lack of harmony and consistency in statutes has led a number of students of crime and delinquency to suggest that criminology should abandon legalistic definitions of its field of inquiry and should replace them by some other units of study which are universal and unchanging. Jeffery has summarized a number of these "sociological" approaches to crime which reject legalistic definitions of the phenomena of study in favor of conduct norms and violations of them.[2] Sutherland and Cressey have also enumerated a number of these views.[3] Similarly Bloch and Geis have commented on approaches to criminology which would replace the investigation of legally defined crime with such phenomena as moral aberrance, parasitism, or deviancy.[4] Cavan notes that one nonlegal definition of the juvenile delinquent is "any child or youth whose conduct deviates sufficiently from normal social usage to warrant his being considered a menace to himself, to his future interests, or to society itself."[5]

The rationale for these definitional innovations is that criminologists ought to concern themselves with the study of antisocial persons, regardless of whether their activities happen to be included within the criminal codes or delinquency statutes. According to this view, criminology would be directed at the study of a homogeneous body of subject matter, rather than at a confused mixture of behavior haphazardly singled out by the criminal laws which, at the same time, ignore other forms of sociological crime or delinquency. Bloch and Geis quite properly criticize these concepts of moral aberrance or parasitism as little more than figures of speech which are devoid of specific meaning. To substitute these concepts for a legalistic definition of the field of inquiry would mire criminology in even more terminological and definitional confusion than would the use of a legalistic criterion of crime. The same point holds for the delinquency definition noted by Cavan. How can we recognize conduct which deviates from social usage and which renders the subject a menace to himself or society? It seems most unlikely that different observers could apply this standard for identifying delinquents with any degree of consistency.

Most criminologists conclude that efforts in the direction of nonlegalistic definitions of crime and delinquency will continue to be fruitless. They agree that, for criminological purposes, crime and delinquency are whatever the statutes declare them to be. The subject

[2] Clarence R. Jeffery, "The Structure of American Criminological Thinking," *Journal of Criminal Law, Criminology and Police Science*, XLVI (January-February 1956), 660–63.

[3] Sutherland and Cressey, *Principles of Criminology*, pp. 15–16.

[4] Herbert A. Bloch and Gilbert Geis, *Man, Crime, and Society* (New York: Random House, Inc., 1962), pp. 10–13.

[5] Ruth Shonle Cavan, *Juvenile Delinquency* (Philadelphia: J. B. Lippincott Co., 1962), p. 17.

matter of criminology is defined by the criminal law,[6] a position with which this book concurs; delinquency is that behavior prohibited by the delinquency laws.

If, in the case of adult criminality, we would settle upon a legalistic approach to the field of study, we could then examine the statutes and find rather specific definitions of particular offenses. For example, we would find that the elements of "burglary in the second degree" were specifically and clearly identified.[7] The same point holds for "embezzlement," "larceny by bailee," "statutory rape," and most of the other offenses enumerated in the criminal codes. However, delinquency laws in the United States are broader and more ambiguous than the penal code, so that they make it difficult to discover the limits of the behavior included within their purview.

The Laws of Delinquency

The development of special laws and special procedures for juvenile offenders has been lengthy; some authorities have seen the beginning of the juvenile court movement in the fifteenth-century English courts of chancery. Tappan has observed that the development of a court of chancery jurisdiction provided special consideration to children. Equity was designed to provide aid to individuals and groups that could find no other remedy under the limitations of the rigid rules that had developed in the common law. Under chancery jurisdiction the crown claimed a power of *parens patriae* over infants and their estates on the assumption that children, as wards of the state, were in need of special protection. However, chancery functioned primarily in the administration of the estates of well-to-do infants.[8]

[6] For a discussion of the elements of criminal law, see Don C. Gibbons, *Society, Crime, and Criminal Careers* (Englewood Cliffs, N.J.: Prentice-Hall, Inc., 1968), pp. 18–23.

[7] One should not suppose that the criminal law in modern societies is conveniently gathered up in a single collection of written statutes called the Penal Code. For example, in the state of California definitions of misdemeanors are to be found in the Welfare and Institutions Code, Fish and Game Code, Education Code, Administrative Code, and other statute books. In addition, the criminal law exists in part in the common law decisions of judges in specific cases.

It is the case that offenders are often convicted for offenses different from the one in the criminal statutes which most closely describes their illegal conduct. In other words, offenders often plead guilty to offenses other than the ones they actually committed. This practice is termed "pleading guilty for considerations" or "plea copping." For a discussion of this activity, see Gibbons, pp. 82–84.

[8] Paul W. Tappan, *Crime, Justice and Correction* (New York: McGraw-Hill Book Co., Inc., 1960), p. 388.

The harsh treatment of youthful offenders began to be mitigated in the United States in the early 1800s. The first juvenile reformatory was established in New York in 1825, followed shortly thereafter by similar institutions in Massachusetts and Pennsylvania. The movement to provide foster homes for neglected and destitute children originated in New York in 1853, while Chicago in 1861 provided a commission to hear cases of petty offenses by boys six to seventeen years of age. A Massachusetts law of 1869 provided that an agent of the state board of charities should attend trials of children to make recommendations for the disposition of these cases, and separate trials for juveniles were instituted in Boston in 1870. Between 1878 and 1898, Massachusetts began a system of state-wide probation which included children, while New York created special hearings for juveniles below the age of sixteen in 1892.[9]

These developments came to full bloom in 1899, when the first juvenile court was established by statute in Cook County, Illinois. Within ten years of the passage of this legislation, twenty states and the District of Columbia had created juvenile court laws; by 1945, court legislation had been extended to all the states.

The philosophy of the juvenile court is supposed to be protective, rather than punitive. With the emergence of the juvenile court, emphasis shifted from the punishment of young criminals to the protection and treatment of them. The Illinois law specified that the treatment given the juvenile offender should "approximate as nearly as may be that which should be given by its parents." To secure these ends, juvenile court procedures evolved which differed markedly from those in criminal courts. In addition, a new category was identified in the laws: the juvenile delinquent.[10]

The statutes which define juvenile delinquency or which identify the conditions over which the juvenile court has jurisdiction are similar in form throughout the United States. They first specify that the court has control over juveniles who have violated federal, state, or local laws or ordinances. In other words, they assert that delinquents are persons under some specified age who commit acts which would

[9] These developments are discussed in *Encyclopaedia Britannica*, V (Chicago: Encyclopaedia Britannica, Inc., 1965), 516; Tappan,*Crime, Justice and Correction*, pp. 388–89; Frederick B. Sussmann, *Law of Juvenile Delinquency*, revised edition (New York: Oceana Publications, Inc., 1959), p. 13.

[10] Delinquency laws in the United States are discussed in Sussmann, *Law of Juvenile Delinquency*, p. 21; Cavan, *Juvenile Delinquency*, pp. 15–22; Sol Rubin, *Crime and Juvenile Delinquency* (New York: Oceana Publications, Inc., 1958), pp. 43–45; Rubin, "The Legal Character of Juvenile Delinquency," in Rose Giallombardo, ed. *Juvenile Delinquency* (New York: John Wiley and Sons, Inc., 1966), pp. 25–32.

constitute crimes if carried out by adults. Although the different state laws vary somewhat in terms of the age limits of juvenile court jurisdiction, the most common upper age limit is eighteen years of age; persons over that age are held accountable as adult criminals and are dealt with in criminal courts.

But the American delinquency laws do not stop at this point. All of them contain an additional "omnibus" clause or provision awarding the court jurisdiction over youths who have behaved in ways which are not forbidden by criminal laws. The omnibus provisions differ somewhat from state to state, but Sussmann and Rubin have both indicated that the various state delinquency statutes collectively specify several dozen vaguely defined conditions for which a juvenile may be adjudicated a delinquent.[11]

The flavor of omnibus provisions can be detected from a partial list of the conditions which are identified as comprising delinquency in these laws. For example, these statutes award juvenile courts the jurisdiction over children who engage in immoral or indecent conduct, who exhibit immoral conduct around schools, who engage in illegal occupations, who knowingly associate with vicious or immoral persons, who grow up in idleness or crime, who patronize or visit policy shops or gaming houses, who wander in the streets at night, who habitually wander about railroad yards or tracks, who are incorrigible, or who deport themselves so as to injure themselves or others.

The extension of court jurisdiction to these forms of conduct has not been uniformly applauded. Instead, a host of critics have suggested that these categories of behavior are so vaguely defined that nearly all youngsters could be made the subject of court attention. Considerable doubt has been expressed as to whether these kinds of conduct are predictive of serious antisocial conduct.Perhaps courts would be better off not to concern themselves with these activities and conditions if they are relatively innocuous. At any rate, the fact that these omnibus provisions are included within delinquency statutes means that these laws lack the clarity and specificity of the criminal codes. Although juvenile delinquency is what the laws say it is, the content of these statutes is not entirely clear.

One detailed example of contemporary legislation defining the scope of juvenile court jurisdiction can be taken from the Welfare and Institutions Code of the state of California. The three parts of the jurisdictional section of that code award the court control over dependent and neglected children (nondelinquents), youngsters who have violated the criminal law, and certain other children who come

---

11 Sussmann, *Law of Juvenile Delinquency*, p. 21; Rubin, "The Legal Character of Juvenile Delinquency," p. 26.

under an omnibus provision.[12] The sections of the code read as follows:

> **600.** Any person under the age of 21 years who comes within any of the following descriptions is within the jurisdiction of the juvenile court which may adjudge the person to be a dependent child of the court:
> **a.** Who is in need of proper and effective parental care or control and has no parent or guardian, or has no parent or guardian willing to exercise or capable of exercising such care or control, or has no parent actually exercising such care or control.
> **b.** Who is destitute, or who is not provided with the necessities of life, or who is not provided with a home or suitable place of abode, or whose home is an unfit place for him by reason of neglect, cruelty, or depravity of either of his parents, or of his guardian or other person in whose custody or care he is.
> **c.** Who is physically dangerous to the public because of a mental or physical deficiency, disorder or abnormality.
>
> **601.** Any person under the age of 21 years who persistently or habitually refuses to obey the reasonable and proper orders or directions of his parents, guardian, custodian or school authorities, or who is beyond the control of such person, or any person who is a habitual truant from school within the meaning of any law of this State, or who from any cause is in danger of leading an idle, dissolute, lewd, or immoral life, is within the jurisdiction of the juvenile court which may adjudge such person to be a ward of the court.
>
> **602.** Any person under the age of 21 who violates any law of this State or of the United States or any ordinance of any city or county of this State defining crime or who, after having been found by the juvenile court to be a person described by Section 601, fails to obey the lawful order of the juvenile court, is within the jurisdiction of the juvenile court, which may adjudge such person to be a ward of the court.

Such omnibus provisions are restricted virtually to the United States. In Canada the Juvenile Delinquents Act of the central Parliament defines delinquency more sharply as criminal acts carried on by juveniles. However, the terms of this law are extended by statutes in the provinces, so as to take control over youngsters who would fall under one of the omnibus provisions in the United States.[13] Throughout Latin America delinquency is defined as violations of the criminal law by persons under certain specified ages; no omnibus clauses are found.[14] Simi-

[12] State of California, *Welfare and Institutions Code, 1965* (Sacramento: Department of General Services, 1965), p. 35.

[13] United Nations, *Comparative Survey of Juvenile Delinquency. Part I. North America* (New York: United Nations, Department of Economic and Social Affairs, 1958), pp.4–6.

[14] United Nations, *Estudio Comparado Sobre Delinquencia Juvenil. Parte III.*

larly, a survey of selected Asian nations shows no legislation explicitly defining "juvenile delinquency" in its behavioral connotations; by common agreement, however, the term is seen as embracing non-adult violations of the criminal law.[15] No special definition of delinquency is provided in the laws of Middle Eastern countries, so that, again, delinquency consists of criminal law violations by juveniles.[16]

How frequently are the omnibus sections of American delinquency laws utilized? In one report on this question, the United States Children's Bureau statistics for 1944–1945 showed that "ungovernability" was the reason for referral in 18 percent of the cases from 380 reporting juvenile courts, while "acts of carelessness or mischief" accounted for another 20 percent of the referrals.[17] More recent evidence can be found in California police departments and juvenile courts, in which arrests and referrals are made for "delinquent tendencies" under section 601 of the Welfare and Institutions Code. These delinquent tendencies include such things as incorrigibility, running away, waywardness, and improper associations. Of 277,649 juvenile arrests reported to the state statistical agency in 1965, 175,760 (63 percent) were for delinquent tendencies, while 101,889 were for major and minor law violations.[18] The police made different dispositions of these separate categories of delinquency. They handled 49.1 percent of all the offenses within the department; of this percentage only 21.6 percent of the major law violations were disposed of, 54.5 percent of the minor law violations were settled, and 54.6 percent of the delinquent tendencies cases were resolved.[19]

One thing is clear from these statistics: delinquency consists of a continuum of behavior, ranging from some very serious acts of law violation to other conditions which are relatively innocuous or benign. When we assemble a total picture of delinquency, we have to be alert to the possibility that much delinquency is not reported,

América Latina (New York: United Nations, Department of Social Affairs, Division of Social Welfare, 1952), p. 26.

[15] United Nations, *Comparative Survey on Juvenile Delinquency. Part IV. Asia and the Far East* (New York: United Nations, Department of Social Affairs, Division of Social Welfare, 1953), p. 1.

[16] United Nations, *Comparative Survey on Juvenile Delinquency. Part V. Middle East* (New York: Department of Social Affairs, Division of Social Welfare, 1953), p. 1.

[17] Rubin, "The Legal Character of Juvenile Delinquency," pp. 26–27.

[18] State of California, *Crime and Delinquency in California, 1965* (Sacramento: Bureau of Criminal Statistics, 1966), p. 147.

[19] *Ibid.*, pp. 144–45.

particularly those instances of juvenile misconduct that are included under the omnibus provisions of the laws.

SUMMARY

This brief chapter has considered some of the erroneous notions about juvenile delinquency held by members of the general public, for example, that delinquency consists solely of juvenile crime committed by a small segment of the juvenile population. But we have seen that the laws of delinquency are broad in scope, and that juvenile misconduct falling within the scope of these statutes varies widely. We must build up a more detailed picture of juvenile lawbreaking in American society, a picture constructed from a variety of kinds of information.

chapter two

ADOLESCENT MISBEHAVIOR IN AMERICAN SOCIETY

INTRODUCTION

How many delinquent youngsters are there in the United States? How many of them get into the hands of the police and the courts? How many are "hidden" or undetected delinquents? Are only the juvenile offenders who fall into the custody of the law enforcement and correctional agencies usually "hard core," career-oriented delinquents? Or, instead, are the hidden deviants similar to the detected ones, only luckier?

The nature of the task before us can be seen in the scheme provided by Howard Becker in Figure 2-1.[1] Becker observes that some persons who engage in deviant behavior are observed by others and tagged as norm violators, while others succeed in carrying out their aberrant actions in secret. Still other individuals are identified as misbehavers even though their actual behavior is conformist. We need to assemble a picture of delinquency which indicates the extent of delinquent conduct, to determine the extent of recognized or perceived delinquency, and to know the size of the secret or hidden lawbreaker group. Finally, we need to examine the ways in which the recognized offenders resemble or differ from the hidden ones.

[1] Howard S. Becker, *Outsiders* (New York: The Free Press, 1963), p. 20.

FIGURE 2-1

	DEVIANT BEHAVIOR	NONDEVIANT BEHAVIOR
PERCEIVED AS DEVIANT	PURE DEVIANT	FALSELY ACCUSED
NOT PERCEIVED AS DEVIANT	SECRET DEVIANT	CONFORMITY

Chapter Two focuses upon epidemiological questions, questions which, when used in connection with delinquency, concern the statistical facts regarding the number and location of juvenile delinquents in society, and their social characteristics;[2] in Chapter Three, attention will turn to an examination of the social processes which lie behind the statistics in the present chapter. Chapter Two will note that police arrests of juveniles far outnumber police referrals to courts, that many cases are handled informally by police officers, that law enforcement agents often dispense "on-the-street" justice to juvenile offenders; Chapter Three will go into the details of the social behavior of policemen, probation officers, juvenile court judges, and others, as they go about processing youths.

OFFICIAL DELINQUENCY

The first thing that is apparent from statistics on officially-handled cases of delinquency is that juvenile lawbreakers constitute a sizable group within American society, but, at the same time, only a fraction of the youths in the nation. For example, in 1965, the population of juveniles over eleven and under eighteen years of age was 29,479,-000. In the same year, the average daily population in institutions for juvenile offenders was only 62,773, while another 285,431 youths were wards of community agencies such as probation departments.[3]

[2] The notion of epidemiology of crime is discussed in Don C. Gibbons, *Society, Crime, and Criminal Careers* (Englewood Cliffs, N.J.: Prentice-Hall, Inc., 1968), pp. 6–7.

[3] *Ibid.*, p. 443.

Juvenile Court Cases

The United States Children's Bureau collects statistics on the number of youngsters appearing in American juvenile courts each year from a nationwide sample of 494 juvenile courts, then estimates the total court cases. In 1967, juvenile court referrals (excluding traffic cases) numbered approximately 811,000 out of a total population of 30,088,000 children eleven to eighteen years old.[4] In other words, less than 3 percent of the youth population appeared in juvenile courts in 1967. Of course, a somewhat larger number of youths get into court sometime during their juvenile years. Still, appearance in a juvenile court is an experience which occurs to relatively few youngsters. The seriousness of the delinquency problem would seem to be further minimized by the observation that in only 47 percent of these 811,000 cases were petitions alleging delinquency filed against the children. Over half of the court referrals were handled informally, without court hearings.[5]

What have the delinquency trends been in recent years, as measured by court referral? Table 2-1 indicates the estimated number of

TABLE 2-1 Juvenile Court Cases and Child Population,
United States, 1950-1967[6]

YEAR	DELINQUENCY CASES*	POPULATION (AGE 11-17)	PERCENT
1950	280,000	17,398,000	1.6
1951	298,000	17,705,000	1.7
1952	332,000	18,201,000	1.8
1953	374,000	18,980,000	2.0
1954	395,000	19,551,000	2.0
1955	431,000	20,112,000	2.1
1956	520,000	20,623,000	2.5
1957	440,000	22,173,000	2.0
1958	473,000	23,443,000	2.0
1959	483,000	24,607,000	2.0
1960	510,000	25,364,000	2.0
1961	503,000	26,029,000	1.9
1962	555,000	26,962,000	2.1
1963	601,000	28,031,000	2.1
1964	686,000	29,189,000	2.4
1965	697,000	29,479,000	2.4
1966	745,000	30,088,000	2.5
1967	811,000	31,000,000	2.3

* Delinquency cases up to 1957 included traffic offenses.

[4] Children's Bureau, *Juvenile Court Statistics,* 1967 (Washington, D.C.: U.S. Department of Health, Education and Welfare, 1969), p. 10.

[5] *Ibid.,* p. 11.

[6] *Ibid.,* p. 10.

FIGURE 2-2 Juvenile Court Cases and Child Population,
United States, 1950-1967.[7]

TREND IN JUVENILE COURT DELINQUENCY CASES AND CHILD POPULATION 10 - 17 YEARS OF AGE, 1940 - 1967 (semi-logarithmic scale)

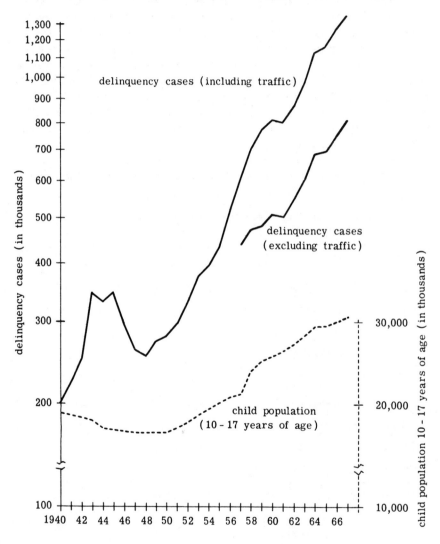

[7] *Ibid.,* p. 8.

court cases in the United States from 1950 to 1967, in relation to the population of youths eleven through seventeen years of age. The increase in court referrals from 1966 to 1967 was 9 percent, while the juvenile population grew by only 2 percent. Moreover, between 1960 and 1967, child referrals increased by 58 percent, but the population of youngsters grew by only 22 percent. These are the figures, represented graphically in Figure 2-2, on which the allegation of a pronounced rise in juvenile delinquency is based.

The grounds for court referral differ markedly for boys and girls. Cavan has noted that throughout United States courts in 1957, 69 percent of the female referrals were charged with malicious mischief, ungovernability, or sex offenses, in contrast to only 34 percent of the boys who were in courts on these complaints. On the other hand, 48 percent of the male referrals were for thefts of various kinds, including automobile theft, burglary, and robbery, but only 15 percent of the girls were charged with property crimes. Finally, 18 percent of the males and 16 percent of the females were referred for personal or miscellaneous offenses.[8] Similar patterns were reported for juvenile courts in Washington state by Gibbons and Griswold.[9]

Police Arrests

Since the police do not turn over all of those children who fall into their hands to the juvenile court, just how large is the group of juveniles they do contact? What portion of these youngsters ends up in juvenile courts? Answers to these questions can be found in the reports of the Federal Bureau of Investigation, which collects nationwide arrest statistics.

The F.B.I. figures for 1967 indicate that 5,518,420 arrests were enumerated by the 4,556 reporting agencies. Persons under the age of fifteen accounted for 9.6 percent of these arrests, while juveniles under eighteen years of age contributed 1,339,578, or 24.3 percent of the arrests. However, persons under eighteen were responsible for 49 percent of the 996,800 reported Crime Index arrests. Index offenses comprise seven serious felonies: murder, forcible rape, robbery, ag-

[8] Ruth Shonle Cavan, *Juvenile Delinquency* (Philadelphia: J.B. Lippincott Co., 1962), p. 28.

[9] Don C. Gibbons and Manzer J. Griswold, "Sex Differences Among Juvenile Court Referrals," *Sociology and Social Research*, XLII (November-December 1957), 106–10; see also William Wattenberg and Frank Saunders, "Sex Differences Among Juvenile Offenders," *Sociology and Social Research*, XXXIX (September-October 1954), 24–31.

gravated assault, burglary, grand larceny, and motor vehicle theft.[10] These figures show that 53.5 percent of the burglary, breaking or entering arrests, 55.0 percent of the grand larceny cases, and 61.8 percent of the motor vehicle arrests involved youths under eighteen years of age.[11]

The police handle a wide variety of complaints, ranging from petty mischief to major felonies. F.B.I. information on arrests of youthful offenders in 1967 indicates that 46.2 percent of the apprehended juveniles were disposed of informally within the department. Most of these children were given admonitions and warnings. The remainder of the cases were dealt with officially; 48.4 percent of all arrested juveniles were referred to juvenile courts, 1.6 percent were turned over to welfare agencies, and 3.7 percent were either referred to other police organizations or to criminal courts.[12]

An indicative sampling of police arrests and dispositions of juveniles can be seen in the state of California. In 1967, California police agencies arrested 323,427 youthful offenders out of a youth population of 2,925,000; arrested juveniles represented about 12 percent of the total group. At the same time, initial referrals to juvenile courts (children appearing in court for the first time) only numbered 123,653. A total of 28,311 youths were placed on probation, and 3,571 youngsters were committed to California Youth Authority custody. In summary, incarcerated juvenile offenders represented only 1.2 percent of the juveniles arrested in this state in 1967.[13]

The varied nature of juvenile arrests can also be seen in California data. Of the 323,427 juvenile arrests, 125,414 were for law violations, while over half of the arrests—198,013—had to do with "delinquent tendencies," i.e., behavior included within the omnibus provision of delinquency laws. The 125,414 law violations involved 64,745 major offenses and 60,669 minor offenses.[14]

Over 70 percent of those major law violations were disposed of officially by referral to a juvenile court; 55.4 percent of the minor offenses were handled informally within the police organizations, as were 57.0 percent of the delinquent tendencies arrests.[15] These figures, as well as the national ones, point to the major screening role

[10] U.S. Department of Justice, *Uniform Crime Reports for the U.S., 1967* (Washington, D.C.: U.S. Government Printing Office, 1968), p. 121.

[11] *Ibid.*, p. 123.

[12] *Ibid.*, p. 110.

[13] Bureau of Criminal Statistics, State of California, *Crime and Delinquency in California, 1967* (Sacramento: Department of Justice, 1968), p. 215.

[14] *Ibid.*, p. 208.

[15] *Ibid.*, p. 208.

of the police, admonishing some juveniles and feeding others into the juvenile court machinery.

Juvenile courts, therefore, receive the most serious cases dealt with by the police; they tend to process "hard core" delinquents. However, the national court data showed that about half of these serious cases were of insufficient importance to warrant official court action. Statistics from California also indicate that many juvenile offenders who are diverted into the court machinery are nonetheless regarded as not serious enough to call for formal court action. In 1967, California juvenile courts disposed of 50.8 percent of the referrals to them by closing the cases at intake or by referring them to other agencies. In only 35.6 percent of the cases were delinquency petitions filed in order to activate the machinery of court hearing and adjudication.[16]

DELINQUENCY HANDLED BY OTHER AGENCIES

The police are in contact with almost twice as many misbehaving youngsters as are juvenile courts. But do the police know about most youthful transgressions of the law? Or instead, are there large numbers of delinquents who are hidden from the view of the police? Goodly numbers of young lawbreakers are handled by public and private social agencies and do not come to the attention of the police. "Hidden delinquency," still another phase, goes unobserved by any agency, public or private.

Many years ago Sophia Robison conducted a major study of delinquents known to agencies other than the juvenile court.[17] In her survey of over forty official and private agencies in New York City which dealt with juvenile delinquents, she discovered that there were 7,090 wards of the Children's Court in New York in 1930, while other agencies had 15,898 cases under their supervision (including the 7,090 court cases).[18] Thus the agencies knew about 8,808 offenders in addition to the 7,090 known to the court. The 15,898 agency cases included 10,374 children who had been referred to them in 1930. Of these cases that had come to agency attention in 1930, 7,090 or 68.3 percent were also known to the juvenile court.[19] What these figures indicate is that the juvenile court has knowledge of many of those

---

[16] *Ibid.*, p. 228.

[17] Sophia M. Robison, *Can Delinquency Be Measured?* (New York: Columbia University Press, 1936).

[18] *Ibid.*, p. 48.

[19] *Ibid.*, p. 52.

youthful lawbreakers who receive some kind of agency intervention, but at the same time, does not detect a significant number of apparently serious cases.

Robison also examined the factors which determine referral to Children's Court or to some other agency. She found that boys were more likely to be turned over to a juvenile court, as were older youths, Negro delinquents, and Catholic youngsters. These differentials reflect the greater availability of non-court resources for dealing with younger children, girls, white youths, and Jewish and Protestant delinquents.[20]

A second study of this sort was carried out by Edward Schwartz.[21] The Council of Social Agencies in Washington, D.C. conducted a registration of all delinquency cases known to the juvenile court, police department, welfare service, or school system during 1943–1944.

The results of this case-finding experiment included the report that only 43 percent of the cases that had come to the attention of agencies had also become known to the juvenile court.[22] As in Robison's report, delinquent boys and misbehaving Negroes were turned over to juvenile courts with great frequency, while girls were handled without court referral.[23] Moreover, the likelihood of court referral was heavily influenced by the kind of delinquency in which the youngster had been engaged. The juvenile court had been apprised of 99 percent of the traffic cases, 80 percent of the stealing cases, and 79 percent of the assault cases known to the other agencies. On the other hand, only 24 percent of the sex offenders, 5 percent of the truants, and 2 percent of the runaways had been reported to the court.[24]

"HIDDEN" DELINQUENCY

When all of the misbehaving youngsters who have been observed by the courts, the police, or other agencies are added up, they still make up a minority of the youth population. But what of undetected or "hidden" delinquents? Are undetected lawbreakers few or abundant? Finally, how do some delinquents remain "hidden" while others get caught up in the machinery of police arrest and court referral? Are

---

[20] *Ibid.*, pp. 49–79.

[21] Edward E. Schwartz, "A Community Experiment in the Measurement of Juvenile Delinquency," *Yearbook, National Probation Association, 1945* (New York: National Probation Association, 1946), pp. 157–81.

[22] *Ibid.*, pp. 164–65.

[23] *Ibid.*, pp. 170–71.

[24] *Ibid.*, p. 173.

hidden delinquents beneficiaries of discriminatory law enforcement, in which their deviant acts are overlooked because they are from favored social class groups or because of other factors of that kind?

The importance of answers to these questions cannot be overemphasized. Research studies dealing with the causation of delinquency are based on assumptions about the true extent of misconduct. If these assumptions are faulty, etiological research based upon them will be vitiated. The most common assumption behind causal inquiries is that most of the youngsters who have escaped the attention of the police, courts, or social agencies are free from involvement in lawbreaking conduct, or at least from persistent and serious misbehavior. The logic of much delinquency research is that these "nondelinquents" can be meaningfully compared to court cases or other recognized "delinquents." The two groups are presumed to be quite unlike in terms of lawbreaking conduct, so that any differences in social characteristics which turn up between them can be viewed as causally significant. But suppose many of the "nondelinquents" are, in fact, frequently involved in undetected but serious and repetitive acts of law violation. In this case, comparison of these persons with officially-recognized delinquents would be causally meaningless. Such comparisons might tell us a good deal about the factors that cause some delinquents to be officially tagged yet allow other youths to remain hidden and undetected.

Early Work

The initial study of hidden delinquency was conducted by Porterfield in Fort Worth, Texas.[25] That investigation examined several thousand juvenile court cases in order to discover the offenses by court wards. These offenses were then incorporated into a questionnaire which was administered to several hundred college students. All of the students reported that they had engaged in a least one of the deviant acts; the average number of admitted delinquencies was 17.6 for males and 4.7 for females.[26] The study also observed that the offenses commonly admitted by the college students were less serious acts than those which reached court. Finally, Porterfield particularly noted that virtually none of the students had been brought to police or court attention, even in those instances in which their delinquent acts were serious in nature.[27]

[25] Austin L. Porterfield, "Delinquency and its Outcome in Court and College," *American Journal of Sociology*, XLIX (November 1943), 199–208.

[26] *Ibid.*, pp. 199–201.

[27] *Ibid.*, pp. 201–2.

Porterfield interpreted his findings as the result of differential application of the law: Children from poor economic areas or from situations of family or neighborhood disorganization are closely observed by the police and are frequently sent off to the juvenile court; juveniles from comfortable backgrounds who commit similar acts are either ignored by the police or are processed informally.[28]

Porterfield's investigation was of value principally as a stimulant to more sophisticated inquiries in part as his questionnaire did not define offenses in detail. (Some student respondents may have admitted to acts of theft, mischief, and the like, which were so petty and innocuous as to be quite unlike the theft and mischief engaged in by court delinquents.) It is possible that some students failed to respond truthfully to the questionnaire items, e.g., one student reported that he had committed a murder and had gone unapprehended for it!

Another early study of hidden delinquency involved a quite different collection of youths. This research was a part of the Cambridge-Somerville Youth Study, a delinquency prevention project conducted in two communities near Boston, Massachussetts.[29] A group of slum area boys regarded as predelinquents moving toward careers in serious lawbreaking were subjected to casework treatment. Caseworkers maintained detailed records of the delinquent acts of these boys over a several year period. The offense behavior of the 101 subjects of the study is shown in Table 2-2;[30] sixty-one delinquents had not been reported to the juvenile court, while forty delinquents had come to court attention. It is readily apparent from this table that all of the youths had been deeply enmeshed in misconduct. Only ninety-five (less than one and one-half percent) of the 6,416 offenses had been reported to the juvenile court.

The delinquent acts which most often resulted in the court referral of these boys were larceny and breaking and entering, while truancy and school offenses were infrequently a matter of court attention. In addition, those boys who had become known to the court were more frequently enmeshed in serious delinquency than the unofficial delinquents; individuals in the officially-known group had committed from five to 323 violations apiece and averaged seventy-nine offenses, in contrast to the hidden group who showed a median of thirty offenses.[31]

The major point on slum area hidden delinquency is the staggering

28 *Ibid.*, pp. 204–8.
29 Fred J. Murphy, Mary M. Shirley, and Helen L. Witmer, "The Incidence of Hidden Delinquency,"*American Journal of Orthopsychiatry*,XVI (October 1946), 686–95.
30 *Ibid.*, p. 688.
31 *Ibid.*, p. 689.

TABLE 2-2 Behavioral Study of 101 Youths in Several Year Period

TYPE OF OFFENSE	UNOFFICIAL DELINQUENTS (NUMBER-61)	OFFICIAL DELINQUENTS (NUMBER-40)	BOTH GROUPS (NUMBER-101)
City ordinance offense	739	655	1,394
Minor offense	1,913	2,493	4,406
Serious offense	174	442	616
Total	2,826	3,590	6,416

amount of it turned up by this study. These data suggest that youthful misconduct may be a way of life for a large number of boys in urban working-class neighborhoods, an observation to be kept in mind when some of the recent studies of hidden delinquents are examined. These show that youths from relatively comfortable social circumstances have often misbehaved, but it may well be that their misadventures are neither as serious nor as repetitive as those of slum-area boys.[32]

Short and Nye's Contributions

Short and Nye have done much to encourage the development of sophisticated studies of hidden delinquency. In his initial inquiry, Short examined a sample of college students and a group of training school subjects in Washington state[33] and asked them to complete a questionnaire about delinquent acts which they had committed of a list of 43 delinquencies. Large numbers of both the students and the training school wards confessed to various illegal acts. However, higher percentages of training school wards were found to have been involved in specific acts. For example, larceny of property worth over $50 was admitted by sixty percent of the training school boys, but by

[32] This finding is paralleled in Albert J. Reiss, Jr., and Albert Lewis Rhodes, "The Distribution of Delinquency in the Social Class Structure," *American Sociological Review*, XXVI (October 1961), 732; Robert H. Hardt and Sandra J. Peterson, "Neighborhood Status and Delinquency Activity as Indexed by Police Records and a Self Report Survey," *Criminologica*, VI (May 1968), 37–47.

[33] James F. Short, Jr., "A Report on the Incidence of Criminal Behavior, Arrests, and Convictions in Selected Groups," *Research Studies of the State College of Washington*, XXII (June 1954), 110–18.

only 1.5 percent of the students. This differential in self-reported delinquency was particularly pronounced for serious offenses; large numbers of training school residents, unlike the students, said they had repeatedly committed these major violations. In general, training school boys more often confessed to specific acts of misbehavior than did training school girls. Finally, the college students indicated that they had rarely been arrested for their deviant acts, although most of those who had been apprehended had subsequently been dealt with in juvenile court.

Short and Nye conducted a second study dealing with high school students in three Washington communities ranging from 10,000 to 30,000 residents, with students in three midwestern towns, and with delinquents in training schools in Washington state.[34] Again, the subjects were asked to complete a questionnaire about the acts of misbehavior in which they had engaged as juveniles. The respondents were also asked to indicate whether they had committed the actions more than once. An abridged version of the results is presented in Table 2-3 in which the delinquencies of the male subjects only are indicated.

The naïve view that youths come only in two distinct types, the "bad" delinquents and the "good" nondelinquents, is most certainly not upheld by the results in Table 2-3. However, these findings do not lend much weight to the equally naïve notion that juveniles get to the training school mainly as a result of discriminatory law enforcement based on social class factors or related criteria, although this does sometime occur. "Nondelinquent" high school students engaged in many relatively petty acts of delinquency for which they could conceivably have been hailed into juvenile court, but the training school youths more frequently admitted to these same acts and, in addition, reported involvement in other, more serious forms of misconduct not common among the students. Finally, the training school boys declared that they had engaged in a large number of delinquencies with considerable frequency. The conclusion to be reached from the Short and Nye study is that *seriousness and frequency of delinquent conduct is one major determinant of the actions taken against juvenile lawbreakers.*

Short and Nye also developed a delinquency scale which allowed them to order youths in terms of degree of involvement in juvenile

---

[34] James F. Short, Jr., and F. Ivan Nye, "Extent of Unrecorded Juvenile Delinquency: Tentative Conclusions," *Journal of Criminal Law, Criminology and Police Science*, XXXXIX (November-December 1958), 296-302. See also James F. Short, Jr., "Psychosomatic Complaints, Institutionalization, and Delinquency," *Research Studies of the State College of Washington*, XXIV (June 1956), 50–159.

TABLE 2-3   Extent of Delinquent Acts Admitted by Students and Training School Boys by Area.[35]

DELINQUENT ACT	ADMIT ACT			ADMIT ACT MORE THAN ONCE OR TWICE		
	Midwest Students	Western Students	Training School Boys	Midwest Students	Western Students	Training School Boys
Driving a car without a license	81.1%	75.3%	91.1%	61.2%	49.0%	73.4%
Skipping school	54.4	53.0	95.3	24.4	23.8	85.9
Fist fighting	86.7	80.7	95.3	32.6	31.9	75.0
Running away	12.9	13.0	68.1	2.8	2.4	37.7
School probation or expulsion	15.3	11.3	67.8	2.1	2.9	31.3
Defying parents' authority	22.2	33.1	52.4	1.4	6.3	23.6
Stealing items worth less than $2	62.7	60.6	91.8	18.5	12.9	65.1
Stealing items worth from $2 to $50	17.1	15.8	91.0	3.8	3.8	61.4
Stealing items worth more than $50	3.5	5.0	90.8	1.1	2.1	47.7
Gang fighting	24.3	22.5	67.4	6.7	5.2	47.4
Drinking beer, wine, or liquor	67.7	57.2	89.7	35.8	29.5	79.4
Using narcotics	1.4	2.2	23.1	0.7	1.6	12.6
Having sex relations	38.8	40.4	87.5	20.3	19.9	73.4

misconduct. [36] This scale was based on seven items of misbehavior:[37]

1. Driving a car without a driver's license or permit.
2. Skipping school without a legitimate excuse.

[35] Nye, *op. cit.*, pp. 13–14. This scale is an omnibus one, in that it includes items of varied kinds, including theft and liquor violations. Scott has developed two delinquency scales which are unidimensional, one dealing with general theft and the second with interpersonal theft. He contends that scores on these two scales are not correlated. See John Finley Scott, "Two Dimensions of Delinquent Behavior," *American Sociological Review*, XXIV (April 1959), 240–43.

[36] Short and Nye, "Extent of Unrecorded Juvenile Delinquency," p. 297.

[37] F. Ivan Nye and James F. Short, Jr., "Scaling Delinquent Behavior," *American Sociological Review*, XXII (June 1957), 326–31; see also Nye, *Family Relationships and Delinquent Behavior* (New York: John Wiley and Sons, Inc., 1958).

3. Defying parents' authority (to their face).

4. Taking little things (worth less than $2).

5. Buying or drinking beer, wine, or liquor.

6. Purposely damaging or destroying public or private property.

7. Having sex relations with the opposite sex.

The individuals were sorted into fifteen scale categories on the basis of the number of these acts they acknowledged and the frequency with which they committed them. The scaling results for high school and training school boys showed that some of the former had higher scale scores than the latter, that the high school boys were "more delinquent" as measured by the scale. However, 86 percent of the high school youths had scores of nine or less on the scale, while only fourteen percent of the incarcerated juveniles had these low scores.[38]

These scaling results again point to the greater involvement in lawbreaking of official delinquents. Note too that the seven items in the scale center upon relatively petty acts. In the development of this scale, several more serious delinquent acts which training school wards frequently admit had to be discarded, because few high school youngsters confessed to them. Thus this scale must be viewed as an instrument which measures the degree of involvement in commonplace but relatively inconsequential forms of juvenile misconduct.[39]

One of the claims often advanced in the delinquency literature is that delinquents are disproportionately lower or working-class youths. Short and Nye, utilizing their scale to examine the social backgrounds of training school and hidden delinquents,[40] reported that nearly all of institutionalized youths were from the lower half of the socioeconomic strata, in contrast to only 53 percent of a group of high school stu-

---

[38] Nye and Short, "Scaling Juvenile Behavior," pp. 299–300.

[39] Some critics of this work have also suggested that scale scores for some undetected offenders may overstate the degree of their involvement in delinquency. The younger, less sophisticated respondents may interpret their own conduct too strictly in terms of these items, so that, for example, an admission of parental disobedience could be based upon acts of defiance of slight importance. Training school wards are not likely to respond in the same fashion, due to their greater sophistication in the ways of delinquency.

[40] James F. Short, Jr., and F. Ivan Nye, "Reported Behavior as a Criterion of Deviant Behavior," *Social Problems*, V (Winter 1957-1958), 207–13; Nye, Short, and Virgil J. Olson, "Socioeconomic Status and Delinquent Behavior," *American Journal of Sociology*, LXIII (January 1958), 381–89. Also see Nye, *Family Relationships and Delinquent Behavior*. This study examines the family and social backgrounds in detail of high school youths who were categorized as "most delinquent" and "least delinquent" on this scale.

dents. But when the high school youths were sorted into delinquency scale types, no relationship was found between delinquency and social class. In other words, students with high or low delinquency scores were found in the four social classes in about the same proportions. This finding suggests that *relatively minor misbehavior* is not class linked. This kind of activity is not restricted to lower-class youths, but, at the same time, it is highly likely that repetitive involvement in serious forms of lawbreaking is most frequent among working-class youths.[41]

Other Recent Studies

A report on theft behavior by adolescents in three Kansas communities has been made by Dentler and Monroe.[42] They studied 912 seventh and eighth graders in three areas: a middle-class suburb, a rural farm town, and a rural nonfarm community. These youths were given a five item questionnaire asking whether they had stolen things worth less than $2, things worth between $2 and $50, things from school desks or lockers, major things such as automobiles, and things worth more than $50. A score of zero was given to those who had not committed any of the acts, while those who had done all five were assigned a score of five. The results showed that 529 of the 912 children had scores of zero, while 304 were designated as engaging in "some theft" (scores of one or two). Only 79 adolescents showed scores between three and five. Those respondents who had the highest theft scores were most frequently males and older children.[43] Additionally, the youngsters who were most involved in theft also declared that they were on poor terms with their parents. Then, too, the thieves reported involvement in other types of delinquency, such as vandalism and truancy, more often than the non-thieves did. [44] In general, serious delinquency did not seem to be endemic in these Kansas communities even though some adolescents were implicated in major forms of theft.

Another recent inquiry dealt with the issue of social class correlates of delinquency.[45] Clark and Wenninger studied 1,154 students in the

[41] A review of the evidence can be found in Gibbons, *Society, Crime, and Criminal Careers.* pp. 274–78.

[42] Robert A. Dentler and Lawrence J. Monroe, "Social Correlates of Early Adolescent Theft," *American Sociological Review* XXVI (October 1961), 733–43.

[43] *Ibid.,* pp. 735–36.

[44] *Ibid.,* pp. 736–39.

[45] John P. Clark and Eugene P. Wenninger, "Socio-economic Class and Area Correlates of Illegal Behavior Among Juveniles," *American Sociological Review,* XXVII (December 1962), 826–34.

TABLE 2-4   Self-Admitted Delinquency in Four
Illinois Communities During A One Year
Period, by Area[46]

OFFENSE	INDUSTRIAL CITY	LOWER-CLASS URBAN	UPPER-CLASS URBAN	RURAL FARM
Disobedience to parents	90%	87%	85%	82%
Minor theft	79	78	80	73
Lying to family, principal, or friend	80	74	77	74
Major theft	37	40	29	20
Vandalism	8	4	2	8
Drug use	3	4	1	3
Arson	3	2	1	3

sixth to twelfth grades in four Illinois communities: a rural farm area, a lower-class neighborhood within a city, an industrial city, and an upper-class area within a city. (See Table 2-4.) Here again, as in the other studies, "nondelinquent" school pupils readily admitted involvement in a variety of relatively insignificant acts of misbehavior; relatively few of them, however, asserted that they had engaged in those more serious kinds of misconduct frequent among juvenile court probationers and training school wards.

Although individual items of lawbreaking varied, Clark and Wenninger found that the lowest incidence for most offenses was in the rural farm area, followed by the upper urban area and then the industrial city; the greatest frequency of offense was in the lower-class urban area. This pattern was particularly apparent in the case of the more serious offenses. After ranking the four communities in terms of the frequency with which various offenses were admitted, Clark and Wenninger summed the ranks to obtain an overall measure of the occurrence of misconduct. The industrial city and the lower-class urban area had the highest overall delinquency rates.[47]

The Clark and Wenninger findings raise the question of social class correlates of delinquency, for they point to differences in misbehavior *between* communities which vary in socioeconomic terms. At the same time, no social class variations in delinquency *within* specific communities were observed, except in the instance of the industrial city.[48]

Still another of the studies of hidden delinquency and its relation to social class was made by Akers; it involved 836 ninth graders in an

[46] *Ibid.*, pp. 829–30.
[47] *Ibid.*, pp. 831–32.
[48] *Ibid.*, pp. 833–34.

Ohio city with a population of 275,000.[49] The students were assigned to one of four social class strata by the occupation of their fathers. Akers' self-report questionnaire concerned fairly innocuous forms of misconduct, so that his study constitutes an examination of social class correlates of petty juvenile misbehavior. (See Table 2-5.) The ninth graders in this study freely admitted involvement in some of the fairly petty activities listed in Table 2-5, but relatively few of them acknowledged participation in the more serious offenses. Finally, Akers reported that the differences among social class groups in incidence of deviant acts were statistically insignificant.

TABLE 2-5 Self-admitted Delinquency By Ninth Grades, By Social Class.[50]

OFFENSE	UPPER CLASS	UPPER-MIDDLE CLASS	LOWER-MIDDLE CLASS	LOWER CLASS
Drive a car without a license	36.3%	32.9%	39.0%	29.5%
Skip school	24.4	23.9	30.4	31.1
Run away	11.4	13.0	12.8	13.3
Defy parents' authority	48.8	49.1	42.0	46.7
Steal items worth less than $2	53.6	49.7	49.6	58.1
Steal items worth from $2 to $50	8.9	7.7	10.9	17.8
Damage property	28.4	32.0	29.1	28.9
Take a car without owner's permission	6.5	9.4	9.3	13.3

Arnold examined hidden delinquency in the sophomore classes of six high schools in a middle-sized Texas city of about 200,000 people.[51] He endeavored to devise delinquency scales of attacks against persons, of vandalism, and of theft. The results of this investigation appeared to show that delinquency was more widespread at the higher levels of socioeconomic status, although this relationship was a weak one.

Voss also conducted a survey in which 629 Honolulu seventh graders (284 boys, 345 girls) completed a questionnaire which asked whether they had been involved in truancy, fist fighting, petty theft, property damage, gang fighting, or driving without a license.[52] When the re-

49 Ronald L. Akers, "Socio-Economic Status and Delinquent Behavior: A Retest," *Journal of Research in Crime and Delinquency,* I (January 1964), 38–46.

50 *Ibid.,* p. 42.

51 William A. Arnold, "Continuities in Research: Scaling Delinquent Behavior," *Social Problems,* XIII (Summer 1965), 59–66.

52 Harwin L. Voss, "Socio-Economic Status and Reported Delinquent Behavior," *Social Problems,* XIII (Winter 1966), 314–24.

sponses of the 284 boys to this scale were divided into "most delinquent" and "least delinquent" categories, ninety-nine of the boys fell
into the first group. However, only thirty-one of the youths were
defined as delinquents when the seriousness and repetitiveness of misbehavior was measured. Voss also sorted the students into social class
groups on the basis of fathers' occupation, but found no pronounced
relationship between delinquency and social status.

A FINAL ASSESSMENT

The conclusions about the extent of delinquency indicated by this
mass of material should be evident. These conclusions, however, must
be stated in terms such as "relatively large numbers" and "somewhat
more," for the available data do not lend themselves to precise
epidemiological statements about juvenile misconduct. A massive and
complex research study would be required in order for us to be able
to assert that some specific percentage of all offenders become known
to the police, or that some specific proportion of lawbreakers receives
a particular disposition from the police or courts. Such an investigation
would have to be longitudinal in form, in which all of the children in
a particular community would be followed over an extended period of
time. Nonetheless, it is possible to state a group of conclusions about
total delinquency in relatively definite terms:

1. Less than three percent of the juveniles in this nation are referred to
   juvenile courts in any single year, although a larger portion of the youth
   population comes to court attention sometime during the adolescent
   years. Only about one-half of these referrals are regarded by court officials as serious enough to warrant the filing of a petition and a court
   hearing, so that the other half are dealt with informally.

2. Police agencies come into contact with almost twice the number of
   children known to the court. In general, they refer the serious cases to
   juvenile courts, while disposing of the less serious offenders informally,
   within the department, by admonitions and warnings.

3. A fairly large number of offenders is dealt with by public and private
   social agencies in the community, but many of the individuals they
   process are also known to the juvenile court. The majority of the cases
   known to agencies but which are unknown to the court are relatively
   petty ones.

4. A large number of youths at all social class levels and in all kinds of
   communities engage in acts of misconduct and lawbreaking which remain hidden or undetected. In this sense, nearly all juveniles are delin-

quent in some degree. However, many of the deviant acts of hidden delinquents are relatively minor ones, the kinds which would often be handled informally or ignored if reported to the juvenile court.

5. Not all of the hidden delinquency in the United States is petty and inconsequential. An indeterminate but important number of serious delinquencies is enacted by juveniles who manage to stay out of the hands of the police or courts.[53]

This last point deserves further comment. Evidence of serious delinquent acts which go undetected has been presented by Karacki and Toby,[54] and by Shanley as well.[55] Furthermore, incidents of hidden

FIGURE 2-3 Delinquency and Nondelinquency in American Society

[53] Further evidence is contained in Maynard L. Erickson and LaMar T. Empey, "Court Records, Undetected Delinquency, and Decision-Making," *Journal of Criminal Law, Criminology and Police Science,* LIV (December 1963), 456–69. They studied fifty high school "nondelinquent" boys, fifty boys who had appeared once in juvenile court, fifty juvenile repeaters, and fifty incarcerated delinquents. The official records of the delinquents were compared against self-reported delinquency. All of the boys admitted acts of delinquency, most of which went undetected. However, the officially-recognized offenders were implicated in delinquency with greater frequency, while the persistent offenders were involved in the most serious delinquencies. In general, those who were engaged in numerous repetitions of delinquency also were the ones who had been in court most frequently.

[54] Larry Karacki and Jackson Toby, "The Uncommitted Adolescent: Candidate for Gang Socialization," *Sociological Inquiry,* XXXII (Spring 1962), 203–15.

[55] Fred J. Shanley, "Middle-Class Delinquency as a Social Problem," *Sociology and Social Research,* LI (January 1965), 185–98.

delinquency come to light in the mass media from time to time, testi-fying to the seriousness of some of this conduct. For example, a subur-ban school district near San Francisco suffers at least $25,000 in damages each year from vandalism—broken windows and other acts of that kind. Virtually none of the culprits are apprehended for these offenses, but they are believed to be middle-class youths who attend schools in the same district.

Probably many of these cases of serious, hidden delinquency go undetected and unattended simply because the police are not able to observe the offenses, just as they are unaware of large numbers of acts of both petty or serious misbehavior in working-class areas. At the same time, differential enforcement of the law allows some of the misbehavior of middle class youths to remain hidden; some juveniles are ignored by the police even though their actions are known to the law enforcement persons and their conduct is serious in character. Conjectural statements about differential enforcement of the law can easily be verbalized, but accurate generalizations about the extent of this phenomenon cannot be made at present; this is a necessary topic for future research investigation.[56]

Figure 2-3 shows another way of picturing the nature of delin-quency in the United States. Different categories of offenders and nondelinquents are portrayed within a circle designating the total youth population. But we must now turn to the study of the social processes and factors which are implicated in these statistics and ob-servations.

---

[56] Another research problem concerns "hidden delinquency" in other countries. For one such study, see Nils Christie, Johs. Andanaes, and Sigurd Skirbekk, "A Study of Self-Reported Crime," *Scandinavian Studies in Criminology*, I (1965), 86–116. This research appears to show that Norwegian youths are less involved in undetected lawbreaking than are American ones.

chapter three

THE POLICE, THE COURT, AND JUVENILE DELINQUENTS

INTRODUCTION

The juvenile justice system in the United States represents grand scale social machinery. Because this people-processing apparatus is manned by many individuals who are involved in making decisions about offenders, its nature cannot be fully captured in a few paragraphs. But a brief summary of this system would note that policemen are most frequently involved in the initial decisions about reported juvenile lawbreakers, for they either observe these youths in acts of deviance or they learn about them from citizens. The police occupy a crucial position in the decision system; they control the initial sorting-out of youths, thus determining which are to be viewed as "bad" or "delinquent" and taken to court, and which do not need court intervention. The policemen take some youngsters directly to the juvenile court, while they give others citations to appear in court at some subsequent time. Although other persons—private citizens, school officials, and others—report youngsters to juvenile court, too, these cases are less frequent than are police referrals.

Those juveniles who end up at the juvenile hall or other court facility are submitted to a variety of decision makers. In larger courts, a probation officer serving in an intake capacity dismisses the referred children whom he concludes do not warrant court attention. Or he determines the referrals as not delinquent enough to deserve formal court action, but still needing some help; many of these youngsters are persuaded to accept informal probation, in which they report periodically to a probation officer even though they have not be formally adjudicated as delinquents. Petitions alleging delinquency are filed on a third group of offenders who are then scheduled for court hearing. Some of these juveniles are detained in juvenile hall while they await a hearing; others are released to their parents. Finally, when a court determines that youngsters are delinquents, this adjudication leads to still other decisions. Some wards are placed on probation, some are turned over to a private agency, and some are sent to custodial institutions for care and treatment.

Sociological interest in the decision-making machinery which processes delinquents is twofold. In the first place, police agencies, juvenile courts, and other structures which deal with juveniles are social organizations. Sociology, which centers on the study of social organizations, can learn much from an examination of these law enforcement and correctional systems. The people-work of these agencies cannot proceed without the development of rules, norms, and other social mechanisms. As in other large-scale organizations, the procedural standards which guide the functionaries of these systems are of several kinds and include both formal and informal rules.The unwritten or informal norms of policemen, juvenile court judges, and probation officers more often determine the ways in which offenders are processed than do the explicit, formal rules of procedure. A considerable number of sociologists are interested in the study of the social workings of the juvenile justice system, quite apart from their specific concern about juvenile delinquency.[1]

The second reason for sociological interest in the social control machinery grows out of recent writings about "labeling" factors. Many commentators are now suggesting that the contact with control agencies and the acquisition of the "delinquent" or "criminal" label is a critical contingency which pushes a number of violators in the direction of repetitive involvement in misbehavior. Those deviants who become publicly identified as "delinquents," or "hoods," find that they are indelibly labeled and stigmatized. In turn, they find avoidance of further deviance to be extremely difficult because other per-

---

[1] A detailed and illuminating statement can be found in Aaron V. Cicourel, *The Social Organization of Juvenile Justice* (New York: John Wiley & Sons, Inc., 1968). Cicourel deals at length with the processes through which the police officers, probation agents, and others arrive at conclusions that juveniles exhibit "defiance of authority," "wrong attitudes," and the like. His analysis also casts considerable doubt upon the use of official records as accurate statements of "what happened" relative to juvenile incidents.

sons continue to respond to them in terms of the stigmatizing label. Those who elude this labeling experience are thought to be less likely to become committed to chronic deviance.[2] Although this hypothesis sounds plausible, hard evidence cannot be easily identified; a firm judgment about its validity must be held in abeyance.[3] A first step in the assessment of the consequences of social labeling can, however, be made by investigation of agency handling of delinquents.

THE OFFENDER AND THE POLICE[4]

Chapter Two observed that the police have a great number of contacts with juveniles which do not result in court referral and that these episodes far outnumber the instances in which the police do decide to take a youth to the court. Some further indication of the magnitude of police work with juveniles has been provided by Bordua,[5] who reported that, in 1964, the Detroit police enumerated 106,000 "encounters" with youngsters. The Youth Bureau of that department conducted "interviews" with 23,645 suspected offenders and also talked to 10,157 other youths for the purpose of gathering evidence. The police termed 9,445 of these contacts, involving only 5,282 juveniles, as "official contacts." The discretionary role of the policeman is well captured by these statistics.

The task then becomes one of ferreting out clues to the social dimensions which lie behind figures of these police decisions. On what basis do policeman decide to ignore cases of misbehavior? How do they decide that some juvenile offenders should be directed to juvenile court? What part does the nature of the offense play in police decisions? What can be said about those common sense hypotheses which suggest that the police are influenced by such things as the social status of youthful lawbreakers?

---

[2] An excellent review of this development, along with the critique of the position, can be found in David J. Bordua, "Recent Trends: Deviant Behavior and Social Control," *Annals of the American Academy of Political and Social Science,* CCCLIX (January 1967), 149–63.

[3] A discussion of this view, along with presentation of scraps of evidence bearing upon it, appears in Don C. Gibbons, *Changing the Lawbreaker* (Englewood Cliffs, N.J.: Prentice-Hall, Inc., 1965), pp. 57–61; Gibbons, *Society, Crime, and Criminal Careers* (Englewood Cliffs, N.J.: Prentice-Hall, Inc., 1968), pp. 236–40.

[4] A general discussion of sociological aspects of police organizations and operations is contained in Gibbons, *Society, Crime, and Criminal Careers,* pp. 47–70. A useful description of juvenile procedures in one police department can be found in Thorsten Sellin and Marvin E. Wolfgang, *The Measurement of Delinquency* (New York: John Wiley & Sons, Inc., 1964), pp. 87–113.

[5] Bordua, "Recent Trends," p. 161.

Bordua suggests that two approaches ought to be taken to the study of police decision making.[6] He points out that police behavior should be examined microscopically, in order to identify the characteristics of offenders to which the police attend in their actions. This kind of study would probe into the influence of factors such as seriousness of offenses, economic status, and racial background in police dispositions. But, in addition, a comparative and historical perspective on police activities is also needed. Perhaps police departments vary as a whole in terms of policies for disposition of offenders. Particular police agencies may also exhibit changes in policies over time which influence their dispositional activities.[7]

Offender Characteristics and Police Decisions

A variety of evidence can be assembled in order to clarify the activities of law enforcement personnel in the area of juvenile decisions. Thus studies by Lyle Shannon[8] and by Charles Guthrie[9] contain material tangential to this subject. Shannon's investigation provided indirect evidence that socioeconomic status of offenders was not a determinant of police disposition of their cases.

One of the best-known pieces of research on police dispositions was done by Nathan Goldman.[10] The study, carried out in 1950 in Allegheny County, Pennsylvania, examined a small mill town, an industrial center, a trade center, and an upper-class residential area. The findings indicated that 64 percent of the youths apprehended by the police were handled without court referral. The police sent 91 percent of the auto thieves to court, while they reported only 11 percent of the mischief cases. A major differential in the reporting practices of the police was that 65 percent of the Negro offenders were referred to court, but only 34 percent of the white juveniles

6 *Ibid.*, pp. 159–61.

7 A brief survey of data on police decision making can be found in the President's Commission on Law Enforcement and Administration of Justice, *Task Force Report: Juvenile Delinquency and Youth Crime* (Washington, D.C.: U.S. Government Printing Office, 1967), pp. 12–14.

8 Lyle W. Shannon, "Types and Patterns of Delinquency Referral in a Middle-Sized City," *British Journal of Criminology*, III (July 1963), 24–36.

9 Charles R. Guthrie, *Law Enforcement and the Juvenile: A Study of Police Interaction with Delinquents,* (unpublished Ph. D. dissertation: University of Southern California, 1963).

10 Nathan Goldman, *The Differential Selection of Juvenile Offenders for Court Appearance* (New York: National Council on Crime and Delinquency, 1963).

were so handled.[11] The matter of differentials in the handling of racial groups, however, is complex; in serious offenses the referral rate was about the same for white and Negro youths. However, Negroes apprehended for minor delinquencies were much more frequently taken to juvenile court than were their white counterparts.

Goldman's results included the observation that sex did not seem to influence the decision for court referral, but that age did; referrals increased with the age of offenders.[12] Somewhat surprisingly, the upper-class residential area had the highest arrest rate of the four communities. But the communities with the lowest arrest rates, the trade center and the industrial center, had the highest proportion of serious offense arrests. The kind of complaints leading to juvenile arrests in the upper-class area and the mill town were usually ignored by people and police in "Trade City" and "Steel City." In short, the police in the latter communities apparently had more serious criminal activities to contend with than juvenile peccadilloes.[13]

Goldman also interviewed police regarding the factors conditioning their decisions about juvenile offenders. The officers exhibited a good deal of variability in the criteria employed, but several factors seemed to loom large in their decisions. They were strongly influenced by the seriousness of the offenses. They were also affected by their views of the juvenile court; those who thought the court had deleterious effects upon youths referred few of them to it. The officers also placed a good deal of emphasis on the demeanor of the juveniles; those who were surly or defiant were more likely to be referred than those youngsters who were polite or contrite.[14]

Another study of police screening of juveniles was conducted by Robert Terry in Racine, Wisconsin, a community with a population of about 100,000.[15] The research dealt with the 9,023 offenses known to the police department's Juvenile Bureau in that community over the five year period from 1958 to 1962. Of the 9,023 offenses, only 755 were referred to the probation department and only 246 of these resulted in a court hearing. It would appear from these figures that delinquency in this community was fairly innocuous, and also that the police department must have had a major policy of handling juvenile offenders internally.

---

[11] *Ibid.*, pp. 35–47.

[12] *Ibid.*, pp. 44–47.

[13] *Ibid.*, pp. 48–92.

[14] *Ibid.*, pp. 93–124.

[15] Robert M. Terry, "Discrimination in the Handling of Juvenile Offenders by Social Control Agencies," *Journal of Research in Crime and Delinquency,* IV (July 1967), 218–30.

Terry found that the police did respond differentially to the delinquents they encountered. Although they released different proportions of the boys and the girls they contacted, this was not a matter of sex discrimination. The males who were referred were involved in serious and repetitive misconduct, while this kind of activity was less frequent among girls.[16] Mexican-American youngsters were more frequently referred to court than were other youths, but, again, this was a function of the kind and severity of the offenses committed. Terry discovered that relationships between economic status of offenders and the dispositions made of them by the police or court authorities were slight or nonexistent. Once more, those relationships which were noted were attributable to variations in the seriousness and repetitiveness of offenses.[17] Terry's general conclusion from his research was that "while males, Mexican-Americans, Negroes, and lower-status offenders are over-represented in correctional institutions, probation departments, courts, and police records, this over-representation does not, on the basis of the evidence examined in this study, appear to be a *direct* result of these characteristics. The over-representation of these individuals is not the result of discrimination by control agencies."[18]

A third investigation of police work with juveniles was carried out by George Bodine in Syracuse, New York.[19] He found that the picture of police intervention was complex. He began with the fact that of juvenile offenders known to the police, low-income area youths were disproportionately referred to juvenile court. After a fairly complex multivariate analysis, his findings were: (1) police dispositions were related to the arrest histories of offenders, so that recidivists were most likely to be referred, (2) arrest histories were related to income, in that recidivists were most frequently from lower-income neighborhoods, and (3) low income area juveniles were disproportionately involved in high referral offenses such as theft. Bodine also observed that (4) age was not a factor in dispositions when arrest history and offense type were taken into account, and (5) no evidence supported the concept that variations in referral rates between income areas were related to race.

Still another study of police dispositions was carried out in the Los Angeles area by A. McEachern and Riva Bauzer.[20] They examined a

---

[16] *Ibid.*, pp. 224–26.

[17] *Ibid.*, pp. 226–28.

[18] *Ibid.*, p. 229. Emphasis added.

[19] George E. Bodine, "Factors Related to Police Dispositions of Juvenile Offenders," paper read at the American Sociological Association annual meeting, Montreal, Canada, August 31, 1964.

[20] A. W. McEachern and Riva Bauzer, "Factors Related to Disposition in

random sample of 1,010 juvenile arrests from the Los Angeles County Sheriff's Department, as well as the records of juvenile-police contacts in Santa Monica from 1940 to 1960. These investigators found that offense seriousness, length of previous record, ethnicity, sex, age, family stability, and probation status were all related to police dispositions. There were important interrelations between these factors, so that when offense was held constant, the influence of family intactness, ethnic status, and sex declined, as did the role of previous record and probation status, but age remained an important consideration in referral decisions.

These four studies add up to a picture of the police operating in a "legalistic" fashion, rather than in terms of prejudices and biases of one kind or another.[21] Apparently the police are more impressed by the nature and seriousness of offenses than by any other factors. The major route to the juvenile court appears to be heavily traveled by those juveniles who are most persistently involved in lawbreaking. The four investigations certainly do not provide much factual underpinning for claims that the principal determinants of police action center about such things as economic status or racial characteristics.

However, there may be more to the picture than has been indicated. The results which we have examined thus far have been drawn from records of various kinds. They seem to show that demographic characteristics of offenders are related to police disposition, but this is because seriousness of offense is correlated with background characteristics. At the same time, we might find that more subtle social factors operate in police decision-making if we were to examine particular instances of officer-offender interaction.

Offender-Police Interaction

One indication that factors additional to the offense enter into police actions was contained in the Goldman study; he found that officers said they were influenced by the demeanor of juveniles.[22] Bordua suggested the same thing in his report on the Detroit police Youth Bureau officers who fill out a section on their report form entitled "Attitude Toward Officer."[23] These officers filed petitions against juveniles in 67 per-

---

Juvenile Police Contacts," in Malcolm W. Klein, ed., *Juvenile Gangs in Context* (Englewood Cliffs, N.J.: Prentice-Hall, Inc., 1967), pp. 148–60.

[21] This conclusion is the same as the one reached by Bordua. See Bordua, "Recent Trends," pp. 158–59.

[22] Goldman, *Differential Selection*, pp. 93–124.

[23] Bordua, "Recent Trends," p. 159. These figures are for court petitions filed

cent of the cases of those identified as showing "honest" attitudes, in 70 percent of the "responsive" cases, in 78 percent of the "evasive" cases, and 80 percent of the "antisocial" attitude cases.

Sellin and Wolfgang have also reported that a number of factors enter into police decisions. They asserted that the police they studied in Philadelphia based their dispositional decisions on a number of factors, including (1) the prior record of the youth, (2) the type of offense and the role of the juvenile in it, (3) the attitude of the victim or complainant, and (4) the family situation of the offender. Other considerations included: (5) the potential community resources which might be utilized for correction, (6) the general appearance and attitude of the offender toward the police, (7) the possible overcrowding at the Youth Study Center, and (8) the police officer's anticipation of juvenile court action should an arrest be made.[24]

Irving Piliavin and Scott Briar have contributed one of the most detailed studies of offender-police interaction.[25] Their report is based on field notes of juvenile encounters with Juvenile Bureau officers over a nine month period in a city with a population of 450,000. These officers deal both with juveniles whom they observe near the scene of reported offenses and with youths whom they detect in acts of misbehavior. They have a number of dispositions available to them: they can release the juvenile outright, reprimand him, cite him to the juvenile court, or arrest him and have him confined in the juvenile hall.

According to Piliavin and Briar, discretion in the handling of juveniles was widely used in this department for most offenses. Many of the officers felt that the juvenile court failed to rehabilitate offenders, so that they were reluctant to turn youths over to it. In addition, discretionary handling and the concept that justice for juveniles should be individualized were departmental policy.

The police in this study dealt with various kinds of misbehavior. The 10 percent of it that was serious in nature was handled uniformly: referral to the court. The nature of the misbehavior was the sole determinant of police action in these cases. But in the remainder of the instances, which involved minor delinquencies and a few serious ones, police decisions tended to be influenced by personal characteristics of the youths rather than by their offenses. The police arrived at characterological assessments of the boys, defining some as "good boys" and

against youths handled as "official contacts." The reader will recall that most police encounters with juveniles are handled informally and do not become official contacts.

[24] Sellin and Wolfgang, *The Measurement of Delinquency*, pp. 95–100.

[25] Irving Piliavin and Scott Briar, "Police Encounters with Juveniles," *American Journal of Sociology*, LXX (September 1964), 206–14.

others as "bad ones," and their decisions followed these assessments. These characterological judgments were made on the spot and were based on scanty information, so that they usually emerged from the immediate interaction between the boy and the officer. Those youths who were identified as "bad guys" were often older boys, Negroes, and youths with greasy hair, black jackets, and dirty Levi's. The conclusion that a juvenile was a "bad boy" who deserved court attention was frequently based upon his failure to display the deference which the policeman felt to be his due.[26]

Piliavin and Briar noted that Negro youths were often stopped by the police and given relatively severe dispositions because they often showed a hostile demeanor toward the police. But it was also noted that the police concentrate much of their attention in urban ghettoes, where they indiscriminately harass citizens. This activity on the part of the police probably has much to do with the hostility demonstrated toward them by delinquent suspects.[27] Thus the vicious circle continues: police harassment of "suspicious" Negro youths leads these youngsters to see police contacts as a routine, taken-for-granted aspect of their lives. In turn, they respond in a hostile or indifferent manner to the police, who then feel little compunction about referring them to court in large numbers. The high arrest and referral rate for Negro youths is then taken by the police as evidence in support of the stereotype of most Negroes as potential criminals.[28]

Additional light is thrown upon the matter of police-juvenile interaction in an essay by Werthman and Piliavin.[29] They present a rich source of descriptive and analytical material showing the nature of police-Negro gang member interaction. Their general premise is that the social perspectives of gang boys are very different from those of the police. The delinquents view neighborhood streets as their "turf" or home, but the police do not honor this perception. The boys regard the police as enemies who enforce laws produced and supported by the power structure of the community. These laws are seen as attempts to suppress minority group members and to perpetuate pat-

---

26 *Ibid.*, pp. 209–13.

27 *Ibid.*, pp. 212–13.

28 Somewhat similar findings to those of Piliavin and Briar are reported in George W. Mitchell, *Youth Bureau: A Sociological Study* (unpublished M.A. thesis, Wayne State University, 1958).

29 Carl Werthman and Irving Piliavin, "Gang Members and The Police," in David J. Bordua, ed., *The Police* (New York: John Wiley & Sons, Inc., 1967), pp. 56–98. A briefer version of their argument can be found in Werthman, "The Function of Social Definitions in the Development of Delinquent Careers," in The President's Commission on Law Enforcement and Administration of Justice, *Juvenile Delinquency*, pp. 166–69.

terns of discrimination. The police regard all residents of the black community as "suspicious" persons.[30] The Negro targets of these police opinions are outraged by being perpetually viewed as criminals or incipient wrongdoers.

Delinquent boys in urban ghettoes employ a number of stratagems to avoid contact with the police; for example, they disperse into smaller units when the police approach, position themselves near girls, wear their club jackets inside out to hide identifying marks, or wear wedding rings so that the police will assume they are married.[31] However, these tactics often fail, so that these youngsters are drawn into encounters with the police. When this happens, the juveniles are prone to display hostility and scorn toward the police, due to their perspectives on the role of law enforcement in the furtherance of discrimination. This interaction produces high rates of arrest and court referral.[32]

Police Organization and Juvenile Dispositions

What about interorganizational variations among police departments? What can be said about changes in departmental policies relating to the handling of juvenile offenders? Several pieces of evidence at hand bear upon questions of this sort. For one, McEachern and Bauzer observed that the Santa Monica police referred to court about 20 percent of the delinquency cases they handled during the years 1940 to 1944; between 1955 and 1960, however, referrals made up over 40 percent of the youths known to the police.[33] Similarly, Bordua noted that the Detroit police referral rate changed markedly between 1951 and 1964.[34] He also presented F.B.I. data for over 2,000 police agencies

[30] Another instance of the police view of "suspicious" persons can be found in Egon Bittner, "The Police on Skid-Row," *American Sociological Review,* XXXII (October 1967), 699–715.

[31] Werthman and Piliavin, "Gang Members and the Police," pp. 83–85.

[32] One other study of police actions toward juveniles which is tangential to the discussion here is William Wattenberg and Noel Bufe, "The Effectiveness of Police Youth Bureau Officers," *Journal of Criminal Law, Criminology and Police Science,* LIV (December 1963), 470–75. They studied delinquent boys, some of whom had become repeaters while the others had not, and also the police officers who had handled them. They wished to identify officers who had been effective or ineffective in their dealings with juveniles. The successful officers had a prominent interest in juveniles, were thorough in their work, were firm in approach, and were neat and clean.

[33] McEachern and Bauzer, "Factors Related to Disposition in Juvenile Police Contacts," pp. 151–52.

[34] Bordua, "Recent Trends," p. 159.

in 1965, showing that 385 of them released less than 5 percent of the juveniles they contacted, sixty agencies turned loose more than 95 percent of the youngsters they encountered, and at least fifty police agencies were found in all of the 5 percent intervals between these extremes, proving that referral rates are extremely varied throughout the nation.[35] Presumably, these rates are the product of variations in the seriousness of delinquency in communities, differences in police policies regarding disposition of cases, differences in the availability of community resources for the handling of youthful lawbreakers, and other factors of this sort.

Wilson conducted the most detailed study of interorganizational variations among police agencies, dealing with "Eastern City" and "Western City," both of which had a population of substantially more than 300,000.[36] Both communities were free from political machine domination. However, their police departments differed; "Western City" had a "professionalized" department, while "Eastern City" showed a "fraternal" law enforcement agency. The "Western City" professional department recruited impartially, practiced consistent enforcement of the law, was not frequented by graft, and was structured in a formal, bureaucratic fashion. In short, it hewed closely to the model of the modern, professional police force. "Eastern City" had a department which recruited entirely from among local residents, practiced differential law enforcement, showed considerable graft, and commonly had informal and fraternal relations in its operation.[37]

The juvenile bureaus of these two police departments showed a number of points of difference. In "Eastern City," the police were moralistic in their outlook, holding that delinquents were the product of faulty personal or family morality. They verbalized restrictive and punitive attitudes toward offenders. In "Western City," on the other hand, the officers were less moralistic and more therapeutic in their opinions. They tended to seek the causes of delinquency in conditions of general social pathology.[38]

What effect do these perspectives have on the handling of delinquent referrals? The effect is the opposite of what one might suspect. The police department of "Western City" processed a larger proportion of its city's juvenile population than did "Eastern City." More-

35 *Ibid.*, p. 160.
36 James Q. Wilson, "The Police and the Delinquent in Two Cities," in Stanton Wheeler, ed., *Controlling Delinquents* (New York: John Wiley & Sons, Inc., 1968), pp. 9–30.
37 *Ibid.*, pp. 10–14.
38 *Ibid.*, pp. 14–19.

over, a larger share of those contacted were arrested in "Western City" than in the other community. These differences were not negligible either; the rate of juveniles contacted or arrested was several times higher in the western city than in the other community.[39] These anomalous results seem to indicate that the police who react most severely toward juveniles are the ones who verbalize nonpunitive and less moralistic views of offenders, while those who speak harshly about lawbreakers are the ones who handle them informally outside the framework of the juvenile court.

Several factors explain these variations between these two cities. There were structural and procedural differences in the two communities. In "Eastern City" the police officer who initially handled the juvenile was obliged to prepare the case and present it to the court; in "Western City" the case was turned over to a probation agent. The opportunity to avoid extra work was an incentive to dealing informally with offenders in "Eastern City."

Wilson also argued that the professional orientation of "Western City" department exerted pressure on officers to take formal action in juvenile cases, while in the fraternal department no such organizational ethos existed. Then, too, the western city had a centralized police department and juvenile bureau, while the eastern city's department and bureau were organized on a precinct station basis. The centralized and bureaucratic pattern of "Western City" led to uniform application of general rules of procedure, consistent enforcement of the law, and routine maintenance of formal records, all of which contribute to the juvenile policies of the department.

Police work in "Eastern City" was conducted quite differently. The use of personal judgment was stressed in the organization. Police officers had greater loyalties to the local neighborhoods, for many of them had lived in the precinct in which they now worked. These policemen engaged in personalized enforcement of the law, which, in the case of juveniles, meant that they turned few of them over to the court.[40]

One final topic of Wilson's study concerned police dealings with Negroes. The "Eastern City" officers had no particularized experience with Negroes, so that they tended to perceive them in a stereotyped manner. Most Negroes were viewed as "suspicious" persons and as individuals from pathological families. Their dealings with Negroes were conditioned by these perspectives. In contrast, the "Western City" officers tended to be more professional and impersonal in their interaction with Negroes.[41]

[39] *Ibid.*, pp. 14–19.

[40] *Ibid.*, pp. 19–27.

[41] *Ibid.*, pp. 26-27. The reader will note the parallel between this observation

Concluding Remarks

The mass of material considered to this point leads to a set of basic conclusions about police interaction with juvenile offenders. These generalizations are:

1. Police officers deal with large numbers of juveniles, most of whom they handle informally without court referral. The decision to take a youngster to the court is often in part a legalistic one. Those offenders who have been engaged in serious or repetitive acts of lawbreaking are most likely to be turned over to the court.

2. Police dispositions tend to be related to demographic characteristics of offenders, such that males, Negroes, lower-income youths, and older boys are most frequently dealt with formally by court referral. These demographic characteristics enter into dispositions in part because males, older boys, Negroes, and lower income youngsters appear to be disproportionately involved in serious, repetitive delinquencies.

3. Police perspectives which hold that some groups, such as ghetto Negroes or other lower-class minorities, are particularly criminalistic probably lead to differential attention directed at them. Serious offenses by members of these groups then have a higher likelihood of being observed by the police and being acted upon. If so, the higher official crime and delinquency rates of these groups may be partially the product of police sentiments, rather than a reflection solely of basic differentials in propensities toward crime.

4. In those instances of less serious delinquency, police officers often base their disposition decisions upon the demeanor of the offender. Youths who affect particular clothing styles or who are defiant and hostile tend to be referred more often than polite and contrite youngsters are. It is probably also true that demeanor bears some relationship to seriousness of offense, such that those youths who have engaged in the most innocuous offenses also are most deferential toward policemen. This may explain why police dispositions show a general association with seriousness of misconduct.

5. Police departments show variations in organizational structure over time. Differences in organizational makeup between police agencies also exist. Accordingly, police dispositions of offenders, including juveniles, are far from uniform throughout the country.

The police represent one of the two most critical units within the juvenile justice machinery, for they screen youths into or out of the juvenile court, which is the second major component of this social apparatus. In order to comprehend the activities of this structure, we

and those of Piliavin and Briar, "Police Encounters with Juveniles"; Werthman and Piliavin, "Gang Members and the Police."

must note both the origins of the court as a social institution and the recent criticisms of its operations.

THE JUVENILE COURT AS A SOCIAL INSTITUTION

A vast amount of literature has been written about the juvenile court. The President's Commission on Law Enforcement and Administration of Justice produced a Task Force Report in 1967 which drew a large amount of this material together; our remarks have been heavily drawn from that publication.[42] However, the reader is urged to examine the entire report, for it discusses many of our points in greater detail than is possible here.

Development of the Juvenile Court

We have already mentioned that the juvenile court emerged out of the English chancery courts of the feudal period, and that the doctrine of *parens patriae* was used to justify the juvenile court, the humanitarian movement in this country in the nineteenth century which led to the Juvenile Court Act of 1899 in Illinois, and the protective and treatment philosophy which was the foundation of the court from its first beginnings.

The President's Commission discussion further pointed out that the first juvenile court law in Illinois brought under one jurisdiction the cases of dependency, neglect, and delinquency (including incorrigibles and children thought to be threatened by immoral associations). This legislation also created a new vocabulary in which juvenile courts employed petitions instead of complaints, initial hearings in place of arraignment, adjudication of involvement in delinquency instead of conviction, and disposition rather than sentence. Courts were also supposed to be informal and solicitous of the juvenile's well-being. Lawyers, transcripts, and other trappings of adult courts were thought to be unnecessary or even harmful, for the court would protect the child. These tribunals were intended to operate in a clinical and therapeutic fashion; misbehaving youngsters were to be investigated, diagnosed, and treated, rather than punished, as in adult courts.

The juvenile court notion took root quickly and by 1925 these tribunals were established in nearly all the states. At the present time,

---

[42] The President's Commission on Law Enforcement and Administration of Justice, *Juvenile Delinquency*, pp. 1–40.

there is a juvenile court act in every American jurisdiction, with approximately 2,700 courts hearing children's cases. But the commission report also made it clear that juvenile courts vary markedly from one place to another in the United States.

Juvenile Courts in Operation

Those courts dealing with youth problems are articulated with the other tribunals in specific sections of the country in a number of different ways. In some the juvenile court is a part of the circuit, district, superior, or municipal court, while in a few jurisdictions separate family courts have been established to deal with youngsters.

The age limits delimiting youth court control are not uniform from one area to another. About two-thirds of the juvenile courts in this country have an upper age limit of eighteen, while in the remaining one-third of the courts, the age limit is sixteen, seventeen, or twenty-one. Often the age limit is different between boys and girls.

The majority of states provide for waiver or transfer of youths to adult courts if they are thought to be unsuitable subjects for juvenile handling. However, the conditions which govern the exercise of this option vary from state to state. In addition, written criteria to guide the judges in deciding whether or not to waive a youth to the criminal court are rare. Most frequently, when criteria are stated, they are in terms such as "not amenable to treatment in juvenile court." Many states require no waiver hearing or legal protection for the accused youths. However, the Supreme Court decision in *Kent v. United States* held that juveniles are entitled to a hearing, assistance of counsel, access to records, and a statement of the reasons for the judge's decision to waive.

Most juvenile court statutes fail to provide detailed procedural directions for the operation of the court machinery. Many laws do state that when a complaint is received from the police, parents, social agencies, or some other source, a preliminary inquiry will be made to determine whether court action is required. In many larger metropolitan areas, this activity is conducted by a probation department intake division presided over by one or more probation officers who dispose of about half of the referrals at intake, without taking further formal action. The intake officer also determines whether juvenile referrals should be detained in the juvenile hall or other detention facility pending court action. Standards for detention vary from one location to another, as does the quality of the facilities for holding juveniles.

If a petition alleging delinquency is filed, the juvenile then appears before the judge for a hearing. Because the court is supposed to be informal and noncombative in nature, rules of evidence are often relaxed, and hearsay and unsworn testimony are introduced. The standard of proof required in order to reach a finding of delinquency is markedly lower than the standard of proof required by the criminal court. Approximately two-thirds of the states have no statutory provision for the right of counsel. Accordingly, most accused juveniles are without legal representation. These informal proceedings usually take place privately and bar reporters and persons without specific interest in them.

In some jurisdictions a disposition hearing is conducted separately from the adjudication proceeding, but in many it is held at the same time as the hearing on the question of delinquency involvement. The social history document prepared by the probation officer to whom the case was assigned looms large in the disposition of the case. This report inquires into the social background of the juvenile and includes "information" and "data," some of which is of indeterminate accuracy. The social history is supposed to be a guide to disposition of the case, but in many courts the report is given to the judge prior to the adjudication hearing.

Juvenile court judges usually have broad discretion regarding disposition of cases; they dismiss the offender, or warn, fine, place him on probation, or send him to a private or public institution.

An Assessment of the Juvenile Court Today

The President's Commission Task Force Report made it abundantly clear that the great hopes originally held for the juvenile court have not been fulfilled. The court stands as an instance of malfunctioning social machinery, even though it was contrived by men motivated by the best of intentions. The list of problems which plague contemporary courts is lengthy.

Juvenile court judges often fall short of the ideal, for they are frequently both inadequately trained and overworked. A recent survey sponsored by the National Council of Juvenile Court Judges of 1560 juvenile court judges threw considerable light upon the characteristics and work styles of these persons.[43] Almost all of these individuals

---

[43] Shirley D. McCune and Daniel L. Skoler, "Juvenile Court Judges in the United States. Part I: A National Profile," *Crime and Delinquency*, XI (April 1965), 121–31.

were males; their average age was 53; nearly all were married; and 71 percent had received law degrees. However, 49 percent of these judges had not received BA degrees, and 24 percent were without legal training. The legal experience prior to assuming a judgeship averaged nine years. Of the full-time judges in the group, 72 percent spent a quarter or less of their time on juvenile matters. Accordingly, the juvenile position was viewed as a minor part of the magistrate's responsibilities in most of the jurisdictions.

The judges in the study showed wide variations in salary, but most were underpaid. The average salary for full-time judges was $12,493, which was less than that for judges of trial courts of general jurisdiction or lawyers in private practice. Not only were many of the judges underpaid, they were also undersupplied with resources. About one-third of them reported that they had no probation officers or social workers to assist them. But although these judges appeared to be undertrained in some cases and underpaid in others, a companion study of juvenile judges did indicate that, compared to police officers and nonjuvenile court judges, the former were more social service oriented and less punitive in posture.[44]

Another problem with the juvenile court centers about the probation officer staff. Juvenile probation is provided for by law in every state; thirty-one states have probation services in each county. But in the 164 counties in four states, no juvenile probation exists. Juvenile probation is administered under a variety of different arrangements within the states, and many jurisdictions fail to provide merit or civil service coverage to employees. In the majority of probation services, salaries are inadequate and caseloads are too high.

Other court resources are also lacking. Statements of juvenile court standards usually suggest that psychiatric services should be a part of the court. The Task Force Report indicated that these clinical services have rarely been provided. Then, too, foster homes and group homes rarely exist. Third, the dispositional alternatives available to the court fall short of the richness and relevance to individual needs envisioned by the court's founders.

The problems of the juvenile court run deeper than just personnel and resources. In the words of the Task Force Report:

> In theory the court's operations could justifiably be informal, its findings and decisions made without observing ordinary procedural

---

[44] Regis H. Walther and Shirley D. McCune, "Juvenile Court Judges in the United States. Part II: Working Styles and Characteristics," *Crime and Delinquency*, XI (October 1965), 384–93; see also Stanton Wheeler, Edna Bonacich, M. Richard Cramer, and Irving K. Zola, "Agents of Delinquency Control: A Comparative Analysis," in Wheeler, *Controlling Delinquents*, pp. 31–60.

safeguards, because it would act only in the best interest of the child. In fact it frequently does nothing more nor less than deprive a child of liberty without due process of law—knowing not what else to do and needing, whether admittedly or not, to act in the community's interest even more imperatively than the child's. In theory it was to exercise its protective powers to bring an errant child back into the fold. In fact there is increasing reason to believe that its intervention reinforces the juvenile's unlawful impulses. In theory it was to concentrate on each case the best of current social science learning. In fact it has often become a vested interest in its turn, loathe to cooperate with innovative programs or avail itself of forward-looking methods.[45]

This passage expressed the growing pessimism in recent decades with the court. The commission did not recommend the jettisoning of the court, but it did suggest that more juveniles should be dealt with by pre-judicial dispositions so that they are kept out of the court machinery. The commission also suggested that procedures designed to assure fair and reliable determinations should be infused into the court. In short, the commission came out forcefully for a return to a legalistic concern for due process and the rights of the child.

Procedural Justice for Juveniles

Much of the commentary and criticism of juvenile courts during the first several decades of their existence centered upon their failure to become anything more than legalistic tribunals which were juvenile courts only in that they handled juveniles. In the initial flush of enthusiasm for the juvenile court idea, few voices were heard raising questions about the possible negative effects the court might have upon some of the persons who were processed by it. Little concern was expressed that its informal procedures might run roughshod over the rights of the individual. Those constitutional challenges which were raised concerning the court's inattention to due process were ignored. The commission report cited an opinion of the Pennsylvania Supreme Court of 1905 as a case in point, wherein that tribunal held that youths in juvenile courts have no rights of due process because they are not charged with crimes and the court is operating for their welfare and benefit. More recently, in the case *in re Holmes* in 1955, the Supreme Court ruled that since juvenile courts are not criminal courts, the constitutional rights accorded to accused adults do not apply to juveniles.[46]

[45] The President's Commission on Law Enforcement and Administration of Justice, *Juvenile Delinquency*, p. 9.
[46] Paul W. Tappan, *Crime, Justice and Correction* (New York: McGraw-Hill

However, in the years since World War II, there has been a growing reaction, termed by one juvenile court judge as a "legal renaissance." The voices of a number of scholarly critics have been raised against the potential unfairness and arbitrariness of juvenile court procedures which fail to attend to requirements of due process.[47] Legislative studies in a variety of states have come to the same conclusion, namely that juvenile court laws have failed to provide sufficient legal safeguards for the accused juvenile. A number of states, including New York and California, have revised or amended delinquency statutes in a legalistic direction, laying down firm guidelines for court proceedings and due process. As we noted, the Supreme Court ruled in 1966 in *Kent v. United States* that juveniles are entitled to a hearing, legal representation, and other rights in the instance of waiver to a criminal court.

The commission report presented a strong case for legal counsel for juveniles,[48] for the use of legally admissable evidence in adjudication stages of court appearance, for bifurcation of adjudication and disposition portions of court hearings, and for reforms in the areas of notice of charges, detention, and confidentiality of court records. Finally, the Supreme Court held in *In re Gault* in 1967 that juveniles are entitled to formal notice of the charges against them, the right of legal counsel, the right of confrontation and cross-examination of witnesses, the privilege of protection against self-incrimination, the right to a transcript of proceedings, and the right of appeal.[49] In short, the Gault case is a far-reaching one, for it promises to extend to juveniles most of the protections of due process now accorded to adults.

It would be a mistake to assume that court decisions or legislative changes will automatically and will quickly bring about reforms in the procedures of individual juvenile courts. These changes may be slow and halting as due process is gradually extended throughout the nation. An essay by sociologist Edwin M. Lemert in the Task Force Report is illuminating on this point.[50] He begins with some cogent criticisms of

---

Book Company, 1960), pp. 390–95.

[47] One excellent summary statement on these views, written by a juvenile court judge, is Orman W. Ketcham, "The Unfulfilled Promise of the Juvenile Court," *Crime and Delinquency*, VII (April 1961), 97–110.

[48] Several contributions to the argument about legal representation are Eugene E. Siler, Jr., "The Need for Defense Counsel in the Juvenile Court," *Crime and Delinquency*, XI (January 1965), 45–58; Margaret K. Rosenheim and Daniel L. Skoler, "The Lawyer's Role at Intake and Detention Stages of Juvenile Court Proceedings," *Crime and Delinquency*, XI (April 1965), 167–74.

[49] The Gault decision is presented in The President's Commission on Law Enforcement and Administration of Justice, *Juvenile Delinquency*, pp. 57–76.

[50] Edwin M. Lemert, "The Juvenile Court— Quest and Realities," in The President's Commission on Law Enforcement and Administration of Justice, *Juvenile Delinquency*, pp. 91–105.

that earlier view of the court which would have it endeavor to be a therapeutic substitute for the family on a mass scale:

> Neither the Spartan gymnasium, nor the Russian creches, nor the Israeli kibbutz nurseries, nor scientifically run children's homes have been found to successfully duplicate the sociopsychological mystique which nurtures children into stable adults. Explicit recognition of this might very well preface the juvenile court codes and statutes of the land. At the same time it would be well to delete entirely from such laws pious injunctions that "care, custody and discipline of children under the control of the juvenile court shall approximate that which they would receive from their parents" which taken literally becomes meaningless either as ideal or reality. Neither the modern state nor an harrassed juvenile court judge is a father; a halfway house is not a home; a reformatory cell is not a teenager's bedroom; a juvenile hall counselor is not a dutch uncle; and a cottage matron is not a mother. This does not mean that the people referred to should not be or are not kindly and dedicated, but rather that they are first and foremost members of organizations, enforcers of superimposed rules. Where conflicts arise between the interests of a youth and those of the organization to which these functionaries are bureaucratically responsible there is no pattern of action which can predict that they will observe an order of value satisfaction favorable to the youth's interest.[51]

Much of Lemert's commentary centers about the implementation of legislative changes that were made in California's juvenile court laws in 1961. It is well worth noting that the impetus for these changes in the direction of due process standards came not from judges and other persons within juvenile corrections, but instead from private attorneys, law school professors, a few judges, and other "outsiders." The legislative changes were resisted and contested by many juvenile court judges and probation officers in the state.

The 1961 revisions of California law made mandatory the practice of bifurcated hearings, with adjudication separated from the disposition stage of court processing. In the case of the adjudication hearing, determination of delinquency was supposed to be on the basis of a "preponderance of evidence legally admissible in the trial of criminal cases." However, Lemert found, in a 1965 survey of California juvenile court judges, that a majority of them (67 percent) were still reading the dispositional (social) report prior to the jurisdictional or adjudication portion of the hearing. The intent of the 1961 revisions was to prevent this practice because of the considerable amount of hearsay evidence contained in these reports.

The 1961 revisions also provided for legal counsel in juvenile cases.

---

[51] *Ibid.*, p. 92.

However, Lemert's research in California shows that while this legislation has increased the use of counsel, wide variations still exist in the utilization of lawyers for accused juveniles. In some counties attorneys appeared in court in three-fourths or more of the cases, while in some others lawyers were almost never found. In general, the utilization of attorneys in different counties was conditioned by such things as the existence of a public defender's office and the attitudes of the judges and probation officers in the county.

Lemert also indicated that the revisions in California state law in 1961 were made to insure that clear rules of evidence would be followed. However, the statement that adjudication shall be based on a preponderance of legally admissible evidence has not ruled out the introduction of hearsay evidence of various kinds. Lemert questioned the view that juvenile court judges are capable of culling through this sort of material in order to reach an equitable and reasonable judgment. For example, they may be as easily misled by unreliable and speculative diagnostic pronouncements of psychiatrists as are laymen.

We do not mean to suggest that the concern for due process ought to be lessened because procedural safeguards are sometimes difficult to implement. Quite the contrary, the findings of Lemert point to the need for continued scrutiny of courts and continued efforts at legislative modification of juvenile court law in the direction of ideal standards.

JUVENILE COURT DECISION MAKING

In those smaller jurisdictions presided over by ill-trained judges and characterized by meager resources in the way of probation officer personnel and dispositional alternatives, the actions of judges are probably fairly easily described. In all likelihood, one of two dispositions is made of cases. The juveniles are either dismissed by the court with an admonition or tongue-lashing, or else they are sent off to state custodial institutions. In larger jurisdictions, such as metropolitan areas or major counties, decision making is probably more complicated. In these courts, probation officers are employed in some number. These individuals prepare social reports and make dispositional recommendations which the judges usually follow.

It is unfortunate that an abundance of material dealing with decision making by probation officers is not at hand. The studies of these persons and their activities that are available are relatively few in number and in some cases are only tangentially related to decision-making processes. Nonetheless, it is possible to assemble a sketch of some of the dimensions of decision behavior from research evidence such as "time and motion" studies of probation workers.

Work Styles and Decision Making
of Probation Officers[52]

The remarks of Lloyd Ohlin, Herman Piven, and Donnell Pappenfort concerning the role-dilemmas of probation and parole officers offer some information on probation decision making.[53] They argue that probation and parole services traditionally have been assigned a number of not entirely compatible functions, so that the general public expects probationers to be punished, assisted, supervised, and treated all at the same time. Also, probation agents must contend with persistent suspicion and hostility directed at them and their charges by the police and other groups in the community. We might suppose that one agent response to this sort of pressure would be to send most of the serious delinquents off to training schools, in order to ward off community criticism of the agency as "soft" on offenders.

These three authors also indicate that probation departments vary in the kinds of workers they engage. Some agencies employ "punitive" officers who are untrained in social work and who view themselves as law enforcement officers. These agents strive to protect the community, so that they recommend institutional commitments and other harsh measures probably more frequently than do the other officers. Some probation organizations are staffed with "protective" agents who have sometimes had training in correction, who regard themselves as responsible for treatment, but vacillate back and forth between protecting the public and helping clients. Finally, a large number of "welfare workers" have entered probation settings in recent years. These persons are trained in social welfare theory and techniques and attempt to apply their training in probation work. They are soon confronted, however, with role problems stemming from the agency demand that they carry out various punitive measures which they perceive as alien to their social worker role iden-

[52] Sociological findings concerning probation and parole departments are discussed at greater length in Gibbons, *Society, Crime, and Criminal Careers*, pp. 484–91.

[53] Lloyd E. Ohlin, Herman Piven, and Donnell M. Pappenfort, "Major Dilemmas of the Social Worker in Probation and Parole," *N.P.P.A. Journal*, XI (July 1956), 211–25.

tity. Presumably, the welfare worker types would be more likely to recommend probation or other noninstitutional dispositions for offenders.

There are several "time and motion" studies of probation officers which tell something about decision making. In one, Gertrude Hengerer found that the officers she studied in several California probation departments spent most of their time writing reports, driving from one place to another, and doing similar other operations.[54] They had large case loads and little time to provide therapy to their wards. It therefore might be expected that these officers would have little interest in working with "hard core" delinquents on probation and would divert them to institutions. Lewis Diana has reported similar findings in an investigation in Allegheny County (Pittsburgh), Pennsylvania.[55] His research showed that the average number of contacts between probationers and probation officers was about five within a sixteen-month period, and that these were, for the most part, quite superficial; only about 14 percent of the wards received any sort of case work treatment. It appeared that these harried probation officers dealt with relatively minor cases of delinquency and disposed of the more serious ones by sending them to training schools.

Several studies give us more direct information on the factors that enter into probation decisions. An investigation by Lemert and Rosberg in Los Angeles County indicated that court-adjudicated Negroes and Mexican-Americans were less likely to be placed on probation than were whites, even when variables such as offense history were controlled.[56] On the other hand, Joseph Eaton and Kenneth Polk found bias against males in Los Angeles County; boys were disproportionately committed to institutions. However, they found no evidence of discriminatory dispositions in the case of ethnic group members.[57]

Shannon's research in Madison, Wisconsin, appeared to indicate that economic status of delinquents was not a factor in the dispositions made of them.[58] However, it should be noted that this city is smaller and quite different in structure from large, industrial, metropolitan

[54] Gertrude M. Hengerer, "Organizing Probation Services," *National Probation and Parole Association Yearbook, 1953* (New York: National Probation and Parole Association, 1954), pp. 45–59.

[55] Lewis Diana, "Is Casework in Probation Necessary?" *Focus*, XXXIV (January 1955), 1–8.

[56] Edwin M. Lemert and Judy Rosberg, "The Administration of Justice to Minority Groups in Los Angeles County," *University of California Publications in Culture and Society*, II (1948), 1–28.

[57] Joseph W. Eaton and Kenneth Polk, *Measuring Delinquency* (Pittsburgh: University of Pittsburgh Press, 1961).

[58] Shannon, "Types and Patterns of Delinquency Referral," pp. 24–36.

communities, in which other patterns of juvenile handling might pre-
vail. Robert Terry reported that in Racine, Wisconsin, probation dispositions were unrelated to ethnic status.[59] He did find that probation
decisions were influenced by the seriousness and repetitiveness of
misconduct, thus males were more harshly dealt with because they
were more deeply involved in delinquency. On the other hand, girls
who were retained for official handling by the court were more likely
to be institutionalized than were boys.[60] Don Gibbons and Manzer
Griswold reported the same pattern for boys and girls in Washington
State juvenile courts.[61]

In another inquiry which related to probation dispositions, Sidney
Axelrad was concerned with the 300 boys who had been committed
to the New York State Training School between 1933 and 1934.[62]
That study disclosed that Negro training school wards had been committed at a younger age, for less serious offenses, with fewer previous
court appearances, and with less prior institutionalization than was
true of whites. Axelrad attributed this differential to the greater incidence of unstable homes and other conditions of social disorganization
characteristic of the Negro wards. In other words, the Negro boys got
to the training school at an earlier age and for less serious delinquencies, not because of ethnic status per se, but because of the social
liabilities in their backgrounds.

A different kind of inquiry is contained in the work of Yona Cohn,[63]
who studied about 200 social investigations of delinquents in the
Bronx Children's Court in New York City in order to identify the
underlying criteria used by probation officers in recommending probation, institutionalization, psychiatric examination, or discharge. The
findings included: there were no significant differences in family
structure or socioeconomic status between wards who were placed on
probation and those who were held for psychiatric examination. Sexual delinquents, offenders thought to manifest personality difficulties,
and children involved in serious acts of misbehavior were rarely
placed on probation. The youngsters who were recommended for institutional commitment were less cooperative than the probation referrals. They were also from incomplete families and from low-income

[59] Terry, "Discrimination in The Handling of Juvenile Offenders," pp. 226–28.
[60] *Ibid.*, pp. 224–26.
[61] Don C. Gibbons and Manzer J. Griswold, "Sex Differences Among Juvenile
Court Referrals," *Sociology and Social Research*, XLII (November-December
1957), 106–10.
[62] Sidney Axelrad, "Negro and White Male Institutionalized Delinquents,"
American Journal of Sociology, LVII (May 1952), 569–74.
[63] Yona Cohn, "Criteria for the Probation Officer's Recommendation to the Juvenile Court," *Crime and Delinquency*, IX (July 1963), 262–75.

backgrounds. Girls and Negroes who were held for official action were more often sent to institutions than were white boys. The high incidence of sexual misconduct on the part of girls was responsible for their commitments, while Negroes were recommended for placement in a correctional institution due to the seriousness of their lawbreaking and their deprived backgrounds.

Still another study of probation decision making, done by Seymour Gross, had to do with seventy juvenile probation officers in Minnesota.[64] These persons were asked to indicate the factors they regarded as most important in their dispositional decisions. They responded that the offender's attitude toward his offense, his family background, and his delinquency history, in that order, loomed most important. The agents were also asked to identify the variables which they perceived as most important in the eyes of the judges. On the whole, the officers thought that judges assigned about the same weight to these factors. However, a subgroup of probation officers asserted that they were more influenced by less objective criteria, such as their estimate of the psychiatric status of the delinquent. The dissenting probation officers were the ones who read the greater number of professional journals, who had more pronounced casework orientations, and who were more similar to the "welfare workers" identified by Ohlin, Piven, and Pappenfort in their study.

Another investigation of this kind was made by Francesca Alexander, who asked a group of female probation officers to choose girls from their caseloads whom they thought had a good or poor prognosis for nondelinquent behavior.[65] She then endeavored to discover the characteristics which differentiated these two groups. Alexander indicated that delinquents regarded as having a favorable prognosis tended to be of better economic status than the poor prognosis cases and were more commonly Caucasian girls, while the poor prognosis delinquents were more often Negroes. The good prognosis cases were thought to be the products of situational causation, while girls judged to be poor risks were seen as emotionally troubled.[66]

[64] Seymour Z. Gross, "The Prehearing Juvenile Report: Probation Officers' Conceptions," *Journal of Research in Crime and Delinquency*, IV (July 1967), 212–17; see also Gross, "Biographical Characteristics of Juvenile Probation Officers," *Crime and Delinquency*, XII (April 1966), 109–16.

[65] Francesca Alexander, "A Preliminary Report on a Pilot Investigation of Some Social-Psychological Variables Influencing the Probation Officer," paper delivered at the Pacific Sociological Associations meetings, 1964.

[66] A speculative article which suggests that social class bias and lack of knowledge about subcultures, life styles, and the like by psychiatric workers in juvenile courts and similar situations may render their psychiatric diagnoses faulty is Carmi Harari and Jacob Chwast, "Class Bias in Psychodiagnosis of Delinquents," *Crime and Delinquency*, X (April 1964), 145–51.

We again arrive at the question: what does all this material show? What are we to conclude from these studies of probation dispositions? The main thread throughout almost all of these investigations relates to the role of offense behavior in dispositions. Youths who have been involved in offenses which arouse members of the community, who commit law violations which result in sizable financial suffering to the victims, and who are repeaters, are the ones who most often get placed on the transmission belt to the training school. Ethnic characteristics, sex, age, and other demographic variables seem to be related to dispositions through their interconnection with offense variations. Thus many girls are sent to institutions because they offend members of the community by displays of sexual promiscuity and other "wild" behavior.

Other factors play a part in probation dispositions, but their role is less easily assessed. Apparently, in some agencies probation officers are attuned to the personality characteristics of wards, so that their decisions are based in part on this consideration. It also appears as though ethnic factors enter more directly into dispositions in some cases, so that, on occasion, minority group members are dealt with more severely than is warranted on the basis of their deviant conduct or social backgrounds. Quite probably, dispositional activities of probation agencies are somewhat different in communities of markedly unequal size. Dispositional variations probably characterize departments that are staffed with probation officers of different calibers as well. What all this means is that more comparative and detailed research is required before firm generalizations about probation dispositions can be advanced.

SUMMARY

Chapter Two concerned the complex questions of delinquency statistics, rates, and patterns, while the present chapter had to do with the operations of the police and courts as they generate the cases which result in delinquency statistics and process these individuals through the court. The true picture of delinquency is a complicated one; offenders come in a wide assortment. The things which happen to them as they get swept up by the police or courts are similarly quite complex and varied. We must turn our attention to issues of delinquency causation. We should not be surprised to find that etiological generalizations are not easily arrived at, given the complex nature of the phenomena under study.

One major point to be kept in mind as we become engaged in

causal analysis is that we need to be wary of the false notion that all those youngsters who are without official records of delinquency are truly nondelinquent in behavior. It would be an error to compare a group of these juveniles with a collection of officially designated offenders in the search for causal factors, without first determining which of the "nondelinquents" are, in fact, implicated in misconduct. Chapters Two and Three do not support the notion that there are no real differences in deviant conduct between those juveniles who have been tagged as delinquents and those who have not. But neither do they bear out the naïve belief that all of those youths who engage in illegal behavior fall into the hands of the police or the juvenile authorities. The study of causation will have to pay attention to all the delinquents, no matter where they are located or whether they have been officially identified.

chapter four

DELINQUENCY CAUSATION: THEORIES AND APPROACHES

INTRODUCTION

Chapter Four takes up some basic issues in causal explanation; succeeding chapters will pursue etiological matters in further detail. We need to begin the study of causation[1] by examining the nature of explanation in behavioral science. What do we mean when we declare that we have discovered some of the causes of delinquency? What are the elements of a "good" theory of juvenile deviance? How are valid theories and generalizations developed? What kinds of theories and hypotheses have been investigated so far in the search for elusive causes? These are the kinds of fundamental questions which must be

[1] General summaries of causal theories and research findings can be found in Milton L. Barron, *The Juvenile in Delinquent Society* (New York: Alfred A. Knopf, Inc., 1955); Herbert A. Bloch and Frank T. Flynn, *Delinquency: The Juvenile Offender in America Today* (New York: Random House, Inc., 1956); Ruth Shonle Cavan, *Juvenile Delinquency* (Philadelphia: J. B. Lippincott Co., 1962); Martin H. Neumeyer, *Juvenile Delinquency in Modern Society*, 3rd ed. (Princeton, N.J.: D. Van Nostrand Co., Inc., 1961); Sophia M. Robison, *Juvenile Delinquency* (New York: Henry Holt and Co., 1960); Henry Manuel Shulman, *Juvenile Delinquency in American Society* (New York: Harper & Row, Publishers, 1961); Paul W. Tappan, *Juvenile Delinquency*, (New York: McGraw-Hill Book Company, 1949); Negley K. Teeters and John Otto Reinemann, *The Challenge of Delinquency* (Englewood Cliffs, N.J.: Prentice-Hall, Inc., 1950); George B. Vold, *Theoretical Criminology* (New York: Oxford University Press, Inc., 1958).

addressed preliminary to an examination of current research findings on delinquency.

Causal thinking is surely not foreign to the layman. Few citizens are totally bewildered by the course of events and believe that "things just happen" by pure chance. Instead, most occurrences in the physical and social worlds are presumed to be caused by something else. The layman conceives the cause of some phenomenon as that event which preceded it and which somehow produced it. Consider the illustration of lung cancer. We all know the cause (or one of the causes) of lung cancer — smoking. Cigarettes cause cancer because their ingredients lead to physical changes in lung tissue. Or, stated another way, cigarettes cause cancer because *if* a person smokes them for an extended period of time, *then* he will very likely end up with cancerous lungs.

Causal thinking in science bears some similarity to etiological reasoning on the part of laymen. In both cases, *relationships* are identified, so that one phenomenon, event, or form of behavior is linked to another event which presumably led to it. In addition, a *time sequence* is usually implied such that the cause of something rests in a factor which preceded it in point of time. In short, both the layman and the scientist deal with causal statements taking an "If X occurs, then Y will probably follow" form. In the case of delinquency, an illustrative etiological claim would be: "If children are reared in family circumstances characterized by parental rejection, most of them will develop into aggressive and antisocial persons." This example shows a third element that is common to the causal perspectives of laymen and scientists alike: *probabilistic thinking.* The example asserts that some event or factor usually or frequently leads to some other occurrence, but it does not contend that X always produces Y. Citizens and scientists both make some allowance for intervening variables, unanticipated events, or other factors which intrude into explanations and predictions.

Although scientific and lay notions of causation show some points of similarity, they are not by any means identical. In Chapter One we noted some commonly held citizen beliefs about the causes of juvenile delinquency. Most of these are of the "evil causes evil" variety, in which some "bad" circumstances, such as inadequate parents, defective moral training, deficient recreational facilities, or other factors of that ilk, are alleged to produce the evil of delinquency. Many of these hypotheses are clearly false; the available empirical evidence unequivocally demonstrates them to be without factual support. But, more important, all of these citizen views are naïve and inadequate. In them, juvenile lawbreaking is attributed to some single evil which is thought to be the only cause of it. This kind of thinking is too simplified to do justice to the real world of delinquent conduct. Although social scientists are not yet able to provide a complete and valid accounting of the concatenation of etiological influences behind delinquency, it is clear that these factors are numerous and are interwoven with one another in complex ways. Something in the way of causal analysis which goes well beyond the structure of common sense notions is called for.

Tappan expresses the orientation to causation which this book follows: *"Cause is the exertion by multiple factors, occurring in varied but specific configurations, of a determing influence upon the deviant behavior that ensues."*[2]

Explicit note should be taken of both of the terms *multiple factors* and *specific configurations* in Tappan's definition. We define causation as the operation of some large but finite set of factors which bear an invariant relationship to delinquency. However, there is another kind of multiple-factor thinking which has some supporters, but which we eschew, which holds that causal analysis must be eclectic, providing room for a multitude of factors of various kinds, all bearing some relationship to delinquency.[3] Exponents of this orientation have often congratulated themselves on their avoidance of dogmatism and rigidity and on their willingness to include myriad factors within some kind of explanatory porridge. Advocates of this version of multiple-factor thinking have suggested that the causes of delinquency vary from individual to individual, so that it is therefore necessary to compile lengthy inventories of these causes in each instance of lawbreaking conduct. According to this line of reasoning, the best that can be accomplished in the way of explanation of juvenile delinquency is the accumulation of a very large set of variables or "categoric risks" all bearing some statistical association to delinquency. Proponents of this viewpoint contend that it is not possible to isolate any factor or group of factors which show an invariant relationship to delinquency.

This kind of causal nihilism must be rejected. If there is to be a scientific explanation of delinquency, causal propositions will have to be developed which aver that some large but specific set of factors interact in particular ways to produce lawbreaking. Conventional forms of multiple-factor thinking assert as an operating principle that such statements are outside the realm of the discoverable; we, however, assume otherwise. We agree with Albert Cohen, who has advanced an incisive critique of multiple-factor perspectives. He points

---

[2] Tappan, *Juvenile Delinquency*, pp. 64–65. Emphasis in the original.

[3] One example of this view can be found in Teeters and Reinemann, *The Challenge of Delinquency.*

out that the supporters of this framework usually confuse explanation by means of a *single theory* with explanation by means of a *single factor*. Few modern criminologists would hold that delinquency is the product of one variable, although many would contend that some large but finite number of factors do combine to produce delinquency.[4]

Our search for causes will also concern relationships that are relatively free from considerations of time, place, or other such limitations. Consider a report which declares: "During 1968, 71 percent of the delinquents in the juvenile court in Redwood City, California were from broken homes, while only 32 percent of the nondelinquent high school youths in that city were from broken homes." This is a descriptive statement, not a causal one, for it makes no claims about delinquents at some other time or in other cities. A more satisfactory etiological contention would be one that asserts the existence of a strong and continued relationship between home factors and juvenile misconduct throughout the United States. Note that the preceding comments referred to causal associations that are relatively, rather than absolutely, unbounded by matters of space and time. In a young and immature field of inquiry, etiological propositions may have to be circumscribed and limited so as to refer to juvenile misconduct in the United States, in large cities, in rural areas, during the past twenty years, and so on.

How should we go about discovering the factors which are implicated in delinquency and the combinations and permutations of them that operate in different forms of juvenile lawbreaking? Shall we engage in simple fact-gathering? If we gather enough discrete observations, will the facts speak for themselves? If we make enough observations, will broad explanatory generalizations leap out at us from these findings? The answer to these questions is negative. In the first place, facts are unlimited in number, so that we can never exhaust the list of observations which could be made about delinquency. Some kind of theory is required which suggests the facts which are the important ones to gather. In addition, facts never speak for themselves, so that their causal significance is never self-evident. The job of the delinquency analyst is to "make sense" out of discrete empirical observations by linking them to other facets of the behavior under study. In short, the explanation of delinquency demands the development of theories, of guidelines which point our observational activities in particular directions.

---

[4] This analysis by Cohen is discussed in Donald R. Cressey, "Crime," in Robert K. Merton and Robert A. Nisbet, eds., *Contemporary Social Problems*, 2nd ed. (New York: Harcourt, Brace & World, Inc., 1966), pp. 171–72.

A prominent example of the sterility of eclectic fact-gathering is found in the massive investigation of offenders and nonoffenders by Sheldon and Eleanor Glueck.[5] These researchers utilized a large research staff and a great amount of money in an explicitly eclectic fact-gathering exploration of delinquent conduct, in which information on several hundred characteristics of lawbreakers and nondelinquents was gathered. The Gluecks were of the view that the causes of delinquency would emerge from this mass of observations. Among these many variables were the educational attainment of the grandparents of the subjects, school subject preferences and dislikes, frequency of movie attendance, dynamometric strength (handgrip), presence of genital pathology, and number of dental caries. As might be anticipated, the delinquents and nonoffenders did not differ on most of these factors; the Gluecks therefore found these factors to be unimportant in etiology. Had the researchers begun with a coherent, persuasive theory, they might have expended their research funds more wisely by not spending them on fact-gathering information on teeth, genitals, and hand-grip! Moreover, when the Gluecks concluded this enormous piece of research, they were compelled to sneak in a theoretical perspective in order to make sense out of the findings. They concluded that "under-the-roof" factors, centered about the family life of the subjects, were the major ones responsible for their behavior. At the same time, other students of delinquency have put a different interpretation upon the results, and contend that the facts point most dramatically to the role of peer group associations and subcultural influences in juvenile lawbreaking.

We must now consider the development of delinquency theory and assess the adequacy of current theoretical perspectives on juvenile misconduct. What are some ingredients of mature, developed theories, against which contemporary orientations in the study of delinquency can be compared? We need to examine not only the different images of the offender which are contained in existing theories, but also the psychological arguments which look for various kinds of mental pathology on the part of these offenders. How important are integrative trends in delinquency study, in which efforts are being made to bring psychological and sociological insights together in delinquency theories?

[5] Sheldon and Eleanor Glueck, *Unraveling Juvenile Delinquency* (Cambridge, Mass.: Harvard University Press, 1950).

THE NATURE OF THEORY

Sociologists are among the most tolerant of men when it comes to permitting the loose usage of words. The term *theory* is one of the most abused words in the sociological lexicon, for it has been attached to the widest possible assortment of claims and arguments. Loose and ambiguous conjectures about some phenomenon or another, vague classification schemes, simple generalizations—all have been dignified by the label of *theory*. In our view, sociologists would do better to hew more carefully to a definition of theory which possesses some rigor and clarity. Richard Rudner has offered one such statement, in which he observes: *"A theory is a systematically related set of statements, including some lawlike generalizations, that is empirically testable."* [6] A parallel but more detailed picture of the nature of theory is evoked by Carl Hempel in the following passage:

> A scientific theory might therefore be likened to a complex spatial network: Its terms are represented by the knots, while the threads connecting the latter correspond, in part, to the definitions and, in part, to the fundamental and derivative hypotheses included in the theory. The whole system floats, as it were, above the plane of observation and is anchored to it by rules of interpretation. These might be viewed as strings which are not part of the network but link certain points of the latter with specific places in the plane of observation. By virtue of these interpretive connections, the network can function as a scientific theory: From certain observational data, we may ascend, via an interpretive string, to some point in the theoretical network, thence proceed, via definitions and hypotheses, to other points, from which another interpretive string permits a descent to the plane of observation. [7]

This statement may have an unfamiliar sound to it because theories of this kind are rarely encountered in the social sciences. Instead, behavioral scientists often put forth conjectural statements dealing with ill-defined phenomena, ambiguous concepts, and logically inconsistent propositions. We may have an intuitive feeling that such arguments may be true in that they sound plausible. But, given the fuzzy character of these "theories," empirical verification of them in the manner described by Hempel is not possible. We cannot prove these arguments because, quite literally, we do not know

[6] Richard S. Rudner, *Philosophy of Social Science* (Englewood Cliffs, N.J.: Prentice-Hall, Inc., 1966), p. 10. Emphasis in the original. The reader is referred to this entire book and particularly to pp. 10–53, for some valuable commentary on theory in social science.

[7] Carl G. Hempel, *Fundamentals of Concept Formation in Empirical Science* (Chicago: University of Chicago Press, 1952), p. 36.

exactly what we are talking about, thus we are unable to figure out the sorts of observations which would prove or disprove the contentions.

It is unlikely that sociologists can abruptly and immediately discard their loquacious and rambling theorizing in favor of rigorous, axiomatic, or formalized brands of theory. Instead, this systematic approach will have to be reached by successive approximations, in which we move from sloppy generalizations to increasingly more precise theories. Clarence Schrag comments on this direction:

> Few if any sociological theories satisfy the criteria used in evaluating the formalized research activities of some of the more mature physical sciences. Undeveloped disciplines like sociology lack the abstract and powerful vocabularies, the precise rules of grammar, and the technical dictionaries that are necessary for translating the philosophy of science into viable procedures for handling their distinctive problems. This means that there are no authenticated methods for resolving controversies over the definition of concepts, the acceptability of assumptions and theories, or even the identification of problems that are unique to sociology as a specialized field of inquiry. It may therefore be unwise for most sociologists to devote their energies to the attempted construction of abstract and comprehensive theories such as those found in the more advanced sciences. Perhaps the greatest need in sociology today is for more of the modest "inference chains," "explanation sketches," and embryo theories that aim primarily at organizing selected research findings and suggesting further avenues of inquiry.[8]

In broad terms, the task before the student of delinquency is a double one of theory construction and empirical research. The endeavor might begin with available empirical findings, from which theoretical statements tying these together might be contrived.[9] These theoretical propositions might also contain speculative claims about aspects of delinquency which have yet to be studied. In turn, investigations might be undertaken to test these contentions, while the results of such research would feed back into the theoretical structure. The empirical findings would produce modifications in the theory or extensions of it. During all of this process, more attention ought to be given to rigorous theoretical rhetoric than has usually been the

[8] Clarence Schrag, "Elements of Theoretical Analysis in Sociology," in Llewellyn Gross, ed., *Sociological Theory: Inquiries and Paradigms* (New York: Harper & Row, Publishers, 1967), p. 244. See this entire essay for some valuable comments regarding theoretical ventures in sociology, pp. 220–53.

[9] A number of guidelines for the inductive development of theoretical generalizations out of existing research can be found in Travis Hirschi and Hanan C. Selvin, *Delinquency Research: An Appraisal of Analytic Methods* (New York: The Free Press, 1967).

case in theoretical venture in the past. Close attention needs to be paid to clear definitions of major concepts and logical structure of claims within the theory.[10]

Schrag has identified one important case illustration of the successive-approximation approach to theoretical development in criminology.[11] This case, concerning gang delinquency, centers about the theorizing and research activities which began in 1955 with the work of Albert Cohen.[12] Cohen drew upon a body of seemingly unrelated research findings dealing with delinquency, social class patterns, socialization, and other matters, that had been produced during several of the preceding decades. From this material he then assembled in brilliant fashion a speculative explication of how working-class gang delinquency might be the product of certain adjustment problems of lower-class youths. That essay led to a number of suggested clarifications and revisions by other students of delinquency. It also provided the stimulus for a competing theory of subcultural delinquency by Richard Cloward and Lloyd Ohlin, which took up a number of issues not covered in the Cohen formulation.[13] The Cloward and Ohlin theory stands as a good illustration of the embryo form of argument noted by Schrag, for it is unusually clear in exposition and rigorous in structure. In turn, that statement has provided the impetus for a number of recent studies of working-class delinquency.[14] These investigations have uncovered a number of defects in the Cloward and Ohlin theory, so that further revisions of it are now in order, including additional work on the formal structure of the thesis. In all of this, there is a cumulative quality that is lacking in orthodox fact-gathering, so that it is clear that much has been learned about subcultural delinquency in the past two decades through the interaction of theory and empirical investigation.

Another signpost indicating the direction of future theoretical work can be seen in the evolution of the differential-association perspective

[10] An illustration of theoretical development from a body of available data can be found in Don C. Gibbons, "Problems of Causal Analysis in Criminology: A Case Illustration," *Journal of Research in Crime and Delinquency*, III (January 1966), 47–52; see also Gibbons, *Society, Crime, and Criminal Careers* (Englewood Cliffs, N.J.: Prentice-Hall, Inc., 1968), pp. 299–308.

[11] Schrag, "Elements of Theoretical Analysis," pp. 244–50.

[12] Albert K. Cohen, *Delinquent Boys* (New York: The Free Press, 1955). This material growing out of Cohen's work is discussed in Gibbons, *Society, Crime, and Criminal Careers*, pp. 263–80.

[13] Richard A. Cloward and Lloyd E. Ohlin, *Delinquency and Opportunity* (New York: The Free Press, 1960).

[14] A sample of this material would include Irving Spergel, *Racketville, Slumtown, Haulburg* (Chicago: University of Chicago Press, 1964); Schrag, "Elements of Theoretical Analysis," pp. 244–50.

of Edwin Sutherland.[15] Sutherland's statement underwent a number of revisions over several decades as he subjected it to continued reexamination in the light of newer findings. In its developed form, the differential-association argument asserts that persons become delinquents or criminals through a process of association with carriers of criminalistic norms. Several investigations of this process have been conducted and in each case these studies have encountered difficulties with vague language. Efforts to tidy up the logical structure of the theory have recently been made by Jeffery,[16] Burgess and Akers,[17] and DeFleur and Quinney.[18] In the process, the theory has gained a good deal in the way of clarity, so that its testability has been considerably improved.

IMAGES OF THE DELINQUENT

What kind of picture of the delinquent is conjured up by social science theories and other perspectives? In the great majority of cases, these views put forth much the same image of the deviant. The major elements of this characterization include the implicit notion that delinquents are basically quite different from nonoffenders, so that a picture is put forth which is not too different from the layman's conception of "bad" delinquents and "good" nondelinquents. In turn, the deviant youths are presumed to be driven into delinquency by the force of adverse or pathological circumstances of one kind or another. Offenders have little choice over their life patterns, given the distorted character of their life situation. The delinquent is either pushed into lawbreaking by something in his physical makeup, by aberrant psychological impulses, or by the meanness and harshness of his social environment. Finally, most images of the offender imply that experiences occurring relatively early in life are the ones which are responsible for his present behavior; little attention is paid to events which occur to him after he has become engaged in misconduct.

This picture of the remorselessly driven delinquent has recently

[15] Edwin H. Sutherland and Donald R. Cressey, *Principles of Criminology*, 7th ed. (Philadelphia: J.B. Lippincott Co., 1966), pp. 81–82.

[16] C. R. Jeffery, "Criminal Behavior and Learning Theory," *Journal of Criminal Law, Criminology and Police Science*, LVI (September 1965), 294–300.

[17] Robert L. Burgess and Ronald L. Akers, "A Differential Association-Reinforcement Theory of Criminal Behavior," *Social Problems*, XIV (Fall 1966), 128–47.

[18] Melvin L. DeFleur and Richard Quinney, "A Reformulation of Sutherland's Differential Association Theory and a Strategy for Empirical Verification," *Journal of Research in Crime and Delinquency*, III (January 1966), 1–22; see also Donald R. Cressey, "The Language of Set Theory and Differential Association," *Journal of Research in Crime and Delinquency*, III (January 1966), 22–26.

come under criticism from several quarters. Much of the material on hidden delinquency which we examined in Chapter Two undermines the dichotomous characterization of offenders and nondeviants. Juvenile lawbreakers of one kind or another are legion and are not sharply set off from juvenile conformists. Another challenge to the conception of the driven offender has centered about the motivational forces which lie behind his behavior. Bordua has noted that most contemporary conceptions of gang delinquency contain an image of the offender as a tortured youth, possessed by stress associated with class position or guilt over law violation.[19] Nonoffenders are thought to be free souls not burdened by the adjustment problems which plague the deviants. In Bordua's opinion, an alternative stance may be in order, in which we acknowledge the possibility that, for many youngsters, delinquency may be an attractive line of activity to which they are drawn rather than driven. In short, delinquency may be perceived as fun by many who engage in it.

The most detailed analysis of competing images of the offender has been made by David Matza,[20] who argues that nearly all of the characterizations in prevailing theories are positivist in form, involving deterministic assumptions about juvenile miscreants. In these, offenders are perceived as radically different in behavior from nonconformists; their backgrounds are also assumed to differ. Both the deviant youths and the nondelinquents are thought to be incapable of behaving differently because their conduct is determined by their different backgrounds.[21] In Matza's words, "From the born criminal to differential association, the explanation of delinquency has rested in the radically different circumstances experienced by delinquent and law-abiding alike. Each is constrained, but by a fundamentally different set of circumstances."[22]

Matza's essay examined the main currents of positivist thinking regarding delinquency causation over the past half century or so. At one time, biological theses were in vogue; offenders were thought to be driven into misconduct by biological defects of one sort or another. More recently, personality theories have become ascendant; delinquency is seen as being derived from early, intimate family experi-

19 David J. Bordua, "Some Comments on Theories of Group Delinquency," *Sociological Inquiry*, XXXII (Spring 1962), 245–60; Bordua, "Delinquent Subcultures: Sociological Interpretations of Gang Delinquency," *Annals of the American Academy of Political and Social Science*, CCCXXXVIII (November 1961), 119–36.

20 David Matza, *Delinquency and Drift* (New York: John Wiley & Sons, Inc., 1964).

21 *Ibid.*, pp. 1–32.

22 *Ibid.*, p. 12.

ences which have warped the personality. Finally, various sociological theories have recently emerged which lay stress on the prominence of situational factors of one kind or another which generate the stresses that propel youths into misconduct.[23] Thus Matza informs us that: "The delinquent has come a long way under the auspices of positive criminology. He has been transformed from a defective to a defector."[24]

Matza maintained that the determinist characterization of the offender does not ring true, that it explains too much rather than too little. It fails to account for maturational reform and for the fact that large numbers of juvenile lawbreakers desist from further misconduct near the end of the adolescent period, without any sort of treatment intervention directed at them. If they are truly driven into deviant acts, if personality defects or deep commitment to antisocial norms have produced their antisocial behavior, how can maturational reform be explained?[25]

Matza's own position on these issues was one of soft determinism, in which *drift* plays a major role. In this argument, offenders are hypothesized to be in tune with and under the control of conventional, anticriminal norms most of the time, so that in this regard they are little different from nondelinquents. Matza declared: "The delinquent transiently exists in limbo between convention and crime, responding in turn to the demands of each, flirting now with one, now the other, but postponing commitment, evading decision. Thus, he drifts between criminal and conventional action."[26]

In Matza's view, many delinquents episodically engage in misconduct, not because they are driven into it, but because their usual attachment to prosocial conduct norms is temporarily broken by various neutralizing techniques. These youths entertain various rationalizations which allow them to exculpate themselves from blame for their misdeeds. But for most offenders this release from moral restraint is temporary; they eventually drift back into law-abiding ways. In all of this process, the deviants exercise some degree of choice in their behavior, so that they are to some extent free to willfully violate the law or to abide by it.[27] Matza asserted that if his portrayal of the offender is realistic, the job of causal analysis becomes one of determining the circumstances and conditions which cause the drift of individuals into or out of misconduct.

23 *Ibid.*, pp.12–21.
24 *Ibid.*, p. 21.
25 *Ibid.*, pp. 21–27.
26 *Ibid.*, p. 28.
27 *Ibid.*, pp. 69–179.

Another voice speaking somewhat differently upon this matter of deviant motivation is that of Lemert.[28] He questions those formulations which maintain that deviant behavior is the work of either aberrant individuals or of men who make deliberate decisions to engage in nonconformity in response to perceived defects in their social environment. Instead, he suggests that in complex societies characterized by value pluralism, many persons drift into misconduct in a process of risk taking. Deviance is one of several possible outcomes of their behavior, but at the time they initiate a line of conduct, the actors are not certain which of the possible outcomes will actually occur. Finally, Lemert has also given much attention to the possibility that events occurring after the onset of deviance have much more to do with the course of deviant careers than has usually been supposed. In the case of delinquency, he suggests that experiences with the police, courts, and correctional agencies may be more influential in the crystallization of delinquent careers than any events that took place prior to them.[29]

This is not the place to adjudicate among these possibilities. In our view, it is likely that delinquent actors frequently do become implicated in deviance in the ways suggested by Bordua, Matza, Lemert, and others. At the same time, there may be other kinds of misbehavior in which the participants more closely resemble the image of the driven person contained in many theories. The point to be drawn is that we need to keep an open mind on the question of motivational forces when we direct our attention to the varied forms of juvenile lawbreaking.

TYPES OF DELINQUENCY THEORY

Two Questions About Causation

Discovery of the causes of juvenile delinquency is the principal business of the criminologist-sociologist; and his major aim is to develop a body of generalizations which account for juvenile misconduct. This task is many-faceted, but it involves two main components which are closely related, but which are analytically separate prob-

---

[28] Edwin M. Lemert, *Human Deviance, Social Problems, and Social Control* (Englewood Cliffs, N.J.: Prentice-Hall, Inc., 1967), pp. 3–12. A resumé of Lemert's views on deviance can be found in Gibbons, *Society, Crime, and Criminal Careers*, pp. 194–98.

[29] The influence of societal reactions upon offenders is discussed in Gibbons, *Society, Crime, and Criminal Careers*, pp. 236–40.

lems. The first has to do with the development of explanations for the *kinds and amounts of delinquency* observed in a society or among different societies, while the other centers about the discovery of the processes involved in the *acquisition of delinquent behavior patterns by specific youths.* Two questions are asked about delinquency: (1) What factors produce the rates and patterns that are observed, and (2) how do specific youngsters become delinquents?[30]

Let us examine some illustrations of these two questions as they might be seen in delinquency analysis. The problem of explaining rates and patterns is the question which Cohen has termed the "sociological" one.[31] It is "sociological," because we ask, "What is it about the structure of social systems that determines the kinds of criminal acts that occur in these systems and the way in which such acts are distributed within the systems?"[32] Suppose that a statistical study of lawbreaking patterns within a specific city shows that certain forms of gang delinquency are heavily concentrated in slum areas, while auto theft and vandalism are frequent in certain other areas of the city. The focus of attention in this case would be upon questions of the sort: "Why are these kinds of delinquency so common in some areas and virtually nonexistent in others?" "Is there something about community social structure, such as social class patterns existing in different areas, which results in these observed patterns of misconduct?"

The sociological question about causation has received much attention in recent years and efforts have been made to uncover the social-structural factors which are responsible for different delinquency rates among nations, for different distributions of misconduct in American cities, and for regional variations in juvenile lawbreaking.

The second causal question is one that we shall call "the social-psychology of delinquent careers," and which has been termed the "psychological" one by Cohen.[33] The focus of interest in this case is upon the processes by which specific youths acquire delinquent attitudes and behavior patterns. The difference between social-psychological generalizations regarding delinquent careers and the sociological problem can be illustrated through the earlier example of

---

[30] These two questions have been discussed in Gibbons, *Society, Crime, and Criminal Careers*, pp. 7–11, pp. 172–213.

[31] Albert K. Cohen, *Deviance and Control* (Englewood Cliffs, N.J., Prentice-Hall, Inc., 1966), pp. 41–47; Cohen, "The Study of Social Disorganization and Deviant Behavior," in Robert K. Merton, Leonard Broom, and Leonard S. Cottrell, Jr., eds., *Sociology Today* (New York: Basic Books, Inc., Publishers, 1959), p. 462; Cohen and James F. Short, Jr., "Juvenile Delinquency," in Merton and Nisbet, *Contemporary Social Problems*, pp. 84–135.

[32] Cohen, "Social Disorganization and Deviant Behavior," p. 462.

[33] Cohen, *Deviance and Control*, pp. 41–47.

different delinquency rates in a specific city. Suppose that we have noticed, in addition to the facts already specified, that there are several patterns of behavior among juveniles in the high-delinquency slum area. Some boys have high occupational aspirations, are highly motivated in school, and are conformist in behavior. Others are "corner boys" who are not heavily caught up in patterns of misconduct, but not given to mobility-striving or achievement either. They are unmotivated, conformist juveniles whose actions center about hedonistic "fun seeking." A third group contains youths whose major social role is that of "tough guy" and "delinquent." What socialization experiences led these specific youths into these different behavioral careers? We might entertain a number of candidate hypotheses on this matter which would include the proposition that the delinquents may be the ones with more personality problems than the conformists. Or perhaps the offenders are from more lax or criminalistic backgrounds than the nondelinquents. Still another hypothesis would be that the lawbreakers were more involved in differential association with criminalistic peer groups than the other youths were.

Clearly, these two broad questions are related, rather than distinct. They represent somewhat different ways of looking at segments of the same general phenomenon. On this point, Cohen observed:

> In general, whatever the properties of the culture or social structure to which we attribute the pattern of deviance, these properties determine the behavior of the members of the system through their impacts upon their personalities, the situations in which they operate, the conjunctions of personality and situation, and the interaction processes between them. In other words, psychological inquiry is concerned with identifying variables and processes involved in the motivation of deviance and conformity, and with constructing exact theories about their interrelationships. Sociological theory is concerned with identifying the variables and processes in the larger social system that in turn shape those that are involved in motivation, and that determine their distribution within the system.[34]

At this point, someone might object to these distinctions on the grounds that truly complete causal analysis ought to explain both the variations in rates of delinquency and the variations in involvement in misconduct or law-abiding behavior on the part of the youths in particular neighborhoods, social classes, or other settings. Moreover, many specific instances of criminological theory and/or research have been jointly concerned with these two problems. Nevertheless, it makes sense to keep these two matters analytically separate.

[34] *Ibid.*, p. 47.

Much of the ambiguity and confusion in contemporary theorizing and commentary regarding delinquency can be traced, in part, to the failure to keep the differences between these two matters clearly in mind, for example, those psychiatric hypotheses which allege that delinquents are pathological persons suffering from various psychological impairments. Are such notions intended to explain rate variations according to social class group? Do they imply that much larger numbers of lower-class persons—delinquents and conformists alike—suffer from personality problems as contrasted to members of other strata? That is the inference if psychogenic hypotheses are advanced as an explanation of rate variations. On the other hand, psychiatric notions which are put forth to account for the development of deviant or nondeviant careers on the part of certain persons *within* a social class group leave the matter of rate variations an open question. As an explanation of career development, the personality disturbance framework is logically compatible with a sociological explanation of rate variations which stresses the workings of such variables as differences in neighborhood organization. Conceivably, high delinquency rates could be compounded out of specific offender careers which might be most commonly found in those areas with community influences conducive to delinquency, and in which, in addition, relatively large numbers of youngsters with personality problems are located and serve as candidates for delinquency. Conversely, in neighborhoods more cohesive in character, youths with personality difficulties may be prone to nondelinquent behavior.

All of this discussion is meant to serve merely as an hypothetical illustration, rather than an exposition of the version of causal theory preferred in this book. The empirical accuracy of these notions is not an issue here.

Types of Causal Answers

The search for clues to delinquency causation has gone in many directions during the past hundred years, so that it is no simple matter to sum up the varied hunches and hypotheses that have been pursued at one time or another.[35] But, in general, three major perspectives have guided delinquency analysts as they have gone about their business: *biogenic, psychogenic,* and *sociogenic* approaches. Each of these declares that the genesis of juvenile misconduct is to be found in factors of a particular kind.

[35] One classification of approaches can be found in Cohen, *Deviance and Control,* pp. 41–44; Cohen and Short, "Juvenile Delinquency," pp. 97–98.

Biogenic answers to etiological questions offer us some version of the lawbreaker as a person whose misconduct is the result of faulty biology. The offender is hereditarily defective; he suffers from endocrine imbalance or brain pathology; his bodily structure and temperament pattern have pushed him toward delinquency, and so forth.

Psychogenic approaches are quite varied in character, but they all tell us in some fashion or another that the offender behaves as he does in response to psychological pathology of some kind. In most of these theories, the maladjusted delinquent is judged to be the product of intimate social experiences in the family or similar situations, so that the workings of social organization are rarely paid much heed.

Finally, the sociogenic arguments explain rate variations by reference to conditions of social structure. They also account for individual offenders by reference to normal learning processes which go on in gangs and other circumstances, to the effects of stigmatizing contacts with social control agencies, and to other variables of that kind.

Biogenic Views of Delinquency[36]

The plain fact is that the many years of biogenic exploration of delinquency have not yielded any valid generalizations about biological factors in deviance. Almost without exception, the biological theories that have been advanced have been scientifically naïve, while the research that has been conducted has been flawed in one way or another. Although it cannot unequivocally be claimed that there are no biogenic influences in delinquency, it is undeniably true that none have so far been shown to exist. For these reasons, the interested reader is referred to other detailed summaries of this work.

The most recent biogenic investigation to be noticed was that of the Gluecks, and concerned the presence of mesomorphic bodily structure among delinquents.[37] They found that mesomorphs, that is, boys with athletic, muscular body type, were more frequent among the offenders they studied than among the nonoffenders. Mesomorphic structure characterized 60.1 percent of the lawbreakers, but only 30.7 percent of the nondelinquents. These findings were the result of careful measurement, so that there is little question as to their accuracy. However, a sociologist would be quick to point out that a

[36] A detailed examination of biogenic theories and research can be found in Gibbons, *Society, Crime, and Criminal Careers,* pp. 115–37. Also see Cohen and Short, "Juvenile Delinquency," pp. 99–101.

[37] Sheldon and Eleanor Glueck, *Physique and Delinquency* (New York: Harper & Row, Publishers, 1956).

process of *social selection*, rather than biological determinism, probably explains the results. In other words, it is not unlikely that recruits to delinquent conduct are drawn from the group of more agile, physically fit boys, just as "Little League" baseball or "Pop Warner" league football players tend toward mesomorphy. Fat delinquents and fat ballplayers are uncommon, because social behavior involved in these cases puts fat, skinny, or sickly boys at a disadvantage. If so, the findings reflect the workings of social factors, not biology.

.PSYCHOGENIC THEORIES
OF DELINQUENCY[38]

Introduction

The central hypothesis guiding psychogenic investigation is that the critical causal factors in delinquency center around personality problems to which juvenile misbehavior is presumed to be a response. August Aichhorn, a pioneering figure in the devolpment of this argument, has asserted: "There must be something in the child himself which the environment brings out in the form of delinquency."[39] Delinquents behave as they do because they are in some way "sick," "maladjusted," or "pathological" persons. Aichhorn's statement also indicates a second assumption of psychogenic perspectives: that the environment may function as a precipitating force, but never as a primary force in causation. But as we shall see in succeeding sections of this discussion, different psychogenic statements accord varying weight to the influence of environmental pressures, so that they have given more or less attention to social or environmental factors.

One thing to be noted about all psychogenic arguments is that they have been mute on the matter of *rates* of deviance. These hypotheses contend that personality problems account for delinquent conduct, but they fail to tell us why juvenile misbehavior is common in some places or areas and less common in others. Such matters as social class patterning of juvenile lawbreaking are ignored in psychogenic theories.

Although the voices of psychogenic commentators by no means speak in unison about delinquency, three general positions can be discerned in the writings of psychiatrists, psychologists, and others of psychogenic persuasion. The *psychoanalytic* position is one of these

---

[38] This section is a briefer version of the discussion in Gibbons, *Society, Crime, and Criminal Careers,* pp. 138–70.

[39] August Aichhorn, *Wayward Youth* (New York: Meridian Books, 1955), p. 30.

variants, growing out of the psychoanalytic theory developed by Freud and extended to crime and delinquency by a number of others. In addition, there are a host of more *general arguments* regarding juvenile misbehavior and personality dynamics which do not stem directly from psychoanalytic thought, such as the writings of Healy and Bronner, Hewitt and Jenkins, the Gluecks, and others. A third argument is that delinquency is linked to a particular form of personality structure, *psychopathy* or *sociopathy*.

We need not devote much space to psychoanalytic writings on delinquency.[40] For one thing, psychoanalytic theories involve contentions about the workings of instinctual sources of psychic energy, and these are incapable of empirical verification. These instinctual mainsprings of lawbreaking are said to be unconscious ones, and that the offenders are unaware of them. More importantly, only a trained psychoanalyst is qualified to investigate these motivational forces, so that other observers are unable to see them in operation. Second, psychoanalytic arguments about lawbreaking are relatively unfashionable at present. Just as psychoanalytic perspectives on other forms of human behavior have been modified in the light of recent developments in cultural and behavioral science, so have psychogenic theories of delinquency. Relatively few persons are to be found at the present time espousing orthodox versions of the psychoanalytic view of delinquency which are complete with instincts, unconscious motivation, and other theoretical baggage of that form.

Emotional Problems and Delinquency

Since 1900, much has been written by psychiatrists and others about personality problems, emotional disturbances, and delinquency, and a great deal of it is independent of Freudian psychoanalytic theory. The emotional dynamics that have been identified have been of many kinds, and the origins of these problems have been alleged to involve a large variety of background experiences, with particular emphasis upon parent-child tensions and distorted primary group relations. Hyman Grossbard provided one example of this view.[41] He averred that most offenders show inefficient or underdeveloped ego mechanisms, so that they tend to act out mental conflicts instead of handling them by rational means or symptom formation, as do nonof-

[40] Psychoanalytic theories of crime and delinquency are discussed at length in Gibbons, *Society, Crime, and Criminal Careers*, pp. 144–51.

[41] Hyman Grossbard, "Ego Deficiency in Delinquents," *Social Casework*, XLIII (April 1962), 71–178.

fenders. Instincts and other psychoanalytic elements are not required in this brand of theory.

The thesis that delinquency is due to emotional problems must be taken seriously. Countless numbers of persons have put this view forward and it has frequently been urged as the basis on which treatment ventures ought to proceed. Numerous correctional rehabilitation programs around the nation have been based upon the argument that delinquents are emotionally troubled individuals. Accordingly, we need to ask whether any factual base is apparent for this brand of causal theorizing.

Some Early Studies

Cyril Burt's claim that 85 percent of the offenders he studied prior to 1938 were emotionally impaired stands as an early example of the general personality problem view.[42] Probably the most important of the early studies of delinquency and emotional problems was the research of William Healy and Augusta Bronner, which compared 105 delinquents with 105 of their nondelinquent siblings in New Haven, Boston, and Detroit. After examining these youngsters, the investigators concluded that "it finally appears that no less than 91 percent of the delinquents gave clear evidence of being or having been unhappy and discontented in their life circumstances or extremely emotionally disturbed because of emotion-provoking situations or experiences. In great contradistinction we found similar evidence of inner stresses at the most in only 13 percent of the controls."[43]

Although these seem to be impressive findings, this investigation has received critical attention as well as acclaim.[44] The critics have noted that the differences between the offenders and nondelinquents were probably exaggerated, because the staff members who reported on personality characteristics of the subjects were psychiatrists and psychiatric social workers, predisposed to the opinion that the major etiological variable in delinquency is emotional disturbance. Also, the clinical judgments were obtained by subjective methods; no effort was made to disguise the identities of the subjects prior to the psychiatric examinations. The assessments may have been biased by the knowl-

[42] Cyril Burt, The Young Delinquent (London: University of London Press, 1938).

[43] William Healy and Augusta F. Bronner, New Light on Delinquency and its Treatment (New Haven: Yale University Press, 1936), p. 122.

[44] Michael Hakeem, "A Critique of the Psychiatric Approach," in Joseph S. Roucek, ed., Juvenile Delinquency (New York: Philosophical Library, 1958), pp. 89–95; Sutherland and Cressey, Principles of Criminology, pp. 173–74.

edge of the delinquent-nondelinquent status of the subjects. Additionally, the psychiatric workers were conducting a treatment program for the offenders and were in greater contact with them than with the nonoffenders. If they had spent an equal amount of time with the nonoffenders, would they have observed emotional problems which were originally overlooked? The critics have constructed such a damaging case against the Healy and Bronner study that its findings cannot be accepted as valid. Other reseach results give only partial support at best to these psychogenic contentions.

Proponents of psychogenic arguments must also contend with the findings of Karl Schuessler and Donald Cressey, who reviewed many studies of personality characteristics of delinquents and criminals. They concluded: "of 113 such comparisons, 42 percent showed differences in favor of the noncriminal, while the remainder were indeterminate. The doubtful validity of many of the obtained differences, as well as the lack of consistency in the combined results, makes it impossible to conclude from these data that criminality and personality elements are associated."[45] This survey of psychogenic studies was recently updated when Gordon Waldo and Simon Dinitz examined a large number of investigations that were conducted between 1950 and 1965.[46] After carefully assessing the results of these inquiries, they were led to conclude that no marked relationships between personality elements and delinquency were reflected in them. However, it should be noted that the research investigations examined by Schuessler and Cressey and by Waldo and Dinitz all concerned heterogeneous samples of offenders and nondelinquents. No effort was made in any of these to discover personality dimensions among offender types within the population of delinquents.

Recent Work

Michael Hakeem has presented another review of studies which involves findings from surveys of emotional disturbance among cases from an adolescents' court, a psychiatric clinic affiliated with a juvenile court, and a juvenile training school.[47] The results show a diversity of diag-

---

[45] Karl F. Schuessler and Donald R. Cressey, "Personality Characteristics of Criminals," *American Journal of Sociology*, LV (March 1950), 476–84.

[46] Gordon P. Waldo and Simon Dinitz, "Personality Attributes of the Criminal: An Analysis of Research Studies, 1950-1965," *Journal of Research in Crime and Delinquency*, IV (July 1967), 185–202. Psychological studies of delinquency are also reviewed in Herbert C. Quay, *Juvenile Delinquency* (Princeton, N. J.: D. Van Nostrand Co., Inc., 1965), pp. 139–69.

[47] Hakeem, "A Critique of the Psychiatric Approach," pp. 86–89.

nostic decisions in each of the investigations. One set of diagnostic labels categorized a number of offenders as suffering from psychoneurosis or neurotic character disturbances, while in the other two studies this category did not appear. Immaturity and mental conflict turn up in one report, but not in the others. Additionally, the three investigations, although handling comparable diagnostic groups, tabulated diverse proportions of delinquents. Hakeem therefore concludes that the results probably tell more about the biases of the psychiatrists than about characteristics of offenders. Also, some of the diagnostic categories in these three studies were of dubious validity. For instance, one study diagnosed about one-third of the cases as "conduct disorders." Were any identifiable characteristics of offenders apart from the facts of involvement in misconduct used to recognize conduct disorders? It is quite likely that a tautological classification was involved, in which the delinquent activity of the juvenile was used to indicate the existence of a conduct disorder. If so, conduct disorder explains nothing.

One of the studies discussed by Hakeem was the investigation of the Gluecks, *Unraveling Juvenile Delinquency.* [48] The offenders and controls in that study were given a psychiatric interview and Rorschach tests, a projective instrument designed to measure basic personality traits. The Gluecks reported: "Considering first those traits in which the delinquents as a group significantly exceed the nondelinquents, we observe that they are to a much greater degree socially assertive, defiant and ambivalent to authority; they are more resentful of others, and far more hostile, suspicious and destructive; the goals of their drives are to a much greater extent receptive (Oral) and destructive-sadistic; they are more impulsive and vivacious, and decidedly more extroversive in their behavior trends."[49] A number of characteristics identified through the Rorschach tests as more common among delinquents are not clearly signs of maladjustment. Assertiveness, impulsiveness, and vivacity could be argued as indicators that the delinquents are better adjusted than the nonoffenders.

Psychiatric diagnoses of the lawbreakers and the nondelinquent controls brought out several points.[50] First, the differences between the two groups were not striking; about half of both groups showed no conspicuous mental pathology. Second, the delinquents classified as showing mental deviations were seen as exhibiting a variety of disorders, while the disturbed nonoffenders were predominately neurotic or showing neurotic trends. This finding varies from many psycho-

[48] Sheldon and Eleanor Glueck, *Unraveling Juvenile Delinquency.*
[49] *Ibid.*, p. 240.
[50] *Ibid.*, pp. 239–43.

genic arguments in the criminological literature which contend that delinquency is a form of neurotic, acting-out behavior.

Another body of research data on the psychogenic thesis comes from studies using the Minnesota Multiphasic Personality Inventory.[51] The M.M.P.I. includes eight scales in which certain responses to items in each scale are diagnostic of particular personality patterns. For example, persons with high scale points on the Pa, paranoia scale, give responses similar to those of individuals clinically diagnosed as suffering from paranoia.

One piece of reseach using this inventory involved its application to over 4000 Minneapolis ninth-grade students during 1948.[52] In 1950, the same youngsters were traced through the Hennepin County Juvenile Court and the Minneapolis Police Department to determine which had acquired records of misconduct. Of the boys, 22.2 percent had become delinquent, while 7.6 percent of the girls had become known to the court or police. In examining the responses of delinquents and nonoffenders, the investigators found such results as these: 27.7 percent of the boys who had high Pd (psychopathic deviate) scale points were delinquent, as were 25.4 percent of those with high Pa (paranoia) scale points. Of the boys with "Invalid" responses, indicating uncooperativeness, lying and so on, 37.5 percent were offenders. Thus there was some tendency for delinquent boys to show disproportionate numbers in some of the scale areas of the M.M.P.I., while substantially parallel results were noted with girls.

Hathaway and Monachesi were modest in the claims they made on the basis of these data. In the main, they argued only that the inventory possesses some discriminatory power. Nonetheless, critics have noted the problems of interpretation involved in the variability of results, and have pointed out that a number of social factors correlate more highly with delinquency than do M.M.P.I. scores.[53]

Guy Swanson's investigation is also relevant.[54] He examined the emotional stability and family adjustment of children from Pittsburgh areas by administering tests to school children from a number of high,

[51] These studies are summarized in Gibbons, *Society, Crime, and Criminal Careers,* p. 155; Waldo and Dinitz, "Personality Attributes of the Criminal."

[52] Starke Hathaway and Elio D. Monachesi, eds., *Analyzing and Predicting Juvenile Delinquency with the Minnesota Multiphasic Personality Inventory* (Minneapolis: University of Minnesota Press, 1953).

[53] Clarence Schrag, review of Hathaway and Monachesi, *American Sociological Review,* XIX (August 1954), 490–91; Waldo and Dinitz, "Personality Attributes of the Criminal"; Sethard Fisher, "The M.M.P.I.: Assessing a Famous Personality Test," *American Behavioral Scientist,* VI (October 1962), 21–22.

[54] Guy E. Swanson, "The Disturbances of Children in Urban Areas," *American Sociological Review,* XIV (October 1949), 676–78.

medium, and low delinquency areas. Two measures were employed, the Woodworth-Mathews Personal Data Sheet and the Child-Parents Relationship Scale. If it is true that children from high delinquency areas are emotionally unstable and dissatisfied with their family relationships, we should expect to find a correlation between rates of misconduct and unfavorable scores on these two instruments—the higher the delinquency rate of an area, the greater the number of children who have unfavorable scores. But such was not the case; instead, the observed correlations were negligible. Swanson's study did not lend support to the emotional disturbance argument.

John Conger and Wilbur Miller have recently engaged in still another inquiry into personality disturbances and delinquency.[55] Their investigation involved samples from among the 2348 tenth-grade students in Denver in 1956. One sample involved all of the youngsters (271, or less than 15 percent of the total) who had become known to the juvenile court in that city. The other sample consisted of nondelinquent youngsters who were matched with the offenders by age, socioeconomic status, IQ, school environment, and ethnic group.

Conger and Miller were able to conduct a longitudinal investigation of personality dynamics and delinquency through the use of the youths' school records, which included teacher comments, ratings of personal-social development, and the like. The boys were also subjected to an eclectic assortment of personality tests at the end of the ninth grade.[56] In general, these tests were designed to uncover personality variations which fall short of marked psychological pathology. They measure such things as impulsiveness, sociability, friendliness, closeness of interpersonal relationships, and dimensions of that kind.

In general, the researchers discovered that even as early as the third grade, the future delinquents were seen by their teachers as less well-adjusted than their classmates. The teachers regarded their social behavior as unacceptable and found the boys lacking in dependability, friendliness, fairness, and other such attributes. These differences persisted through the ninth grade, for the future lawbreakers continued to be poorly regarded by their teachers.

The results of the psychological testing pointed in the same direction. The delinquents, as a group, were more immature, egocentric, inconsiderate, impulsive, suspicious, and hostile than the nonoffenders. Interestingly, the offenders tended to view themselves in ways similar to the opinions held of them by their teachers.[57]

[55] John Janeway Conger and Wilbur C. Miller, *Personality, Social Class, and Delinquency* (New York: John Wiley & Sons, Inc., 1966).

[56] *Ibid.*, pp. 44–60.

[57] *Ibid.*, pp. 110–29.

These findings indicate, first, that the personality problems reported by teachers or in personality tests were of a relatively bland, less serious form than the psychological problems which are hypothesized in many psychogenic theories of delinquency. Second, the Conger and Miller data unquestionably show that official delinquents are less well-adjusted than their nondeviant peers.

The consistency of teacher ratings of the boys over a period of time warrants special mention. The investigators assumed that these reports were accurate reflections of the real behavior of the boys. However, many students of societal reaction experiences in deviant behavior would suggest that the processes through which cumulative biographies of boys are constructed by school teachers ought to be studied in detail. There is more than a slight possibility that once a boy gets pointed out as a "bad one" in school records, subsequent reactions of teachers become heavily colored by this initial judgment. Then, too, the offender's own self-attitudes and views of others may be influenced by his perception of their opinion of him. If so, much of the hostility and defiance that later shows up in personality tests could be a product of these experiences.

The results of this study are not at odds with sociological theories. A number of recent theoretical statements by sociologists hold that delinquent conduct is a response to adjustment problems of various kinds which stem from school experiences, neighborhood influences, and other pressures. Sociologists have often pictured the delinquent as an individual with a relatively cynical and bleak outlook upon life. The aggressive criticism of psychogenic formulations by sociologists has been pointed at those extremes which claim that most offenders are markedly maladjusted individuals, not at results such as the Conger and Miller study.

One more work on personality characteristics of delinquents comes from the Jesness Inventory.[58] This instrument, developed in the California correctional system, involves eight scales and a delinquency prediction score. The eight scales measure defensiveness, value orientation, neuroticism, authority attitude, family orientation, psychoticism, delinquency orientation, and emotional immaturity. Findings from the development and validation studies of this inventory in-

---

[58] Carl F. Jesness, *The Jesness Inventory: Development and Validation*, Research Report No. 29 (Sacramento: California Youth Authority, 1962). See also Jesness, *Redevelopment and Revalidation of the Jesness Inventory*, Research Report No. 35 (Sacramento: California Youth Authority, 1963). The 1963 report presents somewhat different findings from applications of the Jesness Inventory to additional samples. However, the outlines of the Jesness Inventory results from this later study of delinquents and nondelinquents were not materially altered from those of the 1962 report, discussed here.

dicated that offenders and nondelinquents do not differ significantly
in defensiveness, value orientation, neuroticism, or family orientation.
The two groups did vary on authority attitudes; delinquents exhibited
greater hostility toward authority figures. They also differed on psychoticism; the offenders were more suspicious and distrustful of other
persons. Additionally, the offenders were differentiated from the
nondelinquents on the two empirical scales: delinquency orientation
and emotional immaturity. Compared to the nonoffenders, institutionalized delinquents were more concerned about being normal, showed
more marked feelings of isolation, were less mature, lacked insight,
and tended to deny that they had problems. The delinquency proneness prediction scales, built up from items in the separate scales separated the two groups, although they overlapped to some degree. Some
nondelinquents had scores predictive of delinquency proneness, while
some offenders had scores indicative of nondelinquency.

Two interpretations of these results are possible. Perhaps the *institutionalized* delinquents were in their predicament because of personality problems which impelled them toward deviance. But it is also
possible that the attitudes discovered by Carl Jesness were the *result*
of involvement in misconduct. Perhaps the experiences of being
tagged as a delinquent and being processed in the correctional machinery were the sources of the bleak and hostile outlooks of the
lawbreakers. Surely it would be a suprise if we discovered that institutionalized lawbreakers have warm and friendly attitudes toward their
jailers.

Psychopathy and Delinquency[59]

One currently popular psychogenic hypothesis argues that many
delinquents (and criminals) exhibit what is alleged to be a particular
form of mental pathology: psychopathic personality (or sociopathic
personality). The term psychopath is usually employed to designate a
pattern of pathology characterized by egocentricity, asocial behavior,
insensitivity to others, and hostility. Actually, the designation is only
one of a number of synonymous terms employed, including psychopathic personality, constitutional psychopathic inferior, moral
imbecile, semantic dementia, sociopathy, and moral mania, which are
employed at different times.[60]

---

[59] Psychopathy formulations are discussed in greater detail in Gibbons, *Society,
Crime, and Criminal Careers*, pp. 158–64.

[60] Robert M. Lindner, *Rebel Without a Cause* (New York: Grune & Stratton, Inc.,
1944), p. 1.

If such a personality pattern exists, it might bear more than a slight relationship to delinquency, for persons showing these traits might be less governed by the demands of society because they are lacking in inner controls and are insensitive to contemporary conduct norms. But if we are to make any use of the concept of psychopathy, we must first develop some means by which to recognize psychopaths. Here is where the trouble begins—the concept has not been defined in a satisfactory manner. Most of the definitions indicate a rather general and unspecific symptomatology. Paul Preu, in examining the ways this concept has been used in practice, says: "The term, 'psychopathic personality' as commonly understood, is useless in psychiatric research. It is a diagnosis of convenience arrived at by a process of exclusion. It does not refer to a specific behavioral entity. It serves as a scrapbasket to which is relegated a group of otherwise unclassified personality disorders and problems. Delinquency of one kind or another constitutes the most frequently utilized symptomatic basis for diagnosis of psychopathic personality."[61] There is no reason why the term cannot be used in this way, but if it is to be a synonym for delinquency, it cannot be used to explain the same behavior.

Even though the notion of psychopathy is extremely ambiguous, a number of authorities have accepted the argument that sociopaths exist and that they appear in the population of delinquents in inordinate numbers.[62] But in none of these cases is any indication given of the prevalence of such personality problems in the population at large or in the population of offenders.

One recent and rather remarkable piece of research on psychopathy has been produced by Lee Robins, a particularly good illustration of the problems with this concept.[63] The study traced the adult adjustments of 524 child guidance clinic patients in St. Louis thirty years after they had appeared in the clinic. A comparison group of 100 normal school children were similarly subjected to a follow-up study. Most of the guidance clinic juveniles had been sent to the clinic by the juvenile court; over 70 percent had been referred for "antisocial conduct," i.e., runaway behavior, truancy, and theft. The remarkable feature of this study is that the investigators managed to obtain interviews concerning 82 percent of those individuals who had lived to the age of twenty-five, either from the subjects or from their relatives.

---

[61] Paul W. Preu, "The Concept of Psychopathic Personality," in J. McV. Hunt, ed., *Personality and Behavior Disorders,* II (New York: The Ronald Press Company, 1944), pp. 922–37.

[62] Bloch and Flynn, *Delinquency* pp. 144–49; Lewis Yablonsky, *The Violent Gang* (New York: The Macmillan Company, 1962).

[63] Lee N. Robins, *Deviant Children Grown Up* (Baltimore: The Williams & Wilkins Co., 1966).

The clinic patients who had been referred for antisocial conduct showed adult careers filled with frequent arrests for criminality and drunkenness, numerous divorces, occupational instability, psychiatric problems, and dependency on social agencies. For example, 44 percent of the antisocial male patients had been arrested for a major crime, but only 3 percent of the control patients had serious criminal records. In short, the clinic subjects exhibited generally ruined adult lives.

A major part of Robins' research concerned the detailed study of sociopathic personality among the subjects. Sociopaths were defined as persons who exhibited: *"a gross, repetitive failure to conform to societal norms in many areas of life, in the absence of thought disturbance suggesting psychosis"*.[64] The diagnosis of sociopathic personality was made in terms of adult behavior patterns. To be judged a sociopath, an individual had to exhibit symptoms of maladjustment within at least five of nineteen life areas, that is, he had to show some combination of poor work history, financial dependency, use of drugs, sexual misconduct, and so on. The final determination that a subject was a sociopath rested with two psychiatrists, who made clinical judgments from interview material. In all, 22 percent of the clinic subjects and 2 percent of the controls were designated as sociopaths. The clinic cases that were diagnosed as sociopaths had been referred almost exclusively for antisocial behavior, particularly theft.

Robins asserted that there is some kind of "disease" or personality entity behind the symptoms which produces sociopaths, but no convincing evidence of this elusive disease appeared in this report. Instead, the argument looks tautological in form. While the report showed that many youngsters who get into juvenile courts and guidance clinics live fairly disordered lives as adults, making a career of failure, there was little evidence in this research that these individuals were pathological personalities. Indeed, some of the findings tended to undermine the sociopath concept. For example, the data suggested that those antisocial children who avoided the juvenile court or training school were less likely to become sociopaths than those who had been through these organizations. Is it perhaps the crude machinery of these agencies, rather than psychopathy, which contributes to adult misfortune and wrecked lives? About a third of the sociopaths were judged to have given up much of their deviant activity by the time of the follow-up investigation. Since sociopaths are supposed to be especially intractable, how did these people escape?

We regard any attempt to proceed further with the psychopathy-

---

[64] *Ibid.*, p. 79. Emphasis in the original.

delinquency line of inquiry, as presently framed, a futile business. We cannot now answer questions about the relationship of delinquency and sociopathy in the terms in which they are bound.[65]

An Evaluation of Psychogenic Hypotheses[66]

What are we to make of all this material on psychogenic factors in delinquency? Our analysis has rejected psychoanalytic claims and notions about psychopathy as untestable. Viewpoints which are incapable of empirical verification have no place in theories of delinquency causation. We have also seen that those contentions that delinquents are characterized by gross indicators of psychological pathology do not square with the facts. The mass of studies which have searched for these severe emotional disturbances have failed to find them. In short, it appears that delinquents are no more or less ridden with personality pathology than are nonoffenders.

Consider those findings which indicate that institutionalized delinquents or court referrals are more hostile or defiant than nondelinquents. We have suggested that one plausible interpretation of these results is that they may reflect the effects of court appearance or institutionalization. These attitudes may not have preceded involvement in misconduct. A frequent outcome of experiences with correctional agencies may be some deterioration of the actor's self-image as he takes on some of the invidious identity imputed to him by correctional agents and society. Studies usually argue that emotional factors produce deviance, and do not as frequently entertain the reverse possibility. There is, however, much to be said for the hypothesis that contacts with the "defining agencies"—the social control organizations—contribute to the development of deviant personalities or role-conceptions.

[65] Gough's work, utilizing the So Scale of his California Personality Inventory, originally began as a venture in the area of psychopathy. The So Scale consists of 54 items which measure role-taking deficiencies, hostility toward one's family, feelings of despondency and alienation, rebelliousness, and poor scholastic achievement. Gough has administered this scale to diverse collections of nonoffenders and delinquents. His findings tend to show the offenders as less well socialized, more suspicious, etc. These are important data, but Gough's studies cannot be taken as evidence in support of orthodox psychopathy notions. For a discussion of Gough's work, see Gibbons, *Society, Crime, and Criminal Careers*, pp. 158–59; pp. 162–64.

[66] Psychogenic formulations in criminology are discussed in more detail in Gibbons, *Society, Crime, and Criminal Careers*, pp. 164–70.

If correctional experiences have an impact upon the personalities of offenders, it still may be the case that personality factors of a non-pathological form do operate in delinquency. Some of the studies examined previously, such as the Conger and Miller research, compel us to acknowledge the possibilitity that youngsters who get involved in delinquency commonly feel powerless in their social surroundings, alienated, hostile, bored with school, or show other feelings of personal inadequacy. Moreover, we have already observed that such a line of argument is compatible with sociological formulations which stress the adverse effects of social circumstances upon juveniles. As a case in point, certain sociological notions currently fashionable hold that middle-class adolescent males commonly experience a good deal of anxiety about masculinity, and much of their behavior is to be understood as a response to masculinity stresses.[67] Masculinity anxiety has also been advanced as a causal ingredient in the behavior of lower-class delinquents.[68]

This line of thinking suggests that careful theorizing is in order regarding the operation of psychological pressures in delinquency. We need to discontinue the fact-gathering sorties that have been all too common, and turn to research which is designed to test explicit hypotheses concerning postulated relationships between particular psychological patterns, social influences, and delinquent behavior.[69]

One model of the sort of theory and research that needs to be developed is to be found in the work of Richard L. Jenkins.[70] Jenkins and several collaborators have engaged in a series of research investigations of delinquent types, out of which Jenkins has advanced the argument that there are two common forms of misbehavior: adaptive

[67] Talcott Parsons, *Essays in Sociological Theory*, rev. ed. (New York: The Free Press, 1954), pp. 304–5; Gibbons, "Problems of Causal Analysis in Criminology: A Case Illustration."

[68] Walter B. Miller, "Lower Class Culture as a Generating Milieu of Gang Delinquency," *Journal of Social Issues*, XIV, 3 (1958), 5–19; Miller, "Implications of Urban Lower Class Culture for Social Work," *Social Service Review*, XXXIII (September 1959), 219–36.

[69] An illustration of the kind of work that is required can be found in Gibbons, "Problems of Causal Analysis in Criminology: A Case Illustration."

[70] H. Hart, Richard L. Jenkins, Sidney Axelrad, and P. Sperling, "Multiple Factor Analysis of Traits of Delinquent Boys," *Journal of Social Psychology*, XVII (May 1943), 191–201; Jenkins and Sylvia Glickman, "Common Syndromes in Child Psychiatry," *American Journal of Orthopsychiatry*, XVI (April 1946), 244–61; Jenkins and Glickman, "Patterns of Personality Organization Among Delinquents," *Nervous Child*, VI (July 1947), 329–39; Lester E. Hewitt and Jenkins, *Fundamental Patterns of Maladjustment: The Dynamics of Their Origin* (Springfield: State of Illinois Printer, 1947); Jenkins and Hewitt, "Types of Personality Structure Encountered in Child Guidance Clinics," *American Journal of Orthopsychiatry*, XIV (January 1944), 84–94.

and maladaptive delinquency.[71] Jenkins claimed that delinquent conduct is not a form of neurotic behavior, for neuroticism involves a high level of inhibition, sense of duty, and introjected standards and strict superego control, while delinquency is frequently the direct opposite of such a pattern. In addition, only the maladaptive or unsocialized offender has a disturbed personality. This is the aggressive lawbreaker who is poorly socialized, lacking in internalized controls, antagonistic toward his peers, and generally maladjusted. The more frequently encountered adaptive, or pseudosocial, offender is usually the product of lower-class slum areas, and is reasonably well socialized and "normal" among his peers and parents. He is characterized by attenuated inhibitions; his loyalty and group identification do not extend to the wider community beyond his local area and immediate peers. Although his hostile posture toward law enforcement and correctional agents is a source of concern to them, the adaptive delinquent is hardly a pathological person.

Jenkins' idea that there may be different types of delinquents, each showing particular psychological characteristics, has become prominent in recent years. The writings of Sethard Fisher,[72] John Kinch,[73] and Albert Reiss[74] are instances of this orientation. This is the direction toward which psychogenic theorizing and research need to be pointed.

SOCIOGENIC THEORIES OF DELINQUENCY

Delinquency and Social Structure

There has been no dearth of broad arguments about social structure and criminalistic conduct. These views, markedly divergent from psychogenic ones, all advance a picture with roughly the same details: a characterization of criminals and delinquents as normal individuals

---

[71] Richard L. Jenkins, "Adaptive and Maladaptive Delinquency," *Nervous Child*, II (October 1955), 9–11; Jenkins, "Motivation and Frustration in Delinquency," *American Journal of Orthopsychiatry*, XXVII (July 1957), 528–37; Jenkins, *Breaking Patterns of Defeat* (Philadelphia: J.B. Lippincott Co., 1954).

[72] Sethard Fisher, "Varieties of Juvenile Delinquency," *British Journal of Criminology*, II (January 1962), 251–61.

[73] John W. Kinch, "Continuities in the Study of Delinquent Types," *Journal of Criminal Law, Criminology and Police Science*, LIII (September 1962), 323–28; Kinch, "Self-Conceptions of Types of Delinquents," *Sociological Inquiry*, XXXII (Spring 1962), 228–34.

[74] Albert J. Reiss, Jr., "Social Correlates of Psychological Types of Delinquency," *American Sociological Review*, XVII (December 1952), 710–18.

who are reacting to deficiencies of the social organization in which they find themselves.

One of the most influential of these lines of speculation places major emphasis upon the lack of opportunity for achievement of common American success goals. This is Robert Merton's theory of anomie, which contends that delinquency (and other forms of deviance) is a response to the unavailability of conventional or socially approved routes to success, and is characteristic of lower-class persons.[75]

A number of other sociological statements on crime and delinquency focus upon such features of societal structure as the causal mechanisms in lawbreaking. The social disorganization line of thinking is one of these, holding that American society shows ruptured bonds of social relationship, lack of social coordination, teamwork, and morale, and other rents and tears in the social fabric.[76] Some sociologists have attributed delinquency to the clash of values in a pluralistic society, to the impersonality, individualism, disrespect for law and order, exploitiveness, and other ingredients central to the American way of life.[77]

These theories of delinquency, framed in differential social organization terms, have a ring of plausibility. Common sense seems to point to the influence of social organization—including differentials in availability of legitimate means to attainment of cultural goals, the growing bureaucratization of "mass society," racial and ethnic cleavages of nominally democratic society, and alienation—upon juvenile misconduct. These factors seem to make sense out of much of the juvenile lawbreaking in this society.

But the problem with these formulations is that they are extremely broad and vague.[78] Precisely how do these abstract influences "get inside" the delinquent, so to speak, to produce his behavior? Most broad theories are silent on that question. Then, too, the factors these formulations depend upon quite probably apply with more force to some kinds of youthful misconduct than to others. Perhaps the behav-

[75] Robert K. Merton, *Social Theory and Social Structure*, revised and enlarged ed. (New York: The Free Press, 1957), pp. 131–94. This perspective is discussed at some length in Gibbons, *Society, Crime, and Criminal Careers*, pp. 176–81. A number of criticisms of it are also noted there, most of them having to do with the theoretical fuzziness of the argument which renders it virtually untestable.

[76] See Gibbons, *Society, Crime, and Criminal Careers*, pp. 182–86, for a discussion of some of these disorganization arguments.

[77] Barron, *The Juvenile in Delinquent Society*, Donald R. Taft and Ralph W. England, Jr., *Criminology*, 4th ed. (New York: The Macmillan Company, 1964), pp. 277–79; Sutherland and Cressey, *Principles of Criminology*, pp. 101–21; Tappan, *Juvenile Delinquency* pp. 66–72.

[78] For another evaluation of general theories, see Gibbons, *Society, Crime, and Criminal Careers*, pp. 188–90.

ior of working-class, predatory thieves grows out of these influences to a much greater extent than does misconduct on the part of middle-class youths. Perhaps the behavior of some kinds of maladjusted delinquents is due to factors that are ignored in broad sociological claims.

The shortcomings of broad arguments about social structure and "juvenile delinquency" have become generally recognized in recent years. The thrust of the work by many contemporary delinquency theorists has been toward more specific, middle-range theories which deal with subgroups of juvenile offenders and which attempt to outline the influences of social organization more clearly and in greater detail. The theorizing and research concerning subcultural delinquency prominently exemplifies this emerging trend. In that work, anomic influences upon working-class juveniles are identified in detail. Attention has been given to the socialization processes through which these factors presumably exert their impact upon youths. In short, this body of activity has produced embryo theory of much greater sophistication than the general claims.

The Social-Psychology of Delinquent Careers

A good many theoretical essays are now available which concern processes by which deviants become caught in aberrant activity, continue in it, or desist from deviance, and which can be utilized to inform the study of delinquency.[79] One of the most important of these, conducted by Lemert, contains a number of seminal ideas concerning deviant behavior.[80] Much of his presentation focuses upon *processual* aspects of deviant behavior, by which he shows that deviant careers often undergo marked changes over time. In Lemert's opinion, initial acts of deviance are often instances of "risk taking," tentative flirtations with proscribed behavior patterns. This kind of activity is termed *primary deviation,* for, at that point, the deviant views his norm-violating conduct as alien to his true self. *Secondary deviation,* on the other hand, involves cases in which the person reorganizes his social-psychological characteristics around the deviant role. In primary deviation a boy thinks of his acts of theft and vandalism as "hell-raising," and sees himself as a "good boy." Secondary deviation would be reflected in the behavior of a juvenile who is

[79] Much of this material is discussed in Gibbons, *Society, Crime, and Criminal Careers,* pp. 193–213.

[80] Lemert, *Human Deviance;* Lemert, *Social Pathology* (New York: McGraw-Hill Book Company, 1951).

heavily involved in misconduct and who views himself as a "tough kid" and a "delinquent."

According to Lemert, primary deviation sometimes becomes secondary in form, while in other cases it remains primary. Secondary deviation most often arises out of societal reactions; a feedback process occurs in which repetition of misconduct triggers societal reactions to the behavior, which stimulate further deviant acts. The misbehaving person is driven further into deviance by the stigma attached to his pariah status.

Most of Lemert's writings deal with the broad class of social deviants, rather than with detailed specification of how these processes operate in the case of delinquency. We need to take these ideas as sensitizing ones when we begin to examine particular forms of delinquent conduct. The same point holds for other formulations about deviant behavior which lay out some major concepts thought to be useful in the study of deviance.[81] Much of our attention will center about efforts to apply modern perspectives on career processes in deviance to delinquent behavior.

A similar evaluation can be made of other sociological hypotheses about the development of delinquent behavior, such as the view that family processes weigh heavily in juvenile misconduct.[82] For example, it has often been argued that ruptured homes are a major cause of lawbreaking. Jackson Toby has recently shown that broken homes are of differential importance in different kinds of delinquency. Older male offenders are from broken homes no more frequently than nonoffenders from similar neighborhoods. However, the difference between preadolescent male delinquents and nonoffenders in terms of broken homes is rather marked, as it is with delinquent and nondelinquent girls.[83] The influence of various social factors probably varies among different forms of misconduct.

THE FUTURE OF DELINQUENCY THEORY

How are we to handle the discordant lines of thought concerning juvenile lawbreaking which we have examined in this chapter? We

---

[81] Howard S. Becker, *Outsiders* (New York: The Free Press, 1963); Erving Goffman, *Stigma* (Englewood Cliffs, N.J.: Prentice-Hall, Inc., 1963).

[82] Some of this material is discussed in Gibbons, *Society, Crime, and Criminal Careers*, pp. 208–13.

[83] Jackson Toby, "The Differential Impact of Family Disorganization," *American Sociological Review*, XXII (October 1957), 505–12.

have already spoken against that counsel which suggests that we throw all of these varied factors together into some kind of etiological smorgasbord. Instead, some way must be found to judiciously put these influences into some kind of coherent order and to assign different weights to them, depending upon the contribution they make to delinquent conduct.[84]

The most prominent contemporary suggestion as to ways in which convergence of psychogenic and sociogenic arguments might be effected in criminology centers about the development of typologies, of classification schemes which attempt to sort the population of offenders into homogeneous categories or types. In the study both of adult criminality and of juvenile delinquency, the suggestion has been repeatedly heard that criminologists ought to turn their attention to behavioral types and away from examination of heterogeneous collections of "criminals" and "delinquents."[85]

There is a readily apparent common sense basis for the typological orientation in criminology. Clearly, the procedure which throws violent rapists, embezzlers, professional thieves, armed robbers, political criminals, abortionists, and other offenders together into a group called "criminals" disguises more than it clarifies. Who would be bold enough to suppose that these lawbreakers all developed out of the same causal process? Similarly, nearly all would agree that there must be something radically different about gang delinquents, sex offenders, petty "hidden" offenders, juvenile arsonists, hyper-aggressive delinquents, and the other lawbreakers who are lumped together under the term "delinquent." It does not make much sense to collect such a diverse bunch of youths and to compare them with "nondelinquents," in the search for etiological variables.

It is out of considerations of this kind that the typological notions in criminology have grown. Various efforts have been made to organize the findings of criminological investigation in this manner, including an extended statement by Don Gibbons on adult criminal

---

[84] One effort in this direction is John M. Martin and Joseph P. Fitzpatrick, *Delinquent Behavior* (New York: Random House, Inc., 1964), pp. 145–89. These authors have attempted to sketch out the differential influence upon delinquency of properties of the organism; social influences; and motives, attitudes, personality problems, and other intervening problems.

[85] The development of this orientation, along with a listing of many of these statements, is dealt with in detail in Gibbons, *Society, Crime, and Criminal Careers*, pp. 217–23; and also in Gibbons, *Changing the Lawbreaker* (Englewood Cliffs, N.J.: Prentice-Hall, Inc., 1965), pp. 24–39. This line of work is also discussed at length in Theodore N. Ferdinand, *Typologies of Delinquency* (New York: Random House, Inc., 1966); National Clearinghouse for Mental Health Information, *Typological Approaches and Delinquency Control: A Status Report* (Washington, D.C.: U.S. Department of Health, Education, and Welfare, 1967).

role-careers.[86] In addition, he has been involved in the development of typological perspectives on delinquency, and in the generation of a typological classification of delinquent patterns.[87]

However, some remarks are in order concerning the nature of offender typologies. What does a good typology look like? A typological scheme is a system which identifies separate *categories* into which persons or things can be sorted. Ideally, the things which the typology orders can be placed in category *A*, *B*, or *C* of the system, but not in two of the types. Sex is such a system, and, for most purposes at least, individuals are either males or females, but not both. Sex is not quantitative, that is, individuals are not male or female only to some degree or in some amount. A typology is a qualitative device of measurement, not a quantitative one, for it assigns things to discrete categories instead of identifying degrees of some property. In the area of criminality and delinquency, a typology is a classification scheme which identifies two or more discrete categories into which individual offenders are placed.

One requirement of an adequate typology is immediately apparent: the dimensions or variables around which it is constructed must be clearly defined so that observers can recognize types when they conduct observations. Typologies which are so ambiguous that they cannot be verified by research are of no use.

Typologies are the product of human invention; they do not simply leap out at us from raw observations about the real world. For example, sociologists may be able to identify "gang delinquents" or "overly aggressive offenders" as clear-cut types, even though the actors who fall into these types may not recognize the existence of such a classification or may not define themselves in this manner. We shall not take up the thorny question of whether such types are real or not, except to say that useful typologies are those which bear a fairly close correspondence to observations that are made about offenders.

How close must this correspondence be between types and facts in the empirical world? Some typologies are stated in such a way as to claim that real-life subjects are exact duplicates of the categories of the scheme, while other typologies are *heuristic* and deal in exaggerated portraits of types, such that real-life subjects only approximate the categories of the scheme. In this case, persons are judged to be closer to type *A* or to type *B* in the system, but are not carbon copies of either. Those who deal in typologies ought to be prepared to indicate which of these relationships between types and the real world is implied in the scheme of classification they put forward.

---

[86] Gibbons, *Society, Crime, and Criminal Careers*, passim.
[87] Gibbons, *Changing the Lawbreaker*, pp. 43–53.

These remarks about the ingredients of typologies should be kept in mind when we examine various type schemes. Both the adult and juvenile typologies of Gibbons are based upon certain assumptions regarding the nature of deviant conduct in American society.[88] In general, these presuppositions argue that relatively discrete patterns among offenders can be observed when these persons are classified in terms of certain variables or dimensions. The dimensions in question have to do with offense behavior and with social-psychological characteristics of offenders.

Although it is not claimed that offenders restrict their illegal actions to highly specific kinds of lawbreaking, the assumption is made that groups of delinquents or criminals do show certain congeries of offense behavior in common. By way of illustration, certain criminals tend to become involved in naïve check forgery and drunkenness to the exclusion of other kinds of lawlessness. Another group of delinquents carry on various predatory offenses, along with gang fighting, all within an interactional setting of peer group tolerance for deviant conduct. Thus our typologies contend that *offense behavior* and *interactional setting* are two important, related dimensions on which violators can be sorted out.

We also maintain that persons who show certain offense patterns in common usually show similar social-psychological characteristics. For example, gang delinquents exhibit *self-concepts* as delinquents and verbalize hostile *attitudes* toward policemen, school officials, and other representatives of middle-class morality.

Throughout the nine delinquent types and twenty-one adult criminal patterns in our typologies, these four dimensions of offense behavior, interactional setting, self-concept, and attitudes are used jointly as the basis for sorting offenders into the following categories: (1) predatory gang delinquent, (2) conflict gang delinquent, (3) causal gang delinquent, (4) causal delinquent, nongang member, (5) automobile thief —"joyrider," (6) drug user—heroin, (7) overly aggressive delinquent, (8) female delinquent, and (9) "behavior problem" delinquent.[89]

Where did these delinquent and criminal types come from? Why are there nine delinquent patterns rather than five, six, fifteen, or some other number? The answer is that they were drawn out of existing research studies, speculative hunches gained from case records, and such other sources. Many of these claims about certain adult and juvenile types stand as research hypotheses, rather than as empirically established forms of conduct.

[88] Gibbons, *Society, Crime, and Criminal Careers*, pp. 223–26; Gibbons, *Changing the Lawbreaker*, pp. 44–47.

[89] Gibbons, *Changing the Lawbreaker*, pp. 78–97.

Just what is the correspondence between the empirical world and these typologies? It seems likely that some types in the adult scheme have real life duplicates in the population of offenders. Thus it is probable that naïve check forgers who closely resemble the description in the typology do exist in correctional case loads. But there are other types which are not found in pure form among actual offenders, so that real-life criminals only approximate these types. Finally, the behavior of some violators is a mixture of ingredients such that they are not subsumed within the typology at all. A recent investigation in a probation setting by Clayton Hartjen and Don Gibbons produced findings of this kind. Some of the probationers seemed to be members of the types in the adult typology, some appeared to fall into other types which were not included in the typology, and still others could not be classified into any type.[90]

The closeness of fit between delinquent typologies and actual offenders is probably even poorer. Stated differently, typological schemes put more order into juvenile lawbreaking than exists in fact. For one thing, we need to remember that delinquents are juveniles, not full-blown adults. They are relatively unsophisticated individuals; many of them are uninformed on the ways of criminality. We should expect to find few dedicated thieves, armed robbers, or embezzlers among them. Their interests fluctuate, so that we should be surprised if many of them have made strong commitments to particular forms of lawbreaking. Then, too, the vicissitudes of police-offender interaction, court appearance, and the like are such that many of them are able to drift in and out of misconduct. For all of these reasons, clear-cut careers of specialized delinquency are probably uncommon.

Some recent empirical investigations show findings consistent with these claims. In the area of gang delinquency, typological formulations have been set forth in some number, asserting that gang offenders come in several distinct forms. But, as we shall see in Chapter Five, these recent studies indicate that behavioral *versatility*, rather than *specialization*, is most characteristic of gang offenders. Similarly, several pieces of research have appeared which cast doubt upon the claim that auto thief-joyriders are an entirely distinct group.

These remarks do not mean that typological perspectives on delinquency ought to be jettisoned. Some offender types apparently are quite distinct, such as overly aggressive delinquents. Other lawbreakers more or less resemble the types in our typology. Our observations stand as a caveat against the premature acceptance of all the contentions in a typology. Delinquent type schemes should be taken as heu-

---

[90] Clayton A. Hartjen and Don C. Gibbons, "An Empirical Investigation of a Criminal Typology," *Sociology and Social Research*, LIV (October 1969), pp. 56–62.

ristic bench marks against which myriad instances of lawbreaking can be measured. We will therefore deal with the facts of juvenile misbehavior within the general rubrics of working-class gang, or subcultural delinquency; middle-class delinquency; female delinquency; and "behavior problem" delinquency. In addition, we shall look at juvenile lawbreakers from other societies.

The listed offender groups have repeatedly been employed in the delinquency literature. A great many observers have argued that gang offenders constitute a distinct kind of lawbreaker, set off from other misbehaving adolescents in terms of the kind of deviance they engage in, their attitudes, and other characteristics. In addition, the opinion is widespread that these law violators are usually working-class boys, so that the causal question has often been asked: "What is it about working-class social life which generates or produces this kind of youthful lawbreaking?" Many delinquency analysts have suggested that middle-class youngsters who engage in delinquency represent another relatively distinct type whose conduct is in some ways a response to social-structural influences of middle-class status structure. Thus the query has often been posed: "What characteristics of middle-class social life lie behind the delinquency of middle-income youths?" In the same way, many have supposed that girl offenders are a separate type in terms of lawbreaking behavior and psychological characteristics. Here again, the causal question takes the general form: "What is it about the ways in which girls are socialized in American society which leads to the kinds of delinquency in which they engage?"A number of investigators have contended that "behavior problem" offenders stand as still another distinct grouping and that their activities stem from relatively idiosyncratic socialization experiences which cut across social class lines. In other words, the hypothesis in this instance is that distorted primary group relationships which produce "behavior problem" offenders occur in all social class groupings. Finally, a good many students of delinquency have entertained the view that juvenile misconduct in other countries probably shows some behavioral coloration related to the cultural conditions in which it occurs. Stated differently, perhaps English, French, or Japanese delinquents differ in behavior from American offenders because of cultural influences in these countries. These categories do mirror some important variations in the real world of juvenile lawbreakers. However, the possibility that more specific types can be observed within these classes must be explored at some length.

A PERSPECTIVE ON DELINQUENCY

The first four chapters have been designed to define the extent of the delinquency problem and to clear away theoretical underbrush in the study of delinquency causation. A number of propositions about juvenile lawbreaking have either been explicitly set out or clearly implied. These claims constitute a set of basic assumptions which inform the analysis to follow. In other words, these contentions stand as the structure upon which analysis of delinquency in the remainder of the book depends. Let us restate these claims which make up our perspective on juvenile lawbreaking:[91]

1. Behavior which violates delinquency statutes is commonplace; nearly all youngsters engage in at least some delinquent behavior during their juvenile careers. At the same time, marked variations occur among offenders in the extent and seriousness of their involvement in lawbreaking. Some juvenile delinquents engage in repetitive, serious forms of misconduct, while others are implicated only in relatively innocuous kinds of misbehavior.

2. Those offenders who get into the hands of the police and are processed through the juvenile justice system tend to be the more career-oriented delinquents who are involved in serious misconduct. However, the factors which enter into police apprehension, court referral, and other decisions are several, such that the offender's prospects of becoming identified as a "juvenile delinquent" are partially dependent upon characteristics of policemen, police departments, court personnel, and community influences.

3. Relatively stable patterns of delinquent roles, involving recurrent forms of deviant activity accompanied by uniform social-psychological role characteristics (self-concept and attitude patterns) can be observed in the population of offenders. In these terms, it can be said that types of delinquency and delinquent role-careers exist.

4. Most juvenile offenders are relatively normal youths in terms of personality structure, in that they do not exhibit aberrant motives, deep-seated psychological tensions, or other marks of psychological disturbances. Officially processed delinquents often do show hostile attitudes, defiance of authority, and characteristics of that kind. However, these are not personality dimensions which are indicative of psychological maladjustment. In addition, some of these personality characteristics may be the product or result of correctional handling. At the same time, there are some youthful lawbreakers who do show atypical personality patterns to which their delinquency may be a response.

5. Delinquency laws forbid a wide range of conduct, so that there are a

---

[91] These claims are a revised version of material which is found in Gibbons, *Society, Crime, and Criminal Careers,* pp. 224–26.

number of role patterns within the offender population. (Some delinquents restrict their activities to forms of predatory theft and allied conduct, some are mainly involved in car theft, still others are principally caught up in sexual misconduct, while still others exhibit aggressive behavior.)

6. The specific causal process that leads to one particular kind of delinquent role behavior involves a number of etiological variables and differs from that which produces another delinquent pattern. In this sense, delinquent behavior is the product of multiple-causation. At the same time, it is possible to identify the different etiological processes which are involved in the various forms of delinquency.

7. Delinquent behavior is learned behavior, acquired in the processes of socialization. Accordingly, the causes of juvenile misconduct are not to be found in biological factors (even though biological variables may play an indirect role in juvenile lawbreaking).

8. The learning of delinquent roles is maximized in a criminalistic society, and the United States is such a society. Much delinquent behavior in the competitive, materialistic American society is societally generated and takes the form of direct and indirect assaults upon property.

9. Some delinquent roles are mainly the consequence of social class variations in socialization and life experiences, along with other social-structural variables. In particular, situations in which legitimate avenues to the attainment of common American goals and values are blocked are importantly involved in certain forms of crime and delinquency. Those members of disadvantaged social groups and social strata may be relatively commonly involved in deviant behavior which is a response to their situation of social and economic deprivation. Additionally, certain class-related influences in other social strata may operate to produce juvenile offenders in those classes. For example, problems of masculine identity may be more common in middle-class groups than elsewhere, and may be importantly involved in middle-class delinquency.

10. Some delinquent roles are produced by family and other socialization experiences which are not class-linked or class-specific. Among these are "parental rejection," "deviant sexual socialization," and others. These kinds of experiences occur at all social class levels.

11. The "defining agencies" (police, probation services, courts, and so forth) play a part both in the definition of deviants and in the continuation of deviant roles. The result of apprehension and "treatment" may be quite contrary to the expected result. In other words, although one official function of correctional agencies and processes is the reformation of the offender, the actual outcome may often be the isolation of the person, reinforcement of the deviant role, and rejection of society by the offender, the final result being nonreformation.

These notions are not controversial for the most part. They assert that delinquents come in a variety of forms, that most of them are relatively normal youngsters, and that the causes of their behavior are to be located in a variety of places.

This emphasis upon delinquency as role behavior is designed to direct attention to the fact that juvenile misconduct is only one of a large number of forms of activity engaged in by youths. We should be on guard against thinking of offenders in terms of the layman's conception of "delinquents," which implies that this term is descriptive of the total behavior of individuals. Even within delinquent gangs, participation in deviant conduct occupies only a small fraction of the time of the participants; most of their behavior is nondelinquent, consisting of school attendance, normal recreational activities, and the like. There are other forms of juvenile lawbreaking in which the participants spend even less of their time, such that delinquency is episodic, infrequent, and not regarded by the actor as central to his true nature.

Our stress upon role-careers in delinquency is focused upon a related point, namely that many youthful offenders participate in illegal acts only a few times and discontinue these before they get into the hands of the police or the courts. These are lawbreakers who demonstrate short-lived careers in deviance. On the other hand, there are some delinquents who pursue their lawbreaking course of action over an extended period of time. The perspective also suggests that careers in delinquency may be influenced by correctional experiences of one kind or another, that one factor which may contribute to long-term involvement in criminality centers about the individual's experience with law enforcement and correctional agents.

A good deal of commentary has suggested that the motivation for involvement in youthful misconduct probably varies among lawbreakers. Some of these youths probably drift into juvenile misconduct as they respond to peer group pressures to define "raising hell" as proper behavior, or as they are drawn into participation in illegal conduct in other ways, without any firm intention of becoming a "juvenile delinquent." Still other offenders can probably be found who are engaged in lawbreaking in response to perceptions of unequal opportunity, to parent-child tensions in the home, or to other conditions of that sort. In short, the competing drift and driven conceptions of the offender may both have relevance to delinquency.

Perhaps the search for the mainsprings of juvenile misconduct should be directed at elements of the social order, such as social class patterns, the educational system, urban social organization, or elements of middle-class life styles. This perspective places accent upon the sociological view, which supposes that behavior as widespread as delinquency probably develops out of conditions of social structure.

At the same time, these contentions also provide some room for the possibility that some youthful deviance is carried on by psychologically maladjusted youngsters who are the product of atypical socialization experiences. Finally, they suggest that we pay careful attention to the workings of the social control apparatus, for it may play some part in the etiology of delinquency.

These claims represent the operating assumptions upon which most sociological analyses of juvenile lawbreaking proceed. We refrain from calling this perspective a "theory of delinquency," for it is a far cry from the kind of systematic exposition which we earlier identified as theory. But let us now put this perspective to work in the study of particular forms of juvenile misconduct. What kind of sense can be made of the theories and research evidence within the framework of these claims? In the chapters to follow, we shall pull some more specific generalizations out of the delinquency literature. Taken together, these assumptions and the additional contentions will constitute a beginning version of delinquency theory.

chapter five

WORKING-CLASS PATTERNS OF DELINQUENCY

INTRODUCTION

In this chapter we begin to move directly into an examination of sociological explanations of delinquency, beginning with lawbreaking among working-class youths because sociologists have amassed an impressive collection of theories and research on this class of youthful misconduct. They have observed that groups of official delinquents include a large number of youngsters from working-class backgrounds, many of whom have been involved in gang or subcultural delinquency. In addition, most sociologists have been impressed by the role of peer influences in the learning processes through which these youngsters become deviants. In short, working-class delinquency is of particular interest because it appears to be the most common form of youthful criminality. But, in addition, it is of significance because it apparently is carried on by normal youngsters who are responding to "abnormal," that is, socially disorganized, life circumstances. Working-class gang delinquency looks like a pronounced case of the operation of social-structural factors in the genesis of misconduct.

Our discussion begins with some of the earlier writings on working-class delinquency which grew out of "the Chicago School" of sociology in the early 1900s. We shall also examine a number of more recent statistical-ecological studies before we turn to the plethora of subcultural theories and research investigations which have sprung up since 1950. This material is a rich body of sophisticated theorizing and impressive research representing modern sociology at its best.

THE ECOLOGICAL DISTRIBUTION OF DELINQUENCY

Background

The study of crime and delinquency rates by city areas represents one of the oldest interests of American criminologists, so that there is a wealth of research now available on that subject.[1] All of these investigations started off from the common sense observation that delinquency and crime are apparently not distributed equally in community areas. Instead, in some neighborhoods, deviance is endemic, while, in others, it is rarely encountered. That much about the spatial patterning of lawbreaking is obvious.

The first major sociological studies of the ecology of criminality took place in Chicago in the 1930s and 1940s, with the work of Frederic Thrasher,[2] Clifford Shaw and Henry McKay,[3] and others. Shaw and McKay found that official rates (juvenile court referrals) varied widely in areas of Chicago and elsewhere, that highest rates were in neighborhoods of rapid population change, poor housing, poverty, tuberculosis, adult crime, and mental disorders.[4] They regarded all of these correlates of delinquency as reflections of an underlying state of social disorganization. They viewed areas of high delinquency as communities which were lacking in social stability, normative consensus, and social cohesion, which, as as result, freed youngsters from the bind of social control to engage in lawbreaking.

[1] Much of this material is summarized in Edwin H. Sutherland and Donald R. Cressey, *Principles of Criminology*, 7th ed. (Philadelphia: J. B. Lippincott Co., 1966), pp. 192–215.

[2] Frederic M. Thrasher, *The Gang*, abridged and with a new introduction by James F. Short, Jr., (Chicago: University of Chicago Press, 1963).

[3] Clifford Shaw and Henry D. McKay, *Juvenile Delinquency and Urban Areas* (Chicago: University of Chicago Press, 1942); Shaw and McKay, *Social Factors in Juvenile Delinquency*, Report on the Causes of Crime for the National Commission on Law Observance and Enforcement, Vol. II (Washington, D.C.: U. S. Government Printing Office, 1930); see also Shaw, *The Jack Roller* (Chicago: University of Chicago Press, 1930); Shaw and Maurice E. Moore, *The Natural History of a Delinquent Career* (Philadelphia: A. Saifer, Publisher, 1951); Shaw, McKay, and James F. McDonald, *Brothers in Crime* (Chicago: University of Chicago Press, 1938).

[4] Shaw and McKay, *Social Factors in Juvenile Delinquency*, pp. 60–108; Shaw and McKay, *Juvenile Delinquency and Urban Areas*, p. 11.

Shaw and McKay also advanced some other major conclusions about delinquency rates and urban areas.[5] First, delinquency rates varied widely among different neighborhoods, so that in all fifteen cities studied, none of the boys in some areas had been arrested, while in others, more than one-fifth had been apprehended in a single year. The latter neighborhoods were termed "delinquency areas" by Shaw and McKay. Second, high rates were usually found near the industrial areas and deteriorated community sections around the city center. Third, areas of high delinquency also showed high truancy rates and high rates of commitment of adults to county jail. Fourth, the areas of high delinquency in 1930 also had high rates in 1900, even though the nationality composition of the populations there had changed markedly. Finally, delinquency rates for particular ethnic groups showed the gradient tendency, high rates occurred near the city center and low rates toward the city periphery.

What do these patterns reflect? One interpretation is that they demonstrate the phenomenon of *differential law enforcement*. If this is the case, the correlates of delinquency rates are not the causes of lawbreaking. Instead, they are indicators of the characteristics of persons against whom the courts and police are biased. This contention assumes that the true delinquency rates (official and "hidden" cases) are approximately the same from one area to another.

A second interpretation of ecological correlations is that they are related to the *differential distribution of delinquency*. Shaw and McKay thought their findings to be indicative of this pattern, so that they viewed the crime rates as meaningful indices of total delinquency and the ecological correlates as causal factors.

While juvenile misbehavior occurs throughout the community, lawbreaking is most serious and repetitive in certain disadvantaged areas. The data in Chapter Two suggest that the distribution of rates of official delinquency is relatively parallel to the ecological patterning of total delinquency, and particularly of serious lawbreaking. We would reiterate that while official rates may partially reflect differential law enforcement and discrimination on the part of the police, they even more strongly point to the differential distribution of serious delinquency. In short, rates are high in certain areas because serious, repetitive misconduct is most common there.

The deteriorated character of delinquency neighborhoods can be seen on simple "spot maps," in which the cases of official delinquency are designated for neighborhoods by dots or colored pins. The concentration of spots is heaviest in certain areas of low income, physical

[5] These are summarized in Sutherland and Cressey, *Principles of Criminology*, p. 192.

deterioration, and the like. The same picture can be obtained by correlational procedures. Thus, correlation coefficients between single variables and delinquency for census tracts in Baltimore, Detroit, and Indianapolis are shown in Table 5-1.[6]

We can see in the table that six of the seven ecological variables there were fairly strongly related to delinquency; the only exception was the proportion of foreign-born in census tracts, which was associated with juvenile lawbreaking only in Detroit. We would discover sizable correlations if we were to examine a great many other variables and delinquency rates. Taken together, they all suggest that certain areas which have a monopoly on conditions of social wretchedness are also most ridden with juvenile and adult criminality.

All of these correlations raise the question of causal significance. Are some of the factors fundamental producers of delinquency? Are other variables merely associated with lawbreaking, due to their correlation with the fundamental, causal ones? Surely not all of the multitudinous variables which are statistically associated with juvenile misconduct are causal ones. This problem has been attacked in a number of statistical-ecological studies which have brought a group of

TABLE 5-1 Correlation Coefficients, Ecological Variables,
and Delinquency, by City

VARIABLE	BALTIMORE	DETROIT	INDIANAPOLIS
Education	-.51	-.47	-.64
Rent	-.54	-.35	-.57
Owner-occupied dwellings	-.80	-.61	-.64
Foreign-born	-.16	-.44	-.11
Nonwhite	.70	.52	.41
Overcrowding	.73	.65	.85
Substandard housing	.69	.62	.81

[6] These zero order correlation coefficients are reported in Roland J. Chilton, "Continuity in Delinquency Area Research: A Comparison of Studies for Baltimore, Detroit, and Indianapolis," *American Sociological Review*, XXIX (February 1964), 73; the data for Indianapolis are in Chilton, *op. cit.*, pp. 71–83; for Detroit from David J. Bordua, "Juvenile Delinquency and 'Anomie': An Attempt at Replication," *Social Problems*, VI (Winter 1958–1959), 230–38; for Baltimore from Bernard Lander, *Toward an Understanding of Juvenile Delinquency* (New York: Columbia University Press, 1954); these correlations and others in the chapter should be read as meaning that the closer they are to a value of 1.00, the greater the association of that factor with delinquency. Correlations which are negative involve associations in which values of the factor decrease as delinquency rates increase. Thus on the education item, delinquency rates for census tracts are highest in areas where mean educational level is lowest.

sophisticated statistical techniques, including partial correlation, multiple regression analysis, and factor analysis, to bear upon the question of causal significance. Because of their complexity, we can only provide a brief overview of them.

Lander's Study[7]

Bernard Lander, in his study in Baltimore, was the pioneer investigator of ecological interrelationships. He computed delinquency rates for census tracts in that city, using official court cases for the period of 1939–1942. He also employed seven census tract variables as indicators of the ecological structure of neighborhoods. Table 5-1 contains these variables and their zero-order correlations with delinquency rates. Because all of the associations are relatively strong, all seven variables appeared to be related to delinquency.

However, the results from the application of a variety of correlational techniques and factor analysis suggested to Lander that only two of his variables were independent correlates of the delinquency rate. These factors were the percent of nonwhites in tracts and percent of owner-occupied homes. The other five variables did not hold up as correlates of delinquency when partial correlations were computed. Lander also carried out a factor analysis which led him to conclude that delinquency is due to anomie, or social instability, revealed in the nonwhite and owner-occupied home factors, while economic variables were judged to be less important. This conclusion was based upon the association of the nonwhite population and owner-occupied housing variables with the delinquency rate. Lander interpreted the clustering of these items into a factor as an indication of an underlying condition of anomie, in which normative control over behavior is defective or missing. It is this anomic condition, rather than economic deprivation, which causes delinquency, according to Lander.

Replication Studies[8]

Lander's research provoked a variety of responses, including sev-

---

[7] Lander, *Toward an Understanding of Juvenile Delinquency.*

[8] These include Bordua, "Juvenile Delinquency and 'Anomie'"; Chilton, "Continuity in Delinquency Area Research"; William Bates, "Caste, Class, and Vandalism," *Social Problems,* IX (Spring 1962), 349–58; see Chilton, *op. cit.,* p. 71 for a bibliography of other replicative studies.

eral other investigations which attempted to replicate it, that is, to verify its conclusions through repetition of it in other areas. One of these was by Bordua's study of Detroit, which involved court cases of delinquency between 1948 and 1952.[9] Although Lander had found a curvilinear relationship of percent nonwhite population and the delinquency rate, Bordua failed to find this result in Detroit. That is, Lander observed that rates of lawbreaking were highest in areas with approximately half nonwhite residents and lower in neighborhoods with either fewer or more nonwhites. In Detroit, the relationship was a direct one in which the larger the proportion of nonwhites, the larger the delinquency rate.

Bordua reported that home ownership was the factor most strongly related to delinquency, and that economic variables were not correlated with juvenile misconduct when other factors were held constant. Thus Bordua argued that his study generally duplicated Lander's findings, even though not all of the empirical findings were identical.[10] On this point, Bordua also found educational level and overcrowding to be strong predictors of delinquency rates.

Roland Chilton conducted another replication, comparing delinquency rates in Indianapolis with those in Baltimore and Detroit.[11] His investigation utilized rates based on juvenile court referrals for 1948–1950 and employed a number of correlational procedures and factor analysis. He concluded that Lander's claim that anomie is more closely related to delinquency than economic characteristics of neighborhoods was not clearly borne out in Indianapolis. Delinquency in that city seemed most closely associated with transiency, poor housing, and certain economic variables.

Still another of these replications was by Kenneth Polk, who used juvenile court cases in San Diego for 1952.[12] Delinquency rates were correlated with census tract scores on the three status dimensions of Shevky-Bell social area analysis[13] These three sets of variables deal with the economic, family, and ethnic aspects of urban social structure which in Shevky and Bell's view are independent aspects of urban social structure. Polk found that the zero-order correlations with delinquency rates were -.24 for economic status, -.21 for family status, and .45 for ethnic status. However, when partial correlations were com-

[9] Bordua, "Juvenile Delinquency and 'Anomie.'"

[10] *Ibid.*, pp. 236–37.

[11] Chilton, "Continuity in Delinquency Area Research."

[12] Kenneth Polk, "Juvenile Delinquency and Social Areas," *Social Problems,* V (Winter 1957–1958), 214–17.

[13] Eshref Shevky and Wendell Bell, *Social Area Analysis* (Stanford: Stanford University Press, 1955).

puted, economic status disappeared as a factor in delinquency. Thus Polk's study appeared to parallel the results of Lander and Bordua, in showing economic factors to be of slight importance. Polk also contended that the hypothesis that family disorganization produces delinquency was not supported by his results. Ethnicity held up as an important factor, although Polk did not observe the curvilinear pattern reported by Lander in Baltimore.[14]

Criticisms of Ecological Studies

The ecological-statistical investigations of Lander and others have produced a variety of responses, some laudatory and others critical. Among the latter, Lawrence Rosen and Stanley Turner have identified a number of problems with this approach.[15] They pointed out that no clear rules in factor analysis itself point to specific interpretations of factors which are isolated, so that Lander's anomie factor could be interpreted quite differently. They suggested that this factor certainly has an economic dimension to it in part, for low income bears some relation to low rates of owner-occupancy and nonwhite residency. Thus they disagreed with Lander in his contention that delinquency rates are not fundamentally associated with economic factors.[16]

However, the basic issue identified by these authors centers about interaction effects of ecological characteristics. They claimed that socioeconomic influences are not completely independent of familial or other relationships with juvenile misconduct and that sets of factors combine or interact in varied ways in different situations. If so, correlational techniques are not appropriate for the study of these phenomena. They then outlined a procedure of "predictive attribute analysis" to be used in ecological studies and applied it to police arrests of juveniles in Philadelphia in 1960. Rosen and Turner found that percent of nonwhite population was the best predictor of delinquency, but that in white areas income was related to delinquency, whereas in nonwhite communities density of housing occupancy was

---

[14] Polk, "Juvenile Delinquency and Social Areas," 214–15; also see Earl R. Moses, "Differentials in Crime Rates Between Negroes and Whites, Based on Comparisons of Four Socio-Economically Equated Areas," *American Sociological Review*, XII (August 1947), 411–20, for an interpretation of high crime and delinquency rates in predominately Negro areas.

[15] Lawrence Rosen and Stanley H. Turner, "An Evaluation of the Lander Approach to Ecology of Delinquency," *Social Problems*, XV (Fall 1967), 189–200.

[16] *Ibid.*, pp. 191–93.

the second most influential factor. Patterns of this kind are masked by the correlational procedures of Bordua, Lander, and Chilton.[17]

Another detailed assessment of ecological-correlational procedures has been provided by Robert Gordon.[18] He identified a number of serious errors of computation and of procedure in the studies of Lander, Bordua, and Chilton. Thus he showed that partial correlation and other of these statistical tools were inappropriately applied in a number of instances. According to Gordon, when all of these errors are taken into account, the relationship between delinquency and socioeconomic status emerges as unambiguously strong. He maintained that socioeconomic status was actually related to delinquency in Polk's investigation, too.[19]

New Directions in Research

Several observations are in order about these ecological reports. The fact that correlations of different factors and delinquency rates in separate cities do not entirely agree probably means that there are variations in community and social influences upon lawbreaking in cities of different sizes, economic structures, and regional locations. Additionally, it seems likely that the interactional effects cited by Rosen and Turner operate in other cities, as well as Philadelphia. If so, similar investigations are needed to look for interactional effects.

Richard Quinney conducted one such study dealing with crime rates, delinquency rates, and Shevky-Bell social area characteristics for census tracts in Lexington, Kentucky.[20] The correlations among status dimensions and crime and delinquency were these: the crime rate correlation with economic status was -.52, with family status it was -.16, and with ethnicity, it was .47. The area correlations with delinquency rates were -.38 for economic status, -.35 for family status, and .48 for ethnic status.[21] However, when rates were examined for areas divided into low and high economic status and also into low or high family status, some interesting variations emerged. The crime rate was highest for the areas which were lowest on both dimensions, while the low economic-high family area had the next highest rate.

---

[17] *Ibid.*, pp. 193–98.

[18] Robert A. Gordon, "Issues in the Ecological Study of Delinquency," *American Sociological Review*, XXXII (December 1967), 927–44.

[19] *Ibid.*, pp. 941–42.

[20] Richard Quinney, "Crime, Delinquency, and Social Areas," *Journal of Research in Crime and Delinquency*, I (July 1964), 149–54.

[21] *Ibid.*, pp. 150–51.

But the crime rate did not vary between the two high economic areas. Thus, family status affects crime rates in low, but not in high economic areas. On the other hand, delinquency rates were highest in the low income-low family area, next highest in the low economic-high family area, lower in the high economic-low family area, and lowest in the area of high family-high economic status. In the case of delinquency, family status appears to condition the role of economic matters at both levels. The more stable the family, the less likely delinquency is to occur.[22]

Polk has presented findings from another study using social area analysis, from 1960 court referrals in Portland, Oregon.[23] When areas were grouped into larger categories on family and economic dimensions, Polk found that delinquency rates were generally highest for the lower income areas and decreased in areas of better income. Also, delinquency rates were highest within income areas which were characterized by low scores on the family dimensions. But these patterns seemed not entirely consistent; in areas at the lowest level of family status, delinquency rates increased with economic status. Polk also found that Portland's nonwhite population fell into two social area categories which were similarly ranked on the family dimension, but which varied on economic status. The delinquency rate was highest in the higher economic area. It seems clear that the relationships in Portland between ethnicity, income, family status, and delinquency vary for areas characterized by different combinations of these dimensions.[24]

A parallel approach to the matter of ecological characteristics and lawbreaking can be found in Charles Willie's study using census tract information in Washington, D.C.[25] He studied the cases of 6,269 youths referred to the juvenile court between 1959 and 1962. The tracts were sorted into high and low economic status levels on the basis of an index utilizing five variables, and also into racial areas; some were classed as white areas and others as nonwhite areas. These racial areas were relatively homogeneous ones, for 95 percent of the persons in areas classed as white were Caucasian, and over 90 percent of the population in nonwhite areas were nonwhite individuals. The degree of residential segregation of ethnic groups was marked in that city. The tracts were also divided into two types on the basis of the

---

[22] *Ibid.*, pp. 151–52.

[23] Kenneth Polk, "Urban Social Areas and Delinquency," *Social Problems*, XIV (Winter 1967), 320–25.

[24] *Ibid.*, pp. 322–24.

[25] Charles V. Willie, "The Relative Contribution of Family Status and Economic Status to Juvenile Delinquency," *Social Problems*, XIV (Winter 1967), 326–35.

extent of broken homes in them. Delinquency rates were then examined for tracts cross-classified on economic, ethnic, and family dimensions.

In the city-wide examination of delinquency rates, the measure of correlation between delinquency and economic status was -.65, while it was -.64 between delinquency and family instability.[26] However, when white and nonwhite areas, classified on family and economic grounds, were studied, some interesting variations emerged. In the nonwhite areas, delinquency rates were higher in the two lower income areas (one with low and the other with high family instability) than in the two higher income areas. In the case of the white areas, the highest delinquency rate was in the low family-low income area, but the next highest rate was in the high income-low family area. It thus appears that family status had a greater influence upon delinquency rate in the white than nonwhite areas, that is, family stability seemed less able to repress the occurence of delinquency in the nonwhite areas than in the white ones. In Willie's view, poverty among nonwhites in Washington, D.C. is such an overpowering factor in their behavior that family stability is unable to exert much influence upon it.

Economic deprivation or lower income position continues to emerge as a major correlate of official delinquency; the place of this variable in delinquency analysis remains secure. At the same time, many of the investigations we have considered warn us against the acceptance of simple-minded notions about the use of such designations as "lower-class" or "low income." The social class structure is not one single system which is the same throughout the country. Urban areas can be classified in economic terms, but, at the same time, neighborhoods of roughly similar economic characteristics may show a good many points of dissimilarity on ethnic, familial, or other terms. We should expect to find that the patterning of delinquency is influenced by all of these social-economic factors as they interact with each other. Generalizations about urban social structure and delinquency must be stated in detailed and sophisticated terms. Delinquency rates are correlated with economic status levels, but that statement does not do full justice to the complexity of the relationship it summarizes.[27] Judith Wilks has provided an excellent summary of this material:

[26] *Ibid.*, pp. 330–31.

[27] Some valuable, tangential information on this point can be found in Albert J. Reiss, Jr., and Albert Lewis Rhodes, "The Distribution of Juvenile Delinquency in the Social Class Structure," *American Sociological Review*, XXVI (October 1961), 720–32.

Interestingly enough, whether concentric zones, individual census tracts, or census tracts grouped into social areas are investigated, the most frequent finding is that offenses and offenders tend to be concentrated in areas characterized by low income, physical deterioration, mixed land usage, nontraditional family patterns (e.g., homes broken in some manner and/or high percentages of single males, and/or women employed in the labor force), and racial-ethnic concentrations which appear to produce low neighborhood cohesion and low integration of the neighborhood into the larger society. This statement is, of course, a gross oversimplification of the interrelationship of area attributes and crime and delinquency rates. As noted previously, in order to predict and explain an area's crime rate, it is necessary to be aware of the existing social structure, ongoing social processes, and the population composition of the area, and the area's position within the larger urban and societal complex. It is only by taking such a perspective that we can:

1. gain an understanding of why the economic, family, and racial composition of an area are associated with offense and offender rates, and

2. understand why the nature of the association between these area characteristics and offense and offender rates vary over time and over different cities.[28]

One indication of the nature of variations in neighborhood structure which probably influence delinquency patterns is found in a study by Eleanor Maccoby, Joseph Johnson, and Russell Church.[29] These investigators believed that in disorganized neighborhoods, delinquency rates will be high due to the lack of community integration. In these areas, adults will feel little responsibility for the activities of the children of others, will ignore much of their deviant behavior, and will unwittingly encourage them to continue in misbehavior. The researchers selected two low income neighborhoods in Cambridge, Massachussetts, one with a high delinquency rate and the other with a low rate. They hypothesized that the high delinquency area would show less social integration, that the values of citizens would be permissive toward delinquency, and that these persons would be reluctant to intervene in the behavior of others. The low delinquency area was hypothesized as showing greater willingness of adults to take

[28] Judith A. Wilks, "Ecological Correlates of Crime and Delinquency," in The President's Commission on Law Enforcement and Administration of Justice, *Task Force Report: Crime and Its Impact—An Assessment* (Washington, D.C.: U.S. Government Printing Office, 1967), p. 149. See this entire paper, pp. 138–56, for a detailed summary of work on ecological correlates of crime and delinquency.

[29] Eleanor E. Maccoby, Joseph P. Johnson, and Russell M. Church, "Community Integration and the Social Control of Juvenile Delinquency," *Journal of Social Issues,* XIV, 3 (1958), 38–51.

action against lawbreakers, greater integration, and less permissive attitudes toward criminality. The results from interviews with citizens in the two areas confirmed the argument about neighborhood cohesiveness. In the high delinquency area, fewer people liked the neighborhood, fewer knew many neighbors by name, and fewer declared themselves to have interests compatible with those of their neighbors. However, the investigators did *not* find citizens in the high criminality area to have more tolerant or indifferent views of deviance than those in the low delinquency area. Finally, somewhat more of the respondents in the low delinquency area were willing to intervene in instances of lawbreaking not directly involving them, but, in both neighborhoods, the prevailing sentiment was one of reluctance to interfere in "other people's business."

DELINQUENT SUBCULTURES

The investigations of Shaw and others dealt with other matters as well as the ecological correlates of delinquency. These sociologists provided criminologists with a series of rich descriptive accounts of the behavioral careers of the offenders in lower-class delinquency areas which have become classics in sociology.[30] These descriptions indicated that most lawbreakers in these areas were members of gangs and peer associations in which delinquent conduct was defined positively, young boys were inducted into lawbreaking by older youths, and juveniles were taught the skills of delinquency in much the same way that youths in socially-favored circumstances learn to become boy scouts or "good boys" of some other brand. These portrayals of normal, vivacious, well-socialized youngsters learning deviant attitudes and techniques quickly became the cornerstone of a variety of sociological arguments which assert that criminality is learned behavior which is acquired in the same basic way as is conforming conduct.[31]

Numerous debates have concerned the extent of delinquency outside of working-class neighborhoods; a number of persons have argued that the members of other community areas also have juvenile offenders in their midst. The data in Chapter Two indicated that this contention is correct, that hidden delinquency is widespread. However, the accuracy of the accounts of gang delinquency have gone unchal-

---

[30] Shaw, *The Jack Roller;* Shaw and Moore, *The Natural History of a Delinquent Career;* Shaw, McKay, and McDonald, *Brothers in Crime.*

[31] These reports heavily influenced Sutherland in development of differential association theory. See Sutherland and Cressey, *Principles of Criminology,* pp. 81–82; Don C. Gibbons, *Society, Crime and Criminal Careers* (Englewood Cliffs, N.J.: Prentice-Hall, Inc., 1968), pp. 200–8.

lenged. Nearly all authorities agree that persistent, organized, gang forms of juvenile misconduct are concentrated in working-class neighborhoods. The modern statement of this position holds that lower-class areas are characterized by delinquent subcultures, that is, "patterns of values, norms, and behavior which have become traditional among certain groups."[32] Although we observe subcultures in action by looking at the behavior of specific gangs and collectivities, subcultures are wider than these organizational forms. Subcultures are value patterns and behavioral systems which are *shared* by individual gangs and these precede and persist beyond the life span of any single group.[33]

Although gang delinquency has been a subject of persistent interest to sociologists since the 1920s, relatively little theoretical or empirical work was conducted regarding gang misconduct in the period between the Chicago work and the 1950s. Publication in 1955 of Albert K. Cohen's *Delinquent Boys* was a signal event, for it triggered an impressive resurgence of speculative and empirical attention to delinquent gang activity. A massive collection of argument and counterargument has grown out of Cohen's initial insights. Then, too, a large and valuable accretion of research evidence produced in the past fifteen years represents research material initially stimulated by his work.

Cohen and Delinquent Subcultures

In his book on gang delinquency, *Delinquent Boys,* Cohen indicated that he was interested in accounting for the emergence of delinquent subcultures in working-class neighborhoods of American cities.[34] According to Cohen, a delinquent subculture may be defined as "a way of life that has somehow become traditional among certain groups in American society. These groups are the boy's gangs that

[32] James F. Short, Jr., ed., *Gang Delinquency and Delinquent Subcultures* (New York: Harper & Row, Publishers, 1968), p. 11. See his introduction to this collection, pp. 9-16, for a brief but succinct discussion of the nature of delinquent subcultures.

[33] This section on delinquent subcultures is a revised and more detailed version of the discussion which appeared in Gibbons, *Society, Crime, and Criminal Careers,* pp. 263–80.

[34] Albert K. Cohen, *Delinquent Boys* (New York: The Free Press, 1955). On the issue of the social class distribution of subcultural gang delinquency, Cohen argues: "It is our conclusion, by no means novel or startling, that juvenile delinquency and the delinquent subculture in particular are overwhelmingly concentrated in the male, working-class sector of the juvenile population." *(Delinquent Boys,* p. 37).

flourish most conspicuously in the 'delinquency neighborhoods' of our larger American cities."[35] The delinquent subculture centers about behavior which is *nonutilitarian, malicious,* and *negativistic.* That is, Cohen argued that much of the stealing and other behavior of gang offenders is motivated by interests other than rational utilitarian gain, that gang delinquents steal "for the hell of it." The malicious and negativistic character of gang behavior is revealed in a number of ways, most commonly in observations that gang members reap enjoyment from the discomfort they have caused others and find cause for pride in reputations they have acquired for "meanness."[36] Cohen also described subcultural deviance in terms of *short-run hedonism,* indicated by a lack of long-term goals or planning on the part of gang members. Finally, *group autonomy* is a hallmark of subcultural deviance, and delinquent gangs are said to be solidaristic collectivities.[37]

Why did the delinquent subculture develop among lower-class boys? In brief, Cohen's reply was that working-class gang delinquency represents a social movement among juvenile offenders. This subculture arose as a solution to *shared* problems of low status among working-class youths. In his words, "The crucial condition for the emergence of new cultural forms is the existence, *in effective interaction with one another, of a number of actors with similar problems of adjustment."* [38]

The shared problems of low status or esteem among gang boys arise as a consequence of their placement in the social order—working-class boys experience status threats when they are evaluated by a middle-class measuring rod, by a set of social expectations regarding the characteristics of "good boys." These expectations center about such traits as ambition, individual responsibility, talent, asceticism, rationality, courtesy, and control of physical aggression.[39] The exemplary youth, in the eyes of important members of the middle-class such as school teachers, embodies most or all of these social characteristics. But the working-class boy has been inadequately socialized in these notions of proper behavior, so he finds himself at a competitive disadvantage in classrooms and other social arenas as he competes with middle-class peers for recognition by adults. Again, to cite Cohen: "The delinquent subculture, we suggest, is a way of dealing with the problems of adjustment we have described. These problems are chiefly status problems: certain children are denied status in the re-

---

[35] *Ibid.,* p. 13.
[36] *Ibid.,* pp. 25–30.
[37] *Ibid.,* pp. 30–32.
[38] *Ibid.,* p. 59. Emphasis in the original.
[39] *Ibid.,* pp. 84–93.

spectable society because they cannot meet the criteria of the respectable status system. The delinquent subculture deals with these problems by providing criteria of status which these children *can* meet."[40] These boys who withdraw from such situations of social hurt as the school find their way into the subculture of the gang, which provides them with a social setting in which to become insulated against assaults upon their self-esteem.

Cohen drew his original portrayal of gang delinquency with broad strokes and joined relatively small areas of factual data with big swatches of speculation. No wonder a number of critics have detected what they felt to be errors in the initial formulation! Gresham Sykes and David Matza advanced an early criticism in the form of some remarks about "techniques of neutralization."[41] They averred that delinquents are at least partially committed to the dominant social order, experience guilt or shame when they engage in deviant acts, and contrive rationalizations or justifications for their acts of lawbreaking in order to assuage guilt feelings. Sykes and Matza then went on to enumerate some of these techniques of neutralization, which include denial of responsibility for one's behavior, denial of injury, and condemnation of the condemners. These notions represent a useful contribution in their own right, in that they direct attention to some of the ways in which offenders define the situation so as to exculpate themselves from guilt regarding violations of norms they regard as valid "in principle." However, a close reading of Cohen's theory indicates that he was not inattentive to the delinquent boy's sensitivity to middle-class ethical standards; the Sykes and Matza argument is compatible with that of Cohen.

Other defects in the Cohen theory have been noted by Harold Wilensky and Charles Lebeaux,[42] who criticized Cohen's claims about masculine identity problems which he alleged to be involved in middle-class delinquency. Wilensky and Lebeaux claimed that middle-class youths are more concerned with status anxiety surrounding downward drift in status of their fathers. According to these critics, lower-class youths are most likely to be anxious about their adequacy

40 *Ibid.*, p. 121.

41 Gresham M. Sykes and David Matza, "Techniques of Neutralization: A Theory of Delinquency," *American Sociological Review*, XXII (December 1957), 664–70; see also Matza, *Delinquency and Drift* (New York: John Wiley & Sons, Inc., 1964); one empirical test which confirmed much of this argument is Richard A. Ball, "An Empirical Exploration of Neutralization Theory," in Mark Lefton, James K. Skipper, Jr., and Charles H. McCaghy, eds., *Approaches to Deviance* (New York: Appleton-Century-Crofts, 1968), pp. 255–65.

42 Harold L. Wilensky and Charles N. Lebeaux, *Industrial Society and Social Welfare* (New York: Russell Sage Foundation, 1958), pp. 187–207.

as males. Wilensky and Lebeaux also raised a series of questions to be researched, such as the matter of variation in gang structure between cliques, loosely-structured confederations, and larger gangs.

One of the most systematic evaluations of Cohen's theory was produced by John Kitsuse and David Dietrick.[43] who noted several major problems. They charged that Cohen failed to make a compelling case for the argument that working-class boys care about middle-class persons' views of them. Kitsuse and Dietrick maintained that lower-class boys are not oriented to status in middle-class systems. Accordingly, in their view, Cohen's notion of the delinquent subculture as a "reaction formation" is seriously undermined. These same critics also contended that Cohen's description of delinquent subcultures is faulty, in that real-life delinquents are more businesslike in action and less directly malicious toward "respectable" persons than the theory suggests. Finally, they claimed that the theory is flawed because it is ambiguous on the issue of how subcultures are maintained once they come into existence. Kitsuse and Dietrick proposed an alternative formulation to that of Cohen, arguing that the original motives of delinquent actors for participation in gangs are varied. Once they get involved in the subculture, hostile responses by respectable citizens, correctional agents, and others are directed at them. In turn, the offenders reject their rejectors through further deviant conduct. Thus, according to these authors, "the delinquent subculture persists because, once established, it creates for those who participate in it, the very problems which were the bases for its emergence."[44]

Bordua has also raised a series of questions about theories of subcultural delinquency, including the one by Cohen.[45] He noted that, in most of these theories, the image put forth of the delinquent is markedly different from that advanced by Thrasher many years ago. While Thrasher's boys were caught up in the attractiveness of delinquent "fun," the delinquents of contemporary theorists are "driven" by stresses and anxieties emanating from a prejudicial and harsh social environment.[46] In addition, Bordua contended that Cohen's theory

[43] John I. Kitsuse and David C. Dietrick, *"Delinquent Boys:* A Critique," *American Sociological Review,* XXIV (April 1959), 208–15.

[44] *Ibid.,* p. 215.

[45] David J. Bordua, *Sociological Theories and Their Implications for Juvenile Delinquency,* Children's Bureau, Juvenile Delinquency, Facts and Facets, No. 2 (Washington, D.C.: U. S. Government Printing Office, 1960); Bordua, "Delinquent Subcultures: Sociological Interpretations of Gang Delinquency," *Annals of the American Academy of Political and Social Science,* CCCXXXVIII (November 1961), 119–36; Bordua, "Some Comments on Theories of Group Delinquency," *Sociological Inquiry,* XXXII (Spring 1962), 245–60.

[46] Bordua, "Delinquent Subcultures."

places undue emphasis upon the nonutilitarian character of gang misconduct. Bordua also suggested that Cohen, as well as a number of other subcultural theorists, failed to accord sufficient weight to family, ethnic, and certain other social variables in delinquency causation. In particular, he pointed out that class-linked family patterns may be the source of much of the stress experienced by delinquent boys; the relatively loosely structured parent-child relationships, absentee fathers, and other common characteristics of many working class families may have much to do with the development of problems and, subsequently, delinquency in lower-class boys.[47]

Cohen has responded to some of these criticisms of his work. In a paper with James F. Short,[48] rejoinders to a number of critical points were presented, including the assertion that there is more than one form of working-class gang delinquency. Cohen and Short agreed with this view and suggested that lower-class subcultures include the parent-male subculture, the conflict-oriented subculture, the drug addict subculture, and a subculture oriented around semiprofessional theft. The characteristics of the parent-male subculture are enumerated in *Delinquent Boys.* Cohen and Short employed the label of "parent subculture" in order to suggest that other gang forms are specialized offshoots from it, thus "it is probably the most common variety in this country—indeed, it might be called the 'garden variety' of delinquent subculture."[49]

In endeavoring to account for the development of these different subcultural forms in individual neighborhoods, Cohen and Short laid much stress upon an earlier paper by Solomon Kobrin.[50] In that essay, Kobrin pointed out that areas vary in the extent to which conventional and criminal value systems are mutually integrated, so that in some communities criminality is meshed with the local social structure; adult criminals are prestigious citizens and are active in local businesses, fraternal organizations, politics, and so on. They serve as local "heroes" or role models for juvenile apprentice criminals. In other neighborhoods, criminality is individualistic, uncontrolled, and alien to the conventional social organization.

[47] Bordua, "Some Comments on Theories of Group Delinquency," 249–56.

[48] Albert K. Cohen and James F. Short, Jr., "Research on Delinquent Subcultures," *Journal of Social Issues,* XIV, 3 (1958), 20–37.

[49] *Ibid.,* p. 24.

[50] Solomon Kobrin, "The Conflict of Values in Delinquency Areas," *American Sociological Review,* XVI (October 1951), 653–61.

Delinquency and Opportunity
Structures

The delinquency theory of Richard Cloward and Lloyd Ohlin represents a full-scale alternative rather than a qualifying statement, to Cohen's argument.[51] For Cloward and Ohlin, the raw material for delinquent gangs consists of boys concerned about economic injustice rather than with middle-class status. They asserted: "It is our view that many discontented lower-class youth do not wish to adopt a middle-class way of life or to disrupt their present associations and negotiate passage into middle-class groups. The solution they seek entails the acquisition of higher position in terms of lower-class rather than middle-class criteria."[52]

Cloward and Ohlin argued that working-class gang delinquent subcultures are to be understood in the following terms: Lower-class boys share a common American value commitment to "success," measured largely in material terms. But these youths are at a competitive disadvantage compared to their middle-class counterparts. Either they do not have access to legitimate or conventional means to reach these success goals, or, if they do have objective opportunities for achievement, they perceive their chances of success as circumscribed. Accordingly, for many working-class boys, a severe disjunction exists between aspiration levels and expectations, or between what they want out of life and what they anticipate they will receive. Pressures to engage in deviant behavior are generated by this goals-means discrepancy.[53] Cloward and Ohlin summarized their position in the following way:

> Our hypothesis can be summarized as follows: The disparity between what lower-class youth are led to want and what is actually available to them is the source of a major problem of adjustment. Adolescents who form delinquent subcultures, we suggest, have internalized an emphasis upon conventional goals. Faced with limitations on legitimate avenues of access to these goals, and unable to revise their aspirations downward, they experience intense frustrations; the exploration of nonconformist alternatives may be the result.[54]

The particular adaptation assumed by working class youths is heavily influenced by the opportunity structures for deviant behavior. Borrowing from the insights of Kobrin, Cloward and Ohlin argued

---

[51] Richard A. Cloward and Lloyd E. Ohlin, *Delinquency and Opportunity* (New York: The Free Press, 1960).

[52] *Ibid.*, p. 92.

[53] *Ibid.*, pp. 77–143.

[54] *Ibid.*, p. 86.

that some lower-class areas are characterized by integration of criminalistic and conformist patterns of social organization, whereas others
are lacking in stable criminalistic networks. In the organized, criminalistic neighborhood, "criminalistic" gang subcultures develop in which
boys are involved in instrumental acts of theft and in careers which
often lead them into adult criminal behavior. This is the community
which produces the "budding gangster." In areas lacking in criminalistic traditions, gang delinquency tends to take the form of "conflict"
subcultural behavior in which gang fighting ("bopping" and "rum-
bles") predominates. Finally, some boys who are failures in both the
legitimate and illegitimate opportunity structures disengage themselves from the competitive struggle and withdraw into the "retreatist" subculture of the drug addict.

Reactions to the Cloward and Ohlin theory have generally been
extremely favorable; a number of action programs for the prevention
and amelioration of juvenile crime have been formulated on the basis
of opportunity structure theory.[55] Still, a series of critical comments
have been advanced on this theory.[56] It has been noted that the
definition of subcultures employed by Cloward and Ohlin limits applicability of their theory to a minority of all delinquents. Critics have
contended that much gang delinquency in working-class areas is more
spontaneous and unstructured than Cloward and Ohlin would have us
believe. One authority has termed many of these deviant collectivities
"near groups," in order to highlight their shifting membership, ambiguous role definitions, lack of group identifications, and other characteristics.[57] Regarding this objection, it would be possible to relax the
definition of subcultures without abandoning the major ingredients of
the theory.

Bordua and others who have assessed the opportunity structure
formulation have also raised questions about its failure to deal systematically with variations in working-class family structures, racial
factors, and other background variations among different working-
class groups.[58] The major thrust of this body of commentary has been
to suggest that real-life social structure in a society such as the United

---

[55] See Don C. Gibbons, *Changing the Lawbreaker* (Englewood Cliffs, N.J.: Prentice-Hall, Inc., 1965), pp. 179–82.

[56] Bordua, "Delinquent Subcultures," "Some Comments on Theories of Group
Delinquency"; David Matza, review of *Delinquency and Opportunity, American
Journal of Sociology*, LX (May 1961), 631–33; Clarence C. Schrag, "Delinquency
and Opportunity: Analysis of a Theory," *Sociology and Social Research*, XLVI
(January 1962), 167–75.

[57] Lewis Yablonsky, "The Delinquent Gang as a Near-Group," *Social Problems*,
VII (Fall 1959), 108–17.

[58] Bordua, "Some Comments on Theories of Group Delinquency," pp. 250–52.

States is exceedingly complex because it is comprised of interwoven layers of social variables which are combined in varied ways and which produce behavioral outcomes such as delinquency. In short, existing theories of gang delinquency are not yet rich enough or elaborate enough to encompass the varieties of real-life experience.

Lower-Class Focal Concerns and Delinquency

Walter B. Miller has advanced another explanation of gang behavior which is markedly at variance with that of Cohen.[59] For Miller, the structure of lower-class life plays the dominant role in bringing forth gang misconduct. Delinquency is the product of long-established, durable cultural traditions of lower-class life, rather than the result of responses to conflicts with middle-class values.

Miller contended that lower-class culture is most strikingly embodied by those persons Harrington has described as populating "the other America," that is, the world of rural migrants to urban areas, American Indians, Puerto Ricans, and urban Negroes.[60] These persons are at the bottom of the social heap and have little prospect of ascending it. The culture of this segment of the population can be described by a series of structural elements peculiar to it and by a complex pattern of "focal concerns."[61]

One of the major structural patterns in lower class society is what Miller termed a female-based household, in which the stability of the family unit is provided by one or more adult females. The mother and older daughters play multiple roles, providing economic support for the family unit as well as discharging the household and affectional duties. This kind of family structure results from the practice of serial

[59] Walter B. Miller, "Lower Class Culture as a Generating Milieu of Gang Delinquency," *Journal of Social Issues*, XIV, 3 (1958), 5–19; Miller, "Implications of Lower Class Culture for Social Work," *Social Service Review*, XXXIII (September 1959), 219–36; Miller, "Preventive Work with Street Corner Gangs: Boston Delinquency Project," *Annals of the American Academy of Political and Social Science*, CCCXXII (March 1959), 97–106; Miller, "The Impact of a Total-Community Delinquency Control Project," *Social Problems*, X (Fall 1962), 168–91; William C. Kvaraceus and Miller, *Delinquent Behavior: Culture and the Individual* (Washington, D.C.: National Education Association, 1959).

[60] Michael Harrington, *The Other America* (New York: The Macmillan Company, 1962). On this matter, see also Jackson Toby, "The Prospects for Reducing Delinquency Rates in Industrial Societies," *Federal Probation*, XXVII (December 1963), 23–25.

[61] These are discussed at length in Miller, "Lower Class Culture as a Generating Milieu of Gang Delinquency."

monogamy, in which women find themselves involved in repetitive sequences of mate-finding, legal or common-law marriage, and divorce or desertion by the male. One result of this dynamic is that the household may be made up of a number of children, each of whom has the same mother, but a different father.

For the boy who grows up in the female-dominated family, life is fraught with anxieties about sex-role identification. The young male is assaulted on all sides by verbal assertions that men are "no damn good." From this situation, there flows a concern on the boy's part for becoming a "real man" as quickly as possible. The male adolescent peer group, territorially located on city streets, provides the training ground and milieu in which lower-class males seek a sense of maleness, status, and belonging.

These elements, along with the pervasive sense of material and social deprivation common to lower-class members, result in life patterns and experiences organized around what Miller called focal concerns. Focal concerns or values represent a series of broad themes that condition the specific acts of lower-class persons. The focal concerns of lower class society include "trouble," "toughness," "smartness," "excitement," "fate," and "autonomy." Trouble refers to a dominant concern about avoiding entanglements with the police, social welfare agencies, and similar bodies—encounters that are an ever-present possibility in this segment of society—while toughness denotes a concern for continued demonstrations of bravery, daring, and other traits which show that one is not feminine or "soft." Smartness is a label for such things as the ability to dupe or outwit others, live by one's wits, and earn a livelihood through a "hustle" (pimping and the like). Excitement was identified by Miller as a generic concern for seeking out weekend activities which disrupt the monotony of weekday routine jobs, while fate has to do with definitions by lower-class people that their lives are ruled by forces over which they have little control, that "luck" plays a major part in their life chances. Finally, autonomy refers to a profound avoidance of control or domination by others.

These structural elements and focal concerns combine in several ways to produce criminality. Those who respond to some of these focal concerns automatically violate the law through their behavior. In situations where lower-class persons have a choice of lines of conduct, they select a deviant form of activity as the most attractive. Miller's total argument was that to be lower-class in contemporary American society is to be in a social situation which contains a variety of direct influences toward deviant conduct, one form of which is juvenile delinquency.

Miller's notions have not escaped criticism;[62] it has been noted that he failed to account for the varieties of gang delinquency which other students have posited. Some offenders steal, some "rumble," and some "shoot dope," but little explanation has been given for these variations. A second quarrel is over Miller's failure to spell out the detailed variations which can be observed in patterns of lower-class culture. His characterization seems to many to be most applicable to certain urban, slum area groups, particularly Negroes, but hardly descriptive of such other lower-class groups as residents in Italian or Chinese enclaves. Specifically, the picture of serial monogamy and female-based households is accurate principally for Negroes and does not hold for other low income, disadvantaged groups. A third claim centers about the danger of tautology in the focal concerns used to account for delinquent conduct. Miller was not always careful to distinguish between observations about these interests and evidence of the behavior they are designed to explain. Finally, Bordua has observed that Miller did not effectively refute Cohen's contention that working class boys are sensitive to middle-class standards.[63] In Bordua's view, it is possible that both Cohen and Miller are partially correct. Perhaps many lower-class boys do not initially internalize middle-class norms as a part of their socialization, but when they get into schools and other competitive situations, these status-measuring standards are forced upon them. These experiences may then alienate lower-class boys, driving them into involvement in delinquent subcultures. This line of conjecture is similar to that of Kitsuse and Dietrick.[64]

We must agree with Bordua, however, that Miller's description of lower-class focal concerns stands as a detailed ethnography of working-class life which fills in some of the descriptive gaps in the Cohen and Cloward and Ohlin statements.[65]

[62] Bordua, "Some Comments on Theories of Group Delinquency," "Delinquent Subcultures."

[63] Bordua, "Delinquent Subcultures," pp. 129–30.

[64] Another effort to reconcile these discrepant views on lower-class values can be found in Hyman Rodman, "The Lower-Class Value Stretch," Social Forces, 42 (December 1963), 205–15. Rodman argues that lower-class persons have a wider range of values than others within the society. They share general societal values with members of other classes, but, additionally, they have stretched these values or developed alternative ones which help them adjust to their deprived circumstances. See also Herbert H. Hyman, "The Value Systems of Different Classes: A Social Psychological Contribution to the Analysis of Stratification," in Reinhard Bendix and Seymour M. Lipset, eds., Class, Status and Power (New York: The Free Press, 1953), pp. 426–42.

[65] Bordua, "Delinquent Subcultures," p.131.

Other Voices

The three lines of analysis which we have examined are the best-known and most influential theories regarding working-class delinquency, but other views have been put forth. Herbert Bloch and Arthur Niederhoffer claimed that a cross-cultural perspective on youth behavior is needed in order to correct the ethnocentric bias in Cohen's theory.[66] They contended that adolescent crises centered about the transition from childhood to adulthood occur in all societies, and that ganging is the universal response to these problems. In this sense, lower-class delinquent gangs have much in common with middle-class ones, and they, in turn, share many ingredients with peer collectivities in other lands.

Bloch and Niederhoffer made a good deal of sense when commenting on structural similarities among adolescent groups in various locales, however, their thesis is flawed in a number of places by anthropological observations of questionable accuracy, as well as by highly suspect assertions regarding American society, such as the claim that class or status differentials are disappearing in this country.[67] Most important, while they raised some challenges to parts of Cohen's description of gang behavior, the cornerstone of his argument remains unchallenged: that serious, repetitive, organized, subcultural delinquency is a particularly peculiar working-class phenomenon in the United States, qualitatively different from peer behavior in other strata or in most other cultures. In consequence, more is needed than an adolescent crisis theory in order to account for the particular form taken by working class adolescent conduct.

Another discordant voice is that of Lewis Yablonsky. The major tenet of his explanation of working class gang delinquency was that the central figures in these gangs are sociopaths, socially deficient boys who cannot manage the social struggle as adequately as other lower-class youths, but who find in the gang a social structure in which they can survive.[68] Critics of Yablonsky's views have charged that he offered little or no evidence for the sociopathy hypothesis independent of the aggressive delinquency it is supposed to explain.[69]

One final contribution, which represents something of an antidote

[66] Herbert A. Bloch and Arthur Niederhoffer, *The Gang* (New York: Philosophical Library, 1958).

[67] *Ibid.*, p. 175.

[68] Lewis Yablonsky, *The Violent Gang* (New York: The Macmillan Company, 1962).

[69] Solomon Kobrin, review of *The Violent Gang, American Sociological Review*, XXVIII (April 1963), 316–17.

to certain theories of delinquency, is that of David Matza and Gresham Sykes, which stressed the role of "subterranean values" in delinquency.[70] They noted that the view of middle-class culture which emphasizes ascetic devotion to thrift, hard labor at a work task defined as a calling, and so on, is one-sided. There are other respectable, but subterranean or unpublicized values pursued by large numbers of conventional citizens, such as pursuit of hedonistic fun or tolerance for certain kinds of aggression and violence. Thus the delinquent's search for "kicks," his disdain for work, desire for the "big score," and posture of aggressive toughness make him an exaggerated and immature version of many middle-class people. The substance of these ideas is to remind us that delinquency may have considerable positive appeal to youngsters at all class levels, including those in the working class, who for one reason or another are indifferent to or alienated from schools, adult role-preparation, and so forth.

RESEARCH ON DELINQUENT SUBCULTURES[71]

These varied lines of explanation for gang delinquency present a bewildering array of contradictory claims. Each of the theories has a ring of plausibility, at least until the criticisms are heard or we confronted with one of its theoretical competitors. Clearly, a mass of hard evidence which will allow us to adjudicate among these theoretical contenders is needed. Before we look at some of the data which has been produced on questions of working-class delinquency, however, a word of warning is in order. The research findings will not magically reduce the argument about gang delinquency to one set of straightforward propositions. Rather, the evidence is likely to make the matter of gang misconduct even more complex in that it reflects the diversity and richness of real life as experienced by actual deviants.

[70] David Matza and Gresham M. Sykes, "Juvenile Delinquency and Subterranean Values," *American Sociological Review*, XXVI (October 1961), 712–19; Matza, *Delinquency and Drift*.

[71] Several collections of research on delinquent subcultures are available, including Short, *Gang Delinquency and Delinquent Subcultures;* Malcolm W. Klein, ed., *Juvenile Gangs in Context: Theory, Research and Action* (Englewood Cliffs, N.J.: Prentice-Hall, Inc., 1967). See Klein's introduction, pp. 1–12, for a good brief assessment of the current state of affairs regarding subcultural research.

Dimensions of Gang Behavior

The first question to be answered is: what kind of delinquent conduct do lower-class boys engage in? Is subcultural deviance patterned in the ways suggested by Cohen and Short and by Cloward and Ohlin? Gerald Robin, conducting an investigation in Philadelphia, studied the official and unofficial police records of over 700 male Negro members of 27 gangs.[72] Most of these youths came to the attention of the police before they were fifteen years old. They showed progressive movement toward deviant acts of increasing seriousness and, in many cases, these culminated in adult criminal careers. One-fourth of all these delinquencies were property-oriented, 37 percent were general disorderly conduct, and 17 percent were violently person-oriented acts. However, about two-thirds of the boys had engaged in at least one offense involving physical violence. Robin interpreted this finding as support for the claims of Cloward and Ohlin concerning the existence of a conflict subculture in delinquency.[73]

Irving Spergel has provided evidence in several separate studies which seem to confirm the Cloward and Ohlin description of different delinquent subcultures.[74] His research in Chicago indicated that delinquency and crime tended toward a criminalistic form in a relatively stable Negro slum area, while, in a more unstable neighborhood, criminality was untrammeled and violent in character.[75] However, in another study in these areas, Spergel discovered that Negro preadolescents eight to twelve years of age most frequently admitted assaultive acts, rather than theft, in interviews. The deviants in both areas were involved in assaultive conduct to the same extent, so that the Cloward and Ohlin claim that social milieu influences the form of deviance regardless of age was not confirmed.[76] In his New York City investigation, Spergel indicated that conflict behavior was most common in Slumtown, a disorganized area, while criminalistic delinquency was oriented around theft activities in one relatively integrated neigh-

[72] Gerald D. Robin, "Gang Member Delinquency: Its Extent, Sequence and Typology," *Journal of Criminal Law, Criminology and Police Science*, LV (March 1964), 59–69.

[73] *Ibid.*, pp. 64–65.

[74] Irving Spergel, "Male Young Adult Criminality, Deviant Values, and Differential Opportunities in Two Lower Class Negro Neighborhoods," *Social Problems*, X (Winter 1963), 237–50; Spergel, "An Exploratory Research in Delinquent Subcultures," *Social Service Review*, XXXV (March 1961), 33–47; Spergel, *Racketville, Slumtown, Haulburg* (Chicago: University of Chicago Press, 1964).

[75] Spergel, "Male Young Adult Criminality."

[76] Irving Spergel, "Deviant Patterns and Opportunities of Pre-Adolescent Negro Boys in Three Chicago Neighborhoods," in Klein, *Juvenile Gangs in Context*, pp. 38–54.

borhood and around racketeering in another community area which was heavily populated by Italian-Americans.[77] Spergel's material provided a footnote to the Cloward and Ohlin framework by suggesting that criminalistic delinquency comes in several varieties.

Still another report on the unlawful behavior of gang offenders can be found in Walter Miller's work.[78] He uncovered a body of national data pointing to the predominance of theft behavior among juvenile lawbreakers. He also noted that theft was the dominant form of criminal behavior among Midcity (Boston) gangs he studied; during the age period from fifteen to seventeen, 37 percent of all known illegal actions of project subjects and 54 percent of their major offenses involved theft. Acts of theft were two to three times more frequent than assaults.[79] Furthermore, the gang members whom Miller studied were involved in an average of four theft-oriented behaviors per month, and about 60 percent of the thefts involved more than one participant. Larcenies accounted for two-thirds of the thefts, while auto thefts made up most of the remainder.[80]

The richest body of recent empirical evidence on gang delinquency and gang behavior is found in the Chicago studies of Short and others.[81] One such investigation examined the delinquent and nondelinquent conduct of about 600 members of Chicago gangs. Street workers maintained detailed records of the day-to-day activities of these boys, and their findings showed that most of the offenders were involved in a wide range of deviant and nondeviant acts, rather than in the narrowly-focused patterns suggested by Cloward and Ohlin. Short and his colleagues argued that an undifferentiated "parent delinquent subculture" exists from which more specialized deviant groups emerge. In other words, they suggested that the generic form of gang behavior involves behavioral versatility, and that, from this broad form, cliques and subgroups branch off into more specialized careers in deviant conduct.[82]

---

[77] Spergel, *Racketville, Slumtown, Haulburg.* It ought to be noted that this study was based upon very small samples of delinquents and nondelinquents. In addition, some of the procedures utilized by Spergel are not entirely clear, so that the results of the investigation must be treated gingerly.

[78] Walter B. Miller, "Theft Behavior in City Gangs," in Klein, *Juvenile Gangs in Context*, pp. 25–38.

[79] *Ibid.*, p. 28.

[80] *Ibid.*, pp. 33–34.

[81] James F. Short, Jr., "Gang Delinquency and Anomie," in Marshall B. Clinard, ed., *Anomie and Deviant Behavior* (New York: The Free Press, 1964), pp. 98–127: Short and Fred L. Strodtbeck, *Group Process and Gang Delinquency* (Chicago: University of Chicago Press, 1965).

[82] Short, "Gang Delinquency and Anomie," pp. 103–5; Short, Ray A. Tennyson, and Kenneth I. Howard, "Behavior Dimensions of Gang Delinquency," in Short

A final bit of information on gang behavior is found in a study by
Reiss which concerned a group of lower-class delinquent males in
Nashville.[83] Their activities included participation in a complex structure of relationships with adult homosexuals in which the boys submitted to adult fellators in exchange for pay, an interaction pattern they
conceptualize as strictly a business transaction.

These seemingly contradictory characterizations of gang delinquency, indicating the existence of different subcultures in some communities but not in others, can perhaps be reconciled. It may well be
that gang misconduct takes a number of forms, both in terms of degree of organization among the deviants and in the kind of activity in
which they engage. We suggest that relatively crystallized forms of
conflict delinquency may be most common in very large cities, and
quite uncommon in smaller communities. It is possible that gang structure is influenced by ethnic variables, variations in neighborhood organization and community structure, and other contingencies of this
sort. The variability in the descriptive data may be a reflection of the
diversity of behavior in the real world of delinquents.

Social Processes in Gang Delinquency

What does the research evidence show about the different causal
arguments on gang delinquency which we have examined? A series of
ecological investigations indicate that official delinquents, many of
whom are gang offenders, are predominately from lower income backgrounds. In one recent attack upon social class correlates of delinquency, neighborhood characteristics, deviant patterns, and related
topics, Albert Reiss and Albert Rhodes have thrown much light upon
the relationships between delinquent conduct and socioeconomic position.[84] In their study of a large number of juvenile males in the
Nashville, Tennessee, metropolitan area, they found no simple or uniform linkage between social class position and delinquency. While
those boys most frequently encountered in the population of officially
designated offenders were from the lower class, delinquency life
chances or risks were not the same for all working-class youths. Juve-

---

and Strodtbeck, *Group Process and Gang Delinquency.*

[83] Albert J. Reiss, Jr., "The Social Integration of Queers and Peers," *Social Problems,* IX (Fall 1961), 102–20.

[84] Reiss and Rhodes, "The Distribution of Juvenile Delinquency"; see also Reiss
and Rhodes, "Status Deprivation and Delinquency," *Sociological Quarterly,* IV
(Spring 1963), 135–49.

nile misconduct was most common in homogeneous lower-class neighborhoods and less usual in communities of mixed social status. Accordingly, Reiss and Rhodes held that the behavior of working-class boys is conditioned by the social class structure and cultural traditions of the community areas in which they live. Youths whose parents are working-class individuals have a high risk of delinquent involvement if they live in areas populated largely by other lower-class persons, but they are not so likely to become offenders if they live in neighborhoods of mixed or predominately middle-class socioeconomic status. This state of affairs is implied in the theories of Cohen, Cloward and Ohlin, and Miller, who claimed that one requirement for the emergence of delinquent subcultures is the existence of similarly disadvantaged lower-class boys in effective interaction with one another.

A second report on these matters is in Spergel's New York City study, which grew directly out of the Cloward and Ohlin opportunity theory of delinquency. He claimed to have identified separate theft, racketeering, and conflict subcultures, each existing in distinct lower-class neighborhoods.[85] Spergel described Slumtown, the locale of conflict behavior, as an area with a Puerto Rican and Negro population suffering from extremely low socioeconomic status and the highest index of social breakdown as shown by public assistance caseloads, venereal disease rates, and other indicators of social liabilities. Haulburg, the community area in which theft behavior predominated, was populated by second generation Americans of European stock and stood highest of the three in measures of socioeconomic status, occupational structure, and absence of social breakdown. Racketville was intermediate between the other two on most of these measures of community structure. These results generally confirmed the claims of Cloward and Ohlin regarding neighborhood variations in illegitimate opportunity structures, although there was some ambiguity as to how Spergel identified these neighborhoods and the techniques by which he developed these descriptions.

Erdman Palmore and Phillip Hammond present additional information on opportunity structures and delinquency.[86] Their investigation involved youngsters in the Aid to Dependent Children welfare program in Greater New Haven, Connecticut. The records of these youths followed from age six to nineteen, showed that 34 percent of them had become known to the police or juvenile court. Palmore and Hammond argued that the Cloward and Ohlin theory implies that legitimate and illegitimate opportunities have a multiplicative effect

---

[85] Spergel, *Racketville, Slumtown, Haulburg*, pp. 2–28.
[86] Erdman B. Palmore and Phillip E. Hammond, "Interacting Factors in Juvenile Delinquency," *American Sociological Review*, XXIX (December 1964), 848–54.

upon youths. Deviance should be particularly frequent among persons who are cut off from legitimate opportunities and who live in circumstances in which illegal opportunities are numerous. The results agreed with this hypothesis; delinquency was most common among Negro youngsters who were school failures and who lived in situations of high family and neighborhood deviation. Delinquency rates were markedly lower among white youths who were school successes and who were from stable families and neighborhoods relatively free of criminalistic influences.

One test of the Cloward and Ohlin formulation regarding delinquents' hypothesized disjunction between occupational aspirations and expectations, between what boys want and what they expect to get out of life, is found in Spergel's New York City study.[87] He reported that delinquent boys in Slumtown and Haulburg had a marked disparity between aspirations and expectations, while the young Racketville deviants had closely related aspirations and expectations. Thus these results partially confirmed the Cloward and Ohlin theory, although it should be noted that Spergel's cases were so few in number as to require that the findings be interpreted with caution. Delbert Elliott has also reported on the question of perceptions of legitimate opportunities on the part of delinquent boys.[88] He found that both the middle-class and lower-class delinquents in his sample perceived their life chances as more limited than did the nondelinquent youths.

The most detailed and comprehensive data regarding position discontent, delinquent norms and values, and related matters, are found in the Chicago material of Short and others.[89] These findings showed that delinquents exhibited greater discrepancies between occupational aspirations and expectations than did nondelinquents. More delinquent boys viewed educational opportunities as closed to them than did nonoffenders. But these relationships were far from clear, for Negro boys who showed the greatest divergence between their aspirations and expectations, compared to the achievements of their fathers, were at the same time the least delinquent. Also, contrary to the hypotheses in the Cloward and Ohlin theory, those boys who had high educational aspirations but poor school adjustment or who perceived educational opportunities as relatively closed were less delin-

[87] Spergel, *Racketville, Slumtown, Haulburg,* pp. 93–123.

[88] Delbert S. Elliott, "Delinquency and Perceived Opportunity," *Sociological Inquiry,* XXXII (Spring 1962), 216–27.

[89] Short, "Gang Delinquency and Anomie"; Short and Strodtbeck, *Group Process and Gang Delinquency;* see also Ramon Rivera and James F. Short, Jr., "Occupational Goals: A Comparative Analysis," in Klein, *Juvenile Gangs in Context,* pp. 70–90.

quent than those youths with low educational aspirations.[90] Short interpreted these results in the following way: "A possible explanation of findings reported in this paper lies in the hypothesis that for our boys, high aspirations are indicative of identification with conventional values and institutions. The stake in conformity thus indexed serves to protect the boys from delinquency involvement."[91]

Short and his colleagues have also examined the question of value commitments of delinquent boys. They found that, contrary to theories which contend that subcultural delinquents are in rebellion against middle-class ideals, individual offenders verbalized allegiance to such middle-class values as cohesive family life, stable jobs, and conformist behavior.[92] However, the structure of gang life inhibits youngsters from expressing these sentiments openly, so that a state of "pluralistic ignorance" prevailed in which gang members saw each other in distorted terms. Finally, and most important, Short argued that although gang behavior is not a direct revolt against middle-class values or a protest against generalized invidious rankings of the boys by the wider society, status considerations are nevertheless of major importance in comprehending lower-class delinquency. He contended that delinquent activities are often a response to a host of real or imagined status threats experienced by boys, and that most of these status deprivations emanate from the more immediate social world, including threats to the boys' status as males, gang members, and so on.[93]

[90] Short, "Gang Delinquency and Anomie," pp. 105–15.

[91] *Ibid.*, p. 115. On the question of "insulation" from delinquency due to a positive self concept; see also Walter C. Reckless, Simon Dinitz, and Ellen Murray, "Self Concept as an Insulator Against Delinquency," *American Sociological Review*, XXI (December 1956), 744–56; Reckless, Dinitz, and Barbara Kay, "The Self Component in Potential Delinquency and Potential Non-delinquency," *American Sociological Review*, XXII (October 1957), 566–70; Reckless, Dinitz, and Murray, "The 'Good Boy' in a High Delinquency Area," *Journal of Criminal Law, Criminology and Police Science*, XLVIII (May-June 1957), 18–25; Dinitz, Kay, and Reckless, "Group Gradients in Delinquency Potential and Achievement Scores of Sixth Graders," *American Journal of Orthopsychiatry*, XXVIII (July 1958), 598–605; Jon Simpson, Dinitz, Kay, and Reckless, "Delinquency Potential of Pre-Adolescents in High Delinquency Areas," *British Journal of Delinquency*, X (January 1960), 211–15; Frank R. Scarpitti, Murray, Dinitz, and Reckless, "The 'Good Boy' in a High Delinquency Area: Four Years Later," *American Sociological Review*, XXV (August 1960), 555–58; Dinitz, Scarpitti, and Reckless, "Delinquency Vulnerability: A Cross Group and Longitudinal Analysis," *American Sociological Review*, XXVII (August 1962), 515–17.

[92] Short, "Gang Delinquency and Anomie," pp. 115–21. For some parallel findings, see Edward Rothstein, "Attributes Related to High School Status: A Comparison of Perceptions of Delinquent and Non-delinquent Boys," *Social Problems*, X (Summer 1962), 75–83.

[93] Short, "Gang Delinquency and Anomie," pp. 117–27.

Family Patterns and Gang
Delinquency

Some of the ecological studies examined in earlier sections of this chapter suggested that delinquent conduct is particularly likely to occur among working-class youths who are, at the same time, from unstable family situations. The notion that juvenile lawbreakers develop out of unhappy or disordered families has many adherents, even though most of the recent subcultural theories have given relatively little heed to family factors in delinquency.[94]

Hyman Rodman and Paul Grams, reviewing the literature on family patterns and juvenile lawbreaking,[95] concluded that delinquents most frequently develop out of several different patterns of family structure. Thus, juvenile offenders are most often from homes which are poorly managed and in which parents are on poor terms with each other and their children. Parents who utilize corporal punishment rather than love withdrawal also tend to contribute to delinquency. Finally, parental rejection emerges as an important family pattern in juvenile lawbreaking.

One major study of family patterns in delinquency was that of the Gluecks.[96] In their comparison of 500 offenders and 500 nonoffenders, they reported that all the affectional patterns of a home—mother-child, father-child, child-parent, and child-child—bear a significant relationship to delinquency. But the most important factor seemed to be the father's affection for the boy; only 40.2 percent of the delinquents, but 80.7 percent of the controls, had affectionate fathers.

Martin Gold's investigation in Flint, Michigan, also provides some insight into family processes in juvenile misconduct.[97] He examined the backgrounds of samples of "repeated delinquents" and "sometime delinquents" from the police juvenile bureau files, along with the characteristics of a group of nondelinquents. Repeated offenders were ones who had been apprehended for at least two serious acts of law-breaking within the previous three years. Gold reported that the per-

[94] A recent psychiatric statement on these matters is Seymour Rubenfeld, *Family of Outcasts* (New York: The Free Press, 1965). A good review of the role of family processes and the interplay of other variables in delinquency is Hyman Rodman and Paul Grams, "Juvenile Delinquency and the Family; A Review and Discussion," in The President's Commission on Law Enforcement and Administration of Justice, *Task Force Report: Juvenile Delinquency and Youth Crime* (Washington, D.C.: U.S. Government Printing Office, 1967), pp. 188–221.

[95] Rodman and Grams, "Juvenile Delinquency and The Family," pp. 198–200.

[96] Sheldon and Eleanor Glueck, *Unraveling Juvenile Delinquency* (Cambridge, Mass.: Harvard University Press, 1950), p. 125.

[97] Martin Gold, *Status Forces in Delinquent Boys* (Ann Arbor: Institute for Social Research, University of Michigan, 1963).

sistent offenders were relatively free from parental control and were less attracted to their families than the nonoffenders were. The quality of the father's affection and control was most important in the genesis of delinquency. In turn, these matters were influenced by economic factors, for the higher the occupational status of the father, the more likely was the boy to be positively oriented to him. Then, too, fathers who employed physical punishment as a principal means of control were on poor terms with their sons, many of whom were involved in delinquency.[98]

Some further data on family backgrounds of working-class offenders can be found in the McCords' report concerning boys who were subjects of the Cambridge-Somerville Youth Study in the Boston area before the second World War.[99] According to the McCords, delinquent and criminal conduct were influenced by the parental role model projected by the father, by attitudes of both parents toward the child, and by the disciplinary methods employed by them. The interrelationships of these factors were quite complex, and the effect of a criminalistic father in the etiology of juvenile misconduct depends on the family influences. These youths grew up to become criminals most often when the father was involved in criminalistic conduct at the same time that parental rejection or maternal deviance was also present. Then, too, consistent discipline and love from one parent reduced the impact of a criminal role model presented by the father.[100]

Robert Stanfield has recently sifted through these same Cambridge-Somerville Youth Study data in search of family influences in delinquency.[101] His major concern was with the examination of interactional relations between family and gang variables. He suggested that explanation of delinquency only in terms of direct causal relationships oversimplifies the situation. Family experiences and gang activity are related to lawbreaking only when such experiences and activity occur in a cultural context that supports delinquent behavior. Gang activity is less likely to produce delinquent behavior when the gang does not have a culture providing support for criminality.

Stanfield explored these possibilities through the data on boys who

---

[98] *Ibid.*, pp. 123–50.

[99] Joan and William McCord, "The Effects of Parental Role Model on Criminality," in Ruth Shonle Cavan, ed., *Readings in Juvenile Delinquency* (Philadelphia: J.B. Lippincott Co., 1964), pp. 170–80; McCord, McCord, and Irving Zola, *Origins of Crime* (New York: Columbia University Press, 1959).

[100] McCord and McCord, "The Effects of Parental Role Model on Criminality," pp. 179–80.

[101] Robert Everett Stanfield, "The Interaction of Family Variables and Gang Variables in the Aetiology of Delinquency," *Social Problems* XIII (Spring 1966), 411–17.

were in the Cambridge-Somerville project. He found that some of these youths were delinquents, in that they had appeared in the juvenile court, while others were nonoffenders, having remained free of court contact. Further analysis of this information showed that delinquents were most numerous in families of low occupational status which also practiced erratic or lax discipline and least frequent in high economic status families practicing consistent discipline. Offenders were also most common in low economic status families in which boys were at the same time involved in frequent peer interaction. They were least common in high economic status families in which the youths were involved in only occasional peer relationships. However, delinquency was also relatively common in high occupational status families in which boys were engaged in relatively frequent peer contacts. Stanfield interpreted this result as showing that in neighborhoods where criminalistic influences are common, frequent peer interaction is not required in order for a boy to become delinquent. But in higher income, less criminalistic areas, frequent peer interaction is required in order for a youth to be drawn into misconduct.[102] In summary, Stanfield's research appeared to indicate that family influences, economic forces, and peer associations interact in several different combinations to produce delinquency.

Unfortunately, there is one glaring fault in this study by Stanfield. Nearly all of the Cambridge-Somerville Youth Study subjects were heavily involved in juvenile lawbreaking, even though only a few of them had become subjects of court attention. Given this fact, Stanfield's findings have more to do with the patterns of family, peer, and economic factors that result in *official recognition as an offender* than they have to do with causation per se. Stanfield was in error in assuming that the delinquents and nonoffenders in his study were quite different groups in terms of deviant conduct. Our view is that the interrelationships which Stanfield discusses probably do exist, but his data did not demonstrate their existence.

A final bit of evidence on family processes and juvenile lawbreaking can be found in Tennyson's study of 538 members of sixteen gangs in Chicago.[103] He conducted interviews with these youths and with nondelinquent lower-class and middle-class boys which showed

---

[102] *Ibid.*, pp. 414–15.

[103] Ray A. Tennyson, "Family Structure and Delinquent Behavior," in Klein, *Juvenile Gangs in Context,* pp. 57–69; see also Lester D. Jaffe, "Delinquency Proneness and Family Anomie," *Journal of Criminal Law, Criminology and Police Science,* LIV (June 1963), 146–54. In this study in Youngstown, Ohio, Jaffe found that Negro lower-class potential delinquents showed more parent-child value confusion and feelings of powerlessness than did white boys from the same schools or white boys from an upper middle-class suburb.

that the female-dominated home described in Miller's writings was relatively uncommon. In the case of Negro gang delinquents, 26.3 percent came from female-centered households, while only 19.1 percent of the white gang members were from this kind of family situation. The joint husband-wife sharing pattern in which both parents made decisions, carried out discipline, and so on, was the commonest family situation among boys from all class levels and delinquency status categories.

School Experiences and Gang Delinquency

There is one point on which nearly all sociological theories of gang misconduct are in agreement: negative experiences in the schools act as powerful forces projecting youth into delinquency. Walter Schafer and Kenneth Polk have recently drawn a vast quantity of material together on the subject of juvenile lawbreaking and schools.[104] They pointed out that the schools emerge as critical in theories of blocked goal attainment, such as those by Cohen and Cloward and Ohlin. School experiences are also seen as critical in those formulations, such as Miller's, which emphasize lack of commitment on the part of lower-class youths. Then, too, recent theorizing on deviant behavior suggests that the schools may play a major role in delinquency by stigmatizing some youngsters so that they acquire a self-image as a "bad guy."

On the issue of blocked goal attainment, Schafer and Polk assembled a large body of data which showed that lower-class citizens place a high value upon educational success.[105] At the same time, educational failure has repeatedly been shown to be disproportionately common among lower income youths.[106] The manner in which these experiences conjoin to produce delinquency is indicated by Schafer and Polk:

> These findings. . . clearly suggest that as a result of being negatively perceived and evaluated, students who fail tend to be progressively shunned and excluded by other achieving students, by individual teach-

[104] Walter E. Schafer and Kenneth Polk, "Delinquency and the Schools" in The President's Commission on Law Enforcement and Administration of Justice, *Task Force Report: Juvenile Delinquency and Youth Crime*, pp. 222–77.

[105] *Ibid.*, pp. 228–31. One major study cited by these authors is James S. Coleman and others, *Equality of Educational Opportunity* (Washington, D.C.: U.S. Government Printing Office, 1966), in which a nationwide study of 645,000 high school students showed that their parents were highly interested in their educational success.

[106] Schafer and Polk, "Delinquency and the Schools."

ers, and by the "system as a whole." Partly as a result of the internal frustrations generated by blocked goal attainment and partly as a result of the stigma which others tend to attach to educational failure, failing students' own assessments of themselves, their place in the world, and their future tend to progressively deteriorate and, understandably, the school experience becomes highly unsatisfying, frustrating, and bitter. . . . The evidence suggests, then, that educational failure is one experience, especially when combined with a desire for success, that contributes to delinquency. While such failure has been shown to relate to delinquency regardless of family status there are at least two reasons why lower income youth are especially susceptible to this influence toward illegitimate behavior. First, they fail more often, as noted earlier; and, second, students from higher status backgrounds who fail are likely to be "held into" the legitimate system by greater pressures from parents and achieving peers and by less susceptibility to delinquent or criminal subcultures.[107]

The role of the schools in the etiology of delinquency is a complicated one, in which a variety of unfavorable experiences may play some part. Schafer and Polk enumerated a sizable list of these experiences; for example, working-class children begin school at a competitive disadvantage due to their social backgrounds. They enter school less equipped in verbal skills and other learning characteristics. However, Schafer and Polk were most interested in the school conditions which exacerbate the educational problems of disadvantaged children. For one thing, school teachers often assume that lower-class children have a limited potential for scholarship, so that they give them short shrift in the classroom. Additionally, many schools place disadvantaged youngsters in situations in which the academic instruction is irrelevant to the needs and interests of children, at the same time that inappropriate teaching methods are used with them.

Schafer and Polk were also critical of those school programs of testing, grouping, and "tracking," which usually assign disadvantaged children to low ability groupings in which they receive little attention. Working-class youngsters are commonly placed in vocational training programs of dubious merit. These same disadvantaged youths receive little in the way of adequate academic and vocational counseling. Schafer and Polk also pointed out that working-class youngsters infrequently receive adequate compensatory or remedial education, and, in addition, they are often taught by inferior teachers in inadequate facilities in ghetto areas.

One particularly significant experience contributing to delinquency is rarely recognized in much of the literature dealing with schools.

[107] *Ibid.*, pp. 230–31.

Schafer and Polk pointed out that teachers usually perceive educational deficiencies and behavior problems as emanating from within the youngsters, and therefore define them as "stupid," "bad," or "sick" children. The role of the school organization in producing these characteristics is rarely acknowledged. Thus, instead of attacking deficiencies in the learning structure of the schools, school authorities place blame upon the deviant children, and thus further alienate them from school.

Other problems of contemporary schools include the degree of social distance between school officials and community residents in low income areas. Economic and racial segregation also contribute to school experiences which are indirectly involved in delinquency. All in all, Schafer and Polk make a persuasive case for the influence of school experiences upon youthful deviance.

One instructive study of some of these matters comes from Elliott's investigation in San Diego.[108] Following Cohen's theory regarding working-class boys and the status problems created for them by status frustration in the schools, Elliott hypothesized that: (1) the rate of delinquency will be greater for boys while they are in school than when out of school, and (2) delinquents who drop out of school will have a higher in-school delinquency rate than when out of school. His reasoning was that the status difficulties which are generated by school experiences will be attenuated when the youngster extricates himself from the school situation.

In order to test these hypotheses, Elliott studied the 743 tenth grade boys who entered two San Diego high schools in 1959, following them through June 1962 when they had either graduated or dropped out of school. Of the 743 boys in the study, 182 had become dropouts and 561 graduated from high school. Delinquent involvement was measured through official contact reports of the police, sheriff and other law enforcement agencies in the area.

The findings of this study showed that the over-all delinquency rate (graduates and future dropouts combined) of boys while in school was substantially higher than the rate after they had left school. The highest delinquency involvement was found among dropout youths from lower income backgrounds prior to their leaving school. However, delinquency rates were about the same for in-school middle-class boys and for dropouts from this social stratum. Finally, delinquent dropouts showed more offending behavior before they had left school than after having departed from the school situation. In summary, Elliott's results were consistent with his hypo-

---

[108] Delbert S. Elliott, "Delinquency, School Attendance and Dropout," *Social Problems*, XIII (Winter 1966), 307–14.

theses, so that they point to the role of school status problems in the creation of delinquency.

An Evaluation

At this point, the reader may well ask: "What does it all mean?" By way of a brief summation, these things can be said about theories of gang delinquency and the research bearing upon them. First, it is apparent that the ecological habitat of gang behavior is the lower-class neighborhood of the city, although the relationship of spatial factors to juvenile lawbreaking is complex in character.

The subcultural theories presented earlier do not all fare equally well when confronted with recent evidence. Most of Cohen's arguments are seriously undermined by findings which appear to show that lower-class youths do not reject middle-class values. The one portion of Cohen's theory which does survive the test of evidence has to do with the notion of a parent-delinquent subculture. Most of the research evidence on behavioral dimensions of gang delinquency indicates that *versatility,* rather than *specialization,* is most descriptive of gang misbehavior. Most gang members are involved in aggression, vandalism, theft, and various other kinds of lawbreaking. The highly differentiated forms of gang subcultures outlined by Cloward and Ohlin are relatively uncommon.

Miller's theoretical claims also receive relatively little support, so that his arguments about female-dominated households and the major role played by lower-class focal concerns seem overstated. These patterns may operate in some cases of working-class delinquency, but they do not appear to be the major determinants of most of this behavior.

The opportunity theory of Cloward and Ohlin receives the most support in the existing research. However, we have noted that their claims about deviant adaptations (specialized subcultures) are overdrawn. The available data do bear out their arguments concerning the part played by illegitimate opportunity structures in delinquency, and they also lend support to the claims regarding discrepancies between expectations and aspirations. At the same time, in some cases youngsters who showed aspirations and expectations out of key were not delinquent. What appears to be operating in these cases are intervening variables, such as particular family patterns which insulate juveniles against lawbreaking. Finally, the Cloward and Ohlin view that lower-class boys are disinterested in middle-class values is not supported by the evidence we have examined.

Another conclusion which is suggested by the available evidence is that there may be several psychological sources of involvement in youthful deviance. Some lower-class juveniles are in gangs because of social status concerns stemming from their placement at the bottom of the social order. For some youths, the pervasive deprivations of lower-class life provide the psychological fuel which propels them toward gangs. For others, the status problems which lead toward deviant peer groups are more immediate, centering about the need to be protected by gang members from assaults by other boys, masculinity anxieties, and so on. These different motivational dynamics are of varied importance in separate cohorts of lower-class youths, so that boys in Negro slums may face problems different from lower-class whites in smaller cities. There is no one route to the gang.

PERSONALITY PATTERNS OF GANG BOYS

Are there any personality dimensions shared by these working-class boys, additional to the social status ones already mentioned? There are a number of pieces of evidence which do suggest that gang offenders share a constellation of self-image characteristics. For example, Lester Hewitt and R. L. Jenkins identified a delinquent type called the pseudo-social boy in their research in a Michigan child guidance clinic.[109] These delinquents looked like gang offenders, for they were involved in furtive stealing, associated with delinquent companions, and inhabited neighborhoods of low socioeconomic status. Their parents were generally neglectful of them and subjected them to indifferent or lax discipline. Hewitt and Jenkins maintained that pseudo-social boys are well-adjusted and normal youths who get along well with their peers, but tend to be indifferent to persons in the larger social system.

Ruth Topping presented some clinical impressions about pseudo-social boys which closely paralleled the claims of Hewitt and Jenkins.[110] She contended that when these youths are seen in training schools, they project an image of self as "cool," sophisticated, well-socialized individuals. Sethard Fisher has put forth similar claims

[109] R. L. Jenkins and Lester Hewitt, "Types of Personality Structure Encountered in Child Guidance Clinics," *American Journal of Orthopsychiatry,* XIV (January 1944), 84–94.

[110] Ruth Topping, "Treatment of the Pseudo-Social Boy," *American Journal of Orthopsychiatry,* XIII (April 1943), 353–60.

about youths whom he terms "delinquents of the delinquent subcultural perspective."[111]

Another report on the psychological characteristics of working-class boys can be found in a study by Albert Reiss in Chicago.[112] In that investigation, male probationers in the Cook County Juvenile Court were classified into psychological types by psychiatrists and psychiatric social workers attached to the court. Of the 1110 probationers, 65 percent were classed as "relatively integrated delinquents," while 12 percent were labeled as showing "relatively defective superego controls." According to Reiss, "delinquents with markedly defective superego controls have not internalized the social-conforming controls of middle-class society and experience little sense of guilt over their delinquent acts. Typically they identify with an adolescent peer culture which rejects these norms."[113] The defective superego youths were often from poor residential areas; they showed frequent residential mobility, poor scholarship in school, involvement in truancy, and in other ways looked like gang offenders. In addition, many of the relatively integrated delinquents were from lower income areas, so that they appeared to be a second kind of gang delinquent. These data lend support to the characterization of gang offenders as relatively normal youths.

In still another study of this sort John Kinch reviewed wards in a state training school.[114] The boys in that study fell into three groups on the basis of background characteristics; one of these categories was that of anti-social offenders from working-class backgrounds. These boys described themselves on an adjective check list as smart, excitable, cold-hearted, stubborn, dependable, and patient.

These observations about the aloof and suspicious psychological posture of gang delinquents probably reflect the workings of social control and correctional structures, at least in part. Quite probably, many lower-class offenders develop these hostile and defiant views as they get caught up in police arrest, court appearance, and institutional commitment. At any rate, the eradication of these perspectives is a major task of correctional programs directed at gang offenders.

---

[111] Sethard Fisher, "Varieties of Juvenile Delinquency," *British Journal of Criminology,* II (January 1962), 251–61; a research test of some hypotheses which parallel these notions of Fisher is Peter M. Hall, "Identification with Delinquent Subculture and Level of Self-Evaluation," is Lefton, Skipper, and McCaghy, *Approaches to Deviance,* pp. 266–78.

[112] Albert J. Reiss, Jr., "Social Correlates of Psychological Types of Delinquency," *American Sociological Review,* XVII (December 1952), 710–18.

[113] *Ibid.,* pp. 710–11.

[114] John W. Kinch, "Self-Conceptions of Types of Delinquents," *Sociological Inquiry,* XXXII (Spring 1962), 228–34.

SUMMARY

This chapter has examined a large quantity of theory and research dealing with working class, subcultural delinquency. The end result of this examination is a complex picture of this form of juvenile misconduct which is hard to summarize in brief fashion. But some general propositions are these:

1. Although delinquents are found throughout neighborhoods and communities in American society, organized group patterns of subcultural lawbreaking constituting a neighborhood tradition tend to be concentrated in urban, working-class neighborhoods. These neighborhoods share a number of ecological characteristics, such as physical deterioration and blight, the presence of vice, and kindred conditions.

2. The most common form of subcultural misconduct is the "parent subculture" pattern of delinquency, characterized by behavioral versatility rather than specialization. Subcultural gang delinquency varies somewhat between communities of different size or other characteristics, so that in some, offender gangs are small and loosely structured, while in others, they are larger, more organized, and devoted to somewhat different kinds of lawbreaking.

3. Working-class boys become involved in subcultural misbehavior out of a variety of circumstances, but most of the causal influences center about social or economic deprivation experienced by lower income citizens in metropolitan neighborhoods. While there is no single route to involvement in subcultural delinquency, a set of related circumstances stemming from the social class structure conjoin to generate this behavior. Some gang offenders are responding to problems of perceived lack of opportunity and economic deprivation, others are more concerned about immediate status threats, while still others are drawn into delinquency out of adjustment difficulties in school.

4. Subcultural offenders tend to be the products of lower-class families in which criminalistic members are sometimes present, or families which exert relatively slight control over the behavior of the boys. Severe parent-child tension is not usually involved in these cases, but family factors of a less marked form do interact with social class influences in subcultural delinquency.

5. Gang delinquents are not usually characterized by personality problems or emotional tensions, but they do exhibit antisocial attitudes, delinquent self-images, and certain other social-psychological characteristics which develop out of their involvement in delinquent subcultures.

chapter six

MIDDLE-CLASS DELINQUENCY

INTRODUCTION

Among members of the general public, attitudes about delinquent
conduct on the part of middle-class youths tend to take either of
two extreme forms.[1] On the one hand, middle income youngsters
are often assumed to be free from involvement in deviance. This
assumption about the saintliness of middle-class juveniles is faulty,
for many of them confess to a number of acts of misbehavior on
hidden delinquency questionnaires. The other perspective on middle-class lawbreaking contends that these youngsters are involved in
unrestrained wickedness, that most of them are believed to be implicated in a wide assortment of markedly deviant acts including
drug use, sexual promiscuity, heavy and repeated drinking, and serious vandalism.[2] In this view, middle-class youths are more involved
in lawlessness than their working-class counterparts, but are the
recipients of differential handling by the law enforcement officials.
They go unpunished and their acts of lawbreaking go unreported

[1] A comprehensive and useful collection of essays on middle-class delinquency
is Edmund W. Vaz, ed., *Middle-Class Juvenile Delinquency* (New York: Harper
& Row, Publishers, 1967).

[2] An example of this popularized treatment of middle-class lawbreaking is David Loth, *Crime in the Suburbs* (New York: William Morrow & Co., Inc., 1967).

because they have powerful parents and other allies who protect them from the police and courts.

The data in the second chapter do not support these popular notions about generic misconduct in middle status groups, nor do they confirm the belief that these juveniles are free from delinquent involvement. A picture closer to the truth would acknowledge that middle-class juveniles are implicated in a large amount of hidden lawbreaking, much of it being fairly innocuous in form. At the same time, there are instances of serious criminality on the part of these adolescents. Middle-class delinquency is considerably more complex than most lay notions suggest. Accordingly, we must first examine a collection of evidence dealing with the disparate forms of middle income juvenile misconduct.

If it is true that middle-class delinquency is a term for a variety of forms of deviant behavior having little in common with each other, it is quite probably also the case that different theories are needed in order to make sense of these separate kinds of juvenile lawbreaking. A number of theoretical perspectives have been put forth concerning middle-class misconduct. It ought to be noted in passing that most of these have been offered as explanations of *all* middle status misbehavior, as though that rubric designates a single entity, a single form of youthful deviance. One of our tasks will be to link different causal arguments to the behavior about which they make the most etiological sense.

Gang forms of lawbreaking on the part of working-class youths have captured most of the interest of criminologists until relatively recently, and relatively little research has been conducted concerning misconduct on the part of youngsters from more favored economic and social circumstances. Theoretical speculation has outrun the process of empirical investigation. Yet there have been some investigations of middle-class delinquency and these will be noted in the concluding section of this chapter.

EXTENT OF MIDDLE-CLASS DELINQUENCY

Official Delinquency

Official statistics on delinquency from widely separated parts of the nation tend to show much the same thing: most juvenile court referrals are from working-class backgrounds. However, youngsters from relatively comfortable economic circumstances do occasionally find their way into the court machinery.

One indication of the extent of this relationship is found in a study by

Roland Chilton, concerning referrals to the Marion County (Indianapolis) Juvenile Court from 1958 through 1960.[3] When he sorted the census tracts in Indianapolis into five socioeconomic status levels, he found that children in the lowest group of tracts constituted 20 percent of the youth population, but made up 42 percent of the court referrals. On the other hand, juveniles from the top ranked tracts comprised 40 percent of the youthful population but contributed only 17 percent of the court cases.[4] Chilton also examined the patterning of offenses among lower- and middle-class groups. He discovered that the middle status youths were underinvolved in robbery, larceny, truancy, and loitering, yet over-represented in traffic, liquor, curfew, incorrigibility, vandalism, and car theft cases.[5] According to Chilton: "The overall pattern suggests that children from lower income areas are over-represented for offenses involving permanent gain, personal injury to others, or what the police believe to be the threat of injury to property or people. Children from high income areas are more likely to come into court for property offenses that do not lead to personal gain, or for the violation of rules intended to control the driving, drinking, and late hours of teenagers."[6]

What can be said about police contacts with middle-class juveniles? What ratio do these bear to court referrals? In other words, do the police report most of the middle status juveniles they encounter to the court, or do they handle most of them informally?

Carter has recently reported some findings which suggest an answer to the question of police activity with middle income juveniles.[7] His study dealt with two communities within the San Francisco-Oakland metropolitan area, both with a population of about 30,000. One of these, Lafayette, is an unincorporated upper middle-class community with a median income in 1960 of about $15,000. The second, Pleasant Hill, is an incorporated city with a middle-class population, having a median income of about $10,000 in 1960. The files of the sheriff's office in which these communities were located were searched for offense incident data concerning delinquency.

The most common offense reported to the police was petty theft-shoplifting, which made up 30.8 percent of all law enforcement contacts for 1966–1967. Shoplifting, malicious mischief, and runaway behavior together accounted for 56.3 percent of the police contacts,

3 Roland J. Chilton, "Middle-Class Delinquency and Specific Offense Analysis," in Vaz, *Middle-Class Juvenile Delinquency*, pp. 91–101.

4 *Ibid.*, p. 94.

5 *Ibid.*, pp. 95–96.

6 *Ibid.*, p. 96.

7 Robert M. Carter, *Middle-Class Delinquency: An Experiment in Community Control* (Berkeley, School of Criminology, University of California, 1968).

while disturbing the peace and curfew violations were also fairly numerous. The most serious lawbreaking was apparently illegal entry and burglary, which made up 10.9 percent of the police contacts. Finally, these files did not contain data on drug use, but the sheriff's personnel were of the opinion that middle-class drug users were not uncommon in the two cities.[8] In general, it appears that most of the youths known to the police were involved in the relatively innocuous or petty acts which have turned up in other studies of middle income juveniles.

The juvenile offenders known to the police were not randomly distributed in the two communities; clear clusters of delinquents could be seen along certain streets and in specific housing areas. Also, about three-fourths of the violations were committed by juveniles in the company of peers, normally of the same sex.[9]

Probably the most significant finding in this study concerned the handling of offenders. Carter indicated that in 1966, the sheriff's office processed 65.6 percent of all juvenile offenses known to it within the department, while turning 32.6 percent of the contacted youths over to the juvenile court. However, it dealt with 80.8 percent of the Lafayette and 76.9 percent of the Pleasant Hill cases within the department, referring less than 20 percent of these youths to the court. Carter labeled this differential handling as "absorption," by which he meant that parents and other citizens in these communities were allowed to assume responsibility for the deviant youths. Absorption operates at other levels, too, for Carter claimed that in both communities, offenses were often handled without any report to the police. He cited such cases as juveniles throwing dye markers into neighbors' swimming pools, vandalism, or similar acts, which were dealt with by consultation between the involved parents. In the same way, the schools in the two communities dealt internally with behavior problem youngsters and rarely reported them to the police.[10] According to Carter, "absorption by the community, except for the most flagrant law-violations, appeared as the normal method for handling youthful offenders in the middle-class community."[11]

Absorption could be branded as undemocratic, in that working-class youths are not often extended the same benefits of informal handling. But, as Carter states, absorption ought to be democratized by extending it to all juveniles, so that only the hard-core lawbreakers at any social class level would be officially processed.

[8] *Ibid.*, p. 13.
[9] *Ibid.*, p. 17.
[10] *Ibid.*, pp. 19–24.
[11] *Ibid.*, p. 22.

Some fairly serious acts of delinquent conduct are revealed in the studies considered to this point. There are other indications that some fair number of middle-class youths are involved in serious forms of lawbreaking. For example, car thefts accounted for 486,568 of the crimes known to the police in this country in 1965.[12] The police arrested 101,763 persons for auto theft in 1965 and of these, 89,957, or 88.4 percent were persons under 25 years of age. In turn, a large number of these youthful car thieves were under 18 years of age.[13]

In one study of middle-class youths, LaMar Empey and Maynard Erickson identified a group of these adolescents whose delinquent behavior was both serious and repetitive.[14] They compared the official and unofficial delinquency patterns of these youths with the records of lower and upper status boys and found that the middle-class subjects had committed the most serious offenses, including forgery, breaking and entering, destroying property, and arson. Middle income youths comprised two-thirds of all the serious violations.

Fred Shanley and his associates discovered a group of aggressive middle- and upper-class youngsters in a Los Angeles suburban school district which they then compared with a group of nonagressive underachievers and a collection of well-adjusted students.[15] The aggressive youths were boys who showed patterns of severe school disruptiveness. Over three-fourths of these youngsters had police records, while nearly half of them had been involved with the police at least four times. Half of the aggressive boys had petitions filed against them in the court. The delinquent activities of these boys appeared to be closely parallel to those of samples of Negro and Mexican-American delinquents from low status areas in Los Angeles. Finally, the aggressive boys were characterized by poor peer group relationships, inadequate school performance, and poor attendance. The aggressive youngsters certainly looked like

[12] Don C. Gibbons, *Society, Crime, and Criminal Careers* (Englewood Cliffs, N.J.: Prentice-Hall, Inc., 1968), p. 95.

[13] *Ibid.*, p. 103.

[14] LaMar T. Empey and Maynard L. Erickson, *Hidden Delinquency: Evidence on Old Issues* (Provo Experiment, Brigham Young University, 1965).

[15] Fred J. Shanley, D. Welty Lefever, and Roger E. Rice, "The Aggressive Middle-Class Delinquent," *Journal of Criminal Law, Criminology and Police Science*, LVII (June 1966), 145–57; Shanley, "Middle-Class Delinquency as a Social Problem," *Sociology and Social Research*, LI (January 1967), 185–98; Shanley also drew attention to another study of institutionalized delinquents which found that the middle-class incarcerated offenders had committed quite serious acts. This study is Herbert A. Herskovitz, Murray Levene, and George Spivak, "Anti-Social Behavior of Adolescents from Higher Socio-Economic Groups," *Journal of Nervous and Mental Diseases*, CXXV (November 1959), 1–9.

serious delinquents, but they constituted only about five percent of the upper and middle income boys within their own schools.

In another detailed study of aggressive middle-class delinquents, Albert Bandura and Richard Walters dealt with a small group of boys obtained through a probation department in California.[16] These youngsters were involved in truancy and disruptive behavior in school, as well as in antisocial conduct outside of school. At the same time, the subjects did not appear to be abnormally aggressive and hostile, for almost none of them had engaged in physical assaults upon their parents, teachers, or peers. Instead, they tended to be verbally defiant. Most of them were middle-class persons; approximately three-fourths of the families of the boys were skilled laborers or minor white collar workers.

Hidden Delinquency

One of the most ambitious investigations on the petty forms of misconduct which are particularly common among middle status juveniles was by F. Ivan Nye, and involved adolescents in three Washington cities of modest size.[17] Boys and girls in that study completed a self-report questionnaire involving petty delinquent acts such as skipping school, defying parental authority, theft of items worth less than $2, along with a few more serious actions. The responses of the subjects were then arranged into a scale indicating degrees of delinquency involvement. Nye found that 86 percent of the high school youths had low scores on this scale, while only 14 percent of a comparison group of training school youths had similar low scores. Stated differently, nearly all of the incarcerated offenders showed up as markedly more delinquent on the scale than the most "delinquent" of the high school youths.

A parallel study of hidden delinquency among high school youngsters in five Canadian communities was recently carried out by Edmund Vaz,[18] whose findings were similar to those in Nye's study: about two-thirds of the students admitted that they had taken items of little value, but less than one-fourth of them said that they had stolen more than once or twice. Similarly, many of them admitted

[16] Albert Bandura and Richard H. Walters, *Adolescent Aggression* (New York: The Ronald Press Company, 1959).

[17] F. Ivan Nye, *Family Relationships and Delinquent Behavior* (New York: John Wiley & Sons, Inc., 1958).

[18] Edmund W. Vaz, "Juvenile Delinquency in the Middle-Class Youth Culture," in Vaz, *Middle-Class Juvenile Delinquency,* pp. 131-47.

involvement in fist fights, but few said they had been repeatedly engaged in fighting.

Serious Hidden Delinquency

Not all of the hidden delinquency on the part of middle income youths is petty. For example, Larry Karacki and Jackson Toby have discussed a group of delinquent gang members in a large midwestern city who had engaged in serious larcenies, armed robbery, sexual promiscuity, "playing the queers" (submitting to homosexual acts for pay), drinking, traffic violations, and malicious mischief.[19] On a number of measures of social class position, these boys appeared to be middle-class youths. Also, Howard and Barbara Meyerhoff have contributed a loose, descriptive account of some middle-class delinquent groups in Los Angeles which suggested that serious misconduct is not entirely rare in these populations.[20] They claimed that the juveniles they observed were involved in extensive theft, a variety of homosexual and heterosexual acts, and a number of forms of mischief.

Common Beliefs and Hard Evidence

Part of the folk wisdom about middle-class juveniles centers about vandalism, drinking behavior, and sexual misconduct. The frequent claim that vandalism is widespread among middle- and upper-class youths has usually been based on isolated but well-publicized incidents in which a few youths have been apprehended after a rampage of destruction in someone's house. Much the same thing is true of allegations about drinking and sexual promiscuity, for a few dramatic cases are often used to support these more general hypotheses. We might ask what the hard evidence shows concerning these common beliefs.

The matter of vandalism has been addressed in a speculative way by Marshall Clinard and Andrew Wade, who argued that middle-class vandals may be asserting masculinity or taking revenge upon their parents through their destructive acts.[21] However, they did not pro-

[19] Larry Karacki and Jackson Toby, "The Uncommitted Adolescent: Candidate for Gang Socialization," *Sociological Inquiry*, XXXII (Spring 1962), 203-15.

[20] Howard L. Meyerhoff and Barbara G. Meyerhoff, "Field Observations of Middle-Class 'Groups,' " *Social Forces*, XXXXII (March 1964), 328-36.

[21] Marshall B. Clinard and Andrew L. Wade, "Toward the Delineation of Vandalism as a Sub-Type in Juvenile Delinquency," *Journal of Criminal Law, Criminology and Police Science*, XXXXVIII (January-February 1958), 493-99.

vide any data regarding the extent of vandalism among middle-class groups. One study which did focus upon the extent was by Nathan Goldman and dealt with the issue of whether variations in school milieu influence rates of school vandalism.[22] He studied sixteen junior and senior high schools in Syracuse, rating them in terms of the degree of vandalism in each school. The schools which suffered the greatest damage were in lower-class areas rather than in middle-class neighborhoods.

The drinking question has been addressed by George Maddox and Bevode McCall in a study of eleventh and twelfth graders in a midwestern city.[23] Over 90 percent of the students interviewed in that research asserted that they had tasted alcohol at some time in their lives, while 9 percent designated themselves as "drinkers."[24] All of the students, whether self-defined "drinkers" or not, claimed that the most frequent occasion for teenage drinking was at a party, particularly a "wild," "beer," or "unsupervised" party.[25] But again contrary to the notion that middle-class youths are most heavily caught up in drinking, it was the lower-class juveniles who were most involved in drinking behavior.[26] William Wattenberg and John Moir conducted a study of teenagers who had been arrested for drunkenness and turned up parallel findings.[27] The boys and girls in that investigation who were involved in drinking were similar to the other delinquents who had been arrested; they were not predominately middle-class children.

The best evidence on the sexual codes and practices of modern teenagers is found in the work of Ira Reiss.[28] He has argued that the most widespread practice among teen-age girls is petting-with-affection, a modern variant of an older standard of abstinence from intercourse before marriage. That is, the majority of modern teen-age girls engage in kissing and various forms of sexual foreplay, particularly in "going steady" relationships, but they stop short of intercourse. Re-

[22] Nathan Goldman, "A Socio-Psychological Study of School Vandalism," *Crime and Delinquency*, VII (July 1961), 221-30.

[23] George L. Maddox and Bevode C. McCall, "Patterns of Drinking and Abstinence," in Vaz, *Middle-Class Juvenile Delinquency*, pp. 157-78.

[24] *Ibid.*, p. 159.

[25] *Ibid.*, p. 162.

[26] *Ibid.*, pp. 172–74.

[27] William W. Wattenberg and John B. Moir, "A Study of Teen-Agers Arrested for Drunkenness," *Quarterly Journal of Studies on Alcohol*, XVII (September 1956), 426–36.

[28] Ira L. Reiss, "Sexual Codes in Teen-Age Culture," in Vaz, *Middle-Class Juvenile Delinquency*, pp. 64–75: see also Reiss, *The Social Context of Premarital Sexual Permissiveness* (New York: Holt, Rinehart & Winston, Inc., 1967).

cent studies have suggested that less than one-fourth of all teen-age girls have had intercourse in their teens. In Reiss' view, what has emerged in the United States in recent decades is a modified sexual code which allows heavy petting, providing affection is involved. But, this new code does not sanction full sexual relations, so that intercourse among high schoolers is not exceedingly common. Reiss also observed that the sexual standards of teenagers are influenced by racial and religious factors.[29]

Reiss suggested that a quite different sexual code exists among teen-age boys. Among college-bound males, about 40 percent have had coitus in their teens, while among those who terminate their education in high school, about three-fourths experience intercourse in their teens.[30] The disparity in incidence of coitus for boys and girls results from practices in which a relatively large number of males engage in intercourse with individual females over time. Any one particular girl who is available for sexual activities thus becomes serially involved with a number of boys. In this way, the relative scarcity of female sexual partners is circumvented.[31]

The question of alleged increases in promiscuity and teen-age licentiousness has been addressed by Reiss. He suggests that the real increases in adolescent sexual behavior over the last generation are not in the area of sexual intercourse but rather in the area of petting and in the more prominent public display of some of this behavior.[32]

One might still argue that dramatic liberalization of sexual codes among both teenagers and adults has occurred in the past few years and that research studies have not caught up with this change. Impressionistic observations about the so-called "love generation" and hippie behavior can be marshalled to buttress such a claim. Conceivably, we may ultimately find that premarital intercourse became quite common in the period beginning about 1965. But whatever the current extent of teen-age sexual behavior, one thing seems clear: those adolescents at any social class level who carry out petting and sexual activity circumspectly, within the framework of a dating, "going-steady" relationship, run only a very slight risk of falling into the hands of the juvenile court. The majority of official or reported cases of sexual misconduct center about prominent public displays of "wild"

---

[29] Reiss, "Sexual Codes in Teen-Age Culture," pp. 65–67.

[30] *Ibid.*, pp. 67–69.

[31] The status problems which are created for girls who get a public reputation as available sexual partners are discussed in Albert J. Reiss, Jr., "Sex Offenses: The Marginal Status of the Adolescent," *Law and Contemporary Problems,* XXV (Spring 1960), 309–33.

[32] Reiss, "Sexual Codes in Teen-Age Culture," pp. 70–72.

behavior by girls, "gang shags," and other activities which are offensive to adults because they seem to constitute blatant flaunting of public sentiments about sexuality.

On the drug issue, traditional thinking has identified lower-class slum areas as the habitat of most juvenile drug users. Chapter Five took note of the gang delinquent involved in narcotics use, in the discussion of the theory of Cloward and Ohlin, which holds that drug use is a retreatist form of conduct engaged in by a sizable minority of gang offenders.[33] The contentions of Cloward and Ohlin are supported by a considerable quantity of empirical evidence showing that lower-class youthful addicts are drawn from the ranks of relatively maladjusted working-class youths.[34]

However, in recent years, many members of the general population have begun to entertain the hypothesis that drug use, particularly marijuana smoking and the use of various pills, has reached epidemic proportions among middle-class youths. On this matter, one national news magazine has noted that a 1967 National Institute of Mental Health study set the figure of marijuana use among high school youngsters at 10 percent of all youths, but then went on to argue that this figure is too low.[35] Support for that claim was provided by an informal survey in the Palos Verdes school system in the Los Angeles area, where the police estimated that over half of all high school youths used marijuana. Further support for the view that marijuana use has increased markedly among middle-class youths is found in figures from California, showing that marijuana arrests among juveniles numbered only 248 in 1962, but increased to 3869 in 1966, while arrests for other narcotics or dangerous drugs remained about the same over this period.[36]

One of the best discussions of drug use among juveniles is to be found in an article by William Simon and John Gagnon, in which they related the use of marijuana among youths to the growth of other pill-taking behavior patterns among the general public.[37] Simon and Gagnon indicated that hard evidence on the extent of marijuana use

[33] See Don C. Gibbons, *Changing the Lawbreaker* (Englewood Cliffs, N.J.: Prentice-Hall, Inc., 1965), pp. 90–92 for a typological description of the lower-class juvenile heroin user.

[34] For a review of this evidence, see Gibbons, *Society, Crime, and Criminal Careers*, pp. 418–26. See also Isidor Chein, Donald L. Gerard, Robert S. Lee, and Eva Rosenfeld, *The Road to H* (New York: Basic Books, Inc., 1964).

[35] *Time*, XCII (August 30, 1968), 44–45.

[36] James T. Carey, *The College Drug Scene* (Englewood Cliffs, N.J.: Prentice-Hall, Inc., 1968), p. 45.

[37] William Simon and John H. Gagnon, "Children of the Drug Age," *Saturday Review*, LI (September 21, 1968), 60–78.

is not yet available, but they cited findings from a nationwide opinion survey which showed that among parents with substantial incomes and some degree of higher education, one in six reported knowing at least one teenager who used marijuana.[38]

Simon and Gagnon speculated that the growth of marijuana and other drug use has not been uniform throughout the nation. Instead, they claimed that this activity is probably most frequent among middle-class youths, while working-class and lower middle-class youngsters are less frequently implicated in marijuana smoking. Simon and Gagnon also offered an account of the manner in which marijuana smoking has probably grown up in recent years, citing the influence of the mass media in communicating tolerant views of drug use. Additionally, marijuana use has probably diffused downward from college age youngsters to high school youths, so that it has been spread through peer contacts. Finally, Simon and Gagnon argued that marijuana use may be most widespread in major cities, and, in particular, in community areas such as the Haight-Ashbury district in San Francisco and East Village in New York City.

Summary

The evidence on the extent of middle-class delinquency in the passages above lead to conclusions which are closely parallel to those of Chapter Two:

1. Middle-class youngsters are relatively uncommon in the juvenile court compared to youths from lower income backgrounds. Police agencies are aware of a larger number of middle status delinquents, but most of these children have been involved in relatively innocuous acts of lawbreaking. Middle-class delinquents known to the police tend not to be involved in repetitive, career patterns of misconduct. Many of the middle-class offenders who come to the attention of the police are "absorbed" back into the community, without referral to the juvenile court.

2. Hidden middle-class delinquency is widespread; nearly all middle income youths have committed at least a few acts which technically constitute delinquency. However, most hidden delinquency on the part of middle-class adolescents is relatively petty in form.

3. Middle-class youths do engage in some kinds of serious lawbreaking. Those youths who are involved in serious delinquency have a relatively high likelihood of ending up in a juvenile court. Serious forms of middle-class delinquency include automobile theft, "joyriding," and aggressive behavior.[39]

---

[38] *Ibid.*, p. 62.
[39] Juvenile joyriders usually do not damage the cars they steal, nor do they

4. Public stereotypes of middle-class youngsters which assert that many of them are caught up in serious vandalism, widespread use of alcohol, and sexual promiscuity, are not supported by much firm evidence. These kinds of behavior apparently are much less common than is often supposed by citizens.

THEORIES OF MIDDLE-CLASS DELINQUENCY

The upsurge of attention to middle-class delinquency in recent years has produced a considerable number of theories. Fred Shanley has identified eight different lines of argument concerning this behavior.[40] He noted that some observers have linked middle-class misbehavior to anxieties felt by boys over masculinity. Other persons have accounted for middle-class offenses in terms of adolescent rebellion steming from frustrations due to forced postponement of adult status, that is, to the limbo position of juveniles in which they are neither children nor are accorded the rights of adults. Other theories consider status deprivation, inadequate parent-child relations, ineffective school performance, the pernicious influence of deviant peers, and capricious experimentation with unlawful behavior. Finally, middle-class delinquency has been seen by many as an outgrowth of broad changes in American social structure, involving weakening of the deferred gratification pattern.

The current state of affairs provides us with an embarrassment of riches. We have too many theories and too little evidence with which to evaluate them. Surely not all of the formulations are valid, particularly in that the assertions in some contradict the claims of other perspectives. In addition, as research is carried out on middle-class lawbreaking, we will probably discover that certain formulations apply with most accuracy to particular forms of misconduct, rather than to middle-class delinquency in all of its heterogeneous forms.

Most theories of middle class delinquency explicitly or implicitly deal with boys only. Additionally, most of the evidence on the extent of middle-class lawbreaking presented previously concerned males. We shall take up the question of delinquency on the part of middle-class girls in more detail in Chapter Seven.

---

deprive the owner of his automobile for very long. Nonetheless, car theft produces a group of irate citizens who view this kind of delinquency as very serious.

[40] Shanley, *op.cit.*, pp. 187–93. This article provides a good succinct summary of theories, along with a number of suggestions for research on middle-class delinquency.

Anxiety Over Masculine Identity

One thesis that has enjoyed a good deal of popularity is that middle-class boys engage in delinquency in order to publicly assert to others (and to themselves) that they are "tough," "hard" males, rather than sissy-like or feminine figures. Car theft, vandalism, drinking and smoking, and other daring acts are supposed to serve as public pronouncements that the youth is a "real man." These compulsive demonstrations of manhood arise because of structural defects which have emerged in the past several decades in modern middle-class families which deprive boys of opportunities for the gradual learning of the ways of male adulthood. Middle-class teenage girls are not subject to this problem, for they are able to observe their mothers in the role of adult female and to emulate her.

This line of theory regarding middle-class delinquency was first advanced by Talcott Parsons.[41] and subsequently enunciated by Albert Cohen.[42] Parsons and Cohen both maintained that middle-class boys experience masculinity difficulties most severely because of the nature of middle-class family life. On this issue, Parsons asserted:

> Especially in the urban middle classes, however, the father does not work in the home and his son is not able to observe his work or to participate in it from an early age. Furthermore, many of the masculinity functions are of a relatively abstract and intangible character, such that their meaning must remain almost wholly inaccessible to the child. This leaves the boy without a tangible meaningful model to emulate and without the possibility of gradual initiation into the activities of the adult male role.[43]

The ingredients of this set of notions have been succinctly summarized by Cohen in the following remarks:

> Because of the structure of the modern family and the nature of our occupational system, children of both sexes tend to form early feminine identifications. The boy, however, unlike the girl, comes later under strong social pressure to establish his masculinity, his *difference from* female figures. Because his mother is the object of the feminine identification which he feels is the threat to his status as a male, he tends to react negativistically to those conduct norms which have been as-

[41] Talcott Parsons, "Certain Primary Sources and Patterns of Aggression in the Social Structure of the Western World," *Psychiatry*, X (May 1947), 167–81; Parsons, "Age and Sex in the Social Structure of the United States," *American Sociological Review*, VII (October 1942), 604–16.

[42] Albert K. Cohen, *Delinquent Boys* (New York: The Free Press, 1955), pp. 157–69.

[43] Parsons, "Age and Sex in the Social Structure of the United States," p. 605.

sociated with mother and therefore have acquired feminine significance. Since mother has been the principal agent of indoctrination of "good," respectable behavior, "goodness" comes to symbolize femininity, and engaging in "bad" behavior acquires the function of denying his feminity and therefore asserting his masculinity. This is the motivation to juvenile delinquency.[44]

We suggest that this line of theorizing is probably too facile, so that at best, it may apply to only a small portion of middle-class delinquency. For one thing, Walter Miller has contended that masculinity problems are most frequent among lower-class youths, rather than middle-class ones.[45] His position is that the pattern of female-dominated households in lower-class society generates chronic anxiety about masculinity on the part of working-class boys. Little evidence can be brought to bear upon these alternative hypotheses, but Miller's argument is at least as plausible as the claim that masculine anxiety is a middle-class problem.

One set of criticisms of Parsons' notions has been put forth by Ralph England.[46] He asked why masculine indentity anxiety leads to rambunctiousness and deviance, rather than to efforts at the assumption of adult responsibility by troubled boys. Additionally, England argued that Parsons overstated the difficulties experienced by middle-class boys in observing occupational roles. He also suggested that Parsons' claims about commuting, absentee middle-class fathers are exaggerated, that most white collar fathers are available to serve as role-models to their sons. England also questioned how the delinquency of middle-class girls is to be explained. Finally, he asked why there has apparently been a dramatic upsurge of middle-class delinquency since the second World War while the occupational and social structure of which Parsons spoke has not been radically altered.

Our assessment of the maculine identity formulation is that it probably is not a satisfactory explanation of most middle-class delinquency. Quite probably, most middle-class boys, delinquent or otherwise, are not markedly troubled by these concerns. At the same time, there may be a collection of middle income boys who are anxious about masculinity and who do engage in deviance out of this anxiety. But, if so, there are probably some intervening variables as well. Specifically, this line of argument may have some applicability to joyriding automobile theft.

[44] Cohen, *Delinquent Boys*, p. 164. Emphasis in the original.

[45] Walter B. Miller, "Lower Class Culture as a Generating Milieu of Gang Delinquency," *Journal of Social Issues*, XIV, 3 (1958), 5–19; Miller, "Implications of Lower Class Culture for Social Work," *Social Service Review*, XXXII (September 1959), 219–36.

[46] Ralph W. England, Jr., "A Theory of Middle Class Juvenile Delinquency," in Vaz, *Middle-Class Juvenile Delinquency*, pp. 242–44.

Youth Culture and Delinquency

A second formulation which has attracted favorable attention holds that a youth culture has grown up in the United States which draws middle-class adolescents into deviant conduct, much of it delinquent in form. Jessie Bernard has enumerated a number of the characteristics of this teen-age culture, including value stress upon cars, clothing, records, teenage magazines, special language forms, and other features.[47] All those who speak of a youth culture contend that juveniles consititute a nationwide group of individuals who perceive themselves to be a kind of minority group. These youngsters have evolved a shared set of definitions of proper conduct, common values, and other characteristics of a relatively separate culture divorced from prevailing adult cultural patterns. Although adolescents are acknowledged to be under the control of and influenced by demands and expectations of their elders to some degree, the pull of youth culture is such as to create frictions and tensions between youths and adults. One current statement of these ideas can be found in discussions of a generation gap presumed to exist, in which many teenagers are alienated from their parents.

One prominent expression of youth culture notions applied to delinquency can be found in an essay by Cohen.[48] He contended that this cultural system has grown up due to sweeping changes in the labor market and educational practices over the past half century. As the occupational system has altered so that youths are no longer absorbed into it at a relatively early age, schools have been forced to retain jurisdiction over all teenagers, whether they perform well in school or not. Educational institutions have watered down the standards for educational performance, so that youngsters are now able to obtain good grades with minimum effort. These changes in American social structure have also been accompanied by growing affluence; middle-class juveniles are now financially able to behave in the manner of a leisure class, enjoying the benefits of ample spending money.

In Cohen's view, the alterations in social structure have weakened the deferred gratification pattern, in which middle-class adolescents formerly perceived that they had to sacrifice many pleasures of the moment if they were to achieve success and upward mobility in the future. In earlier times, most middle-class youngsters did not view themselves as having time to engage in frivolous acts of delinquency. But, at present, increasing numbers of juveniles entertain a picture of

---

[47] Jessie Bernard, "Teen-Age Culture: An Overview," in Vaz, *Middle-Class Juvenile Delinquency*, pp. 23–38.

[48] Albert K. Cohen, "Middle-Class Delinquency and the Social Structure," in Vaz, *Middle-Class Juvenile Delinquency*, pp. 203–7.

the world in which attainment of future goals does not rest heavily upon ascetic, scholarly behavior while one is young. According to Cohen, "to the extent to which these changes have occurred, there has resulted a weakening of one of the principal insulators against juvenile delinquency. It becomes possible to be middle-class in terms of aspirations and at the same time to 'hang around the corner.'"[49]

The values of youth culture center about the hedonistic pursuit of fun and pleasure in the company of one's peers. Most of the behavior of members of the youth culture is nondelinquent in form, but pleasure-seeking on the part of immature persons often has the potential to develop into delinquency. Cohen tells us: "The simulation and compulsive exaggeration of certain patterns which are symbolically adult, especially these connected with liquor, sex and automobiles, also lend themselves to the requirements of the youth cultures and easily take a delinquent form."[50]

Cohen's contentions concerning teenage culture are echoed by England, who also observed that American youths have been removed from functional roles and have been placed in an ambiguous status niche in which they are neither children nor adults.[51] England was particularly concerned with post World War II developments which have contributed to the pronounced growth of youth culture. He suggested that post war affluence has much to do with providing the conditions for the growth of a nationwide group of adolescents who see themselves as constituting a like-minded collectivity. Most modern youngsters have automobiles available to them which provide them with a motorized boudoir. They make up an identifiable market to which a great deal of modern advertising is directed. Then, too, a number of mass media developments have contributed to the we feeling among adolescents, including the proliferation of disc jockeys and young people's magazines as spokesmen for teenagers. England, like Cohen, contended that youth culture emphasis upon irresponsible hedonism results in the transformation of adult values by juveniles so that these take on a delinquent shading. Cars are perceived as playthings, so that they are driven recklessly and at high speed. In a similar way, the unsophisticated members of youth culture get caught up in hedonistic and delinquent elaborations of the drinking and sexual behavior of adults.

Joseph Scott and Edmund Vaz have also discussed the growth of youth culture at considerable length, attributing it to the decline of ascetic mobility-striving on the part of middle-class persons, due to

49 *Ibid.*, p. 206.
50 *Ibid.*
51 England, "A Theory of Middle Class Juvenile Delinquency."

changes in American economic life since the early 1900s.[52] They note
that in past decades parental emphasis upon ambition, achievement,
and character-building behavior patterns such as saving for college
and working at part-time jobs insulated middle-class juveniles from
delinquent involvement. But developments in the economic system,
changes in family structure in the direction of permissive, democratic
organization, and alterations in the school system have all contributed
to the rise of an adolescent leisure class.

One of the strengths of the analysis by Scott and Vaz is that it
indentified a number of symbiotic links between youth culture and
the larger social structure. They pointed out: "In a limited, yet significant, way the adult community creates structured opportunities for
adolescents to engage in youth culture activities, that is, in 'whole-
some' recreation. Organized dances, high school 'formals' and informal 'hops', church 'socials', and athletic events reflect this structural
link between the youth culture and the adult community, and reveal
especially cherished values and expectations sustained by adults."[53]
In other words, most of the deviant acts of adolescent members of
youth culture are exaggerations of the activities which are encouraged
by adults. Parentally approved dating sometimes results in sexual misconduct, parentally sponsored parties sometimes involve excessive
teenage drinking, and so on. If this is so, a special set of motives
probably is not required in order to explain delinquent behavior
within middle-class youth culture.

The youth culture formulation sounds quite convincing, particularly
as an explanation for much of the boisterous and "adult" activities of
middle-class youths, such as drinking and smoking. Nonetheless, this
view is in need of empirical scrutiny through research.

One bit of evidence on youth culture notions is to be found in a
study by Frederick Elkin and William Westley in a suburb of Montreal, Canada.[54] They took issue with the "storm and stress" view of
adolescence which holds that because of uncertainties about his status
and obligations, the teenager identifies with a peer group system
which is in opposition to the standards of the adult world. In the
suburb they examined, children belonged to closely knit families,
shared the same career aspirations as their parents, were involved in
deferred gratification; the peer groups in which they interacted

[52] Joseph W. Scott and Edmund W. Vaz, "A Perspective on Middle-Class Delinquency," in Vaz, *Middle-Class Juvenile Delinquency*, pp. 207–22.

[53] *Ibid.*, p. 220.

[54] William A. Westley and Frederick Elkin, "The Protective Environment and
Adolescent Socialization," in Vaz, *Middle-Class Juvenile Delinquency*, pp. 9–22;
Elkin and Westley, "The Myth of Adolescent Culture," *American Sociological
Review*, XX (December 1955), 680–84.

tended to reinforce these values and behavior patterns. The peer group norms approved of part time jobs, membership in school organizations, and the pursuit of good grades in school. Westley and Elkin acknowledged that the community they studied was small, relatively isolated, tightly knit, and self-contained, so that it may have been rather unlike many other middle-class areas. Still, their results stand as a warning against the premature acceptance of youth culture notions.

Lack of Commitment and Delinquency

Another interpretation of middle-class delinquency has been advanced by Karacki and Toby, growing out of their study of a middle-class gang engaged in serious acts of lawbreaking.[55] They argued that deprivation notions could not be applied to the members of this gang, for these boys were from relatively comfortable social circumstances. Instead, Karacki and Toby offered the hypothesis that lack of commitment was involved in the behavior of the gang. They claimed that a more plausible explanation seemed to be that their academic failures, their disinterest in conventional occupational roles, and their emergence as a delinquent gang were all attributable to the same underlying factor: a failure to develop commitments to adult roles and values.

Further evidence for the part played by lack of commitment was found in the fact that as these boys grew older and more mature, they reentered school or became involved in occupational training. In short, they acquired a degree of commitment which they had previously lacked. As adolescents, the boys were guided by desires for immediate gratification, loyalty to their peers, and the need to assert masculinity through aggressive acts. But this lack of commitment to the standards of the adult world was transitory, and as the interest in adult patterns was revived, involvement in deviance dissipated.

Status Inconsistency and Delinquency

Another plausible, speculative thesis on middle-class delinquency has been put forth by Robert Bohlke, centered about status inconsistency.[56] He argued that lawbreaking may be most common among the

[55] Karacki and Toby, "The Uncommitted Adolescent."

[56] Robert H. Bohlke, "Social Mobility, Stratification Inconsistency, and Middle Class Delinquency," in Vaz, *Middle-Class Juvenile Delinquency*, pp. 222–32. See this article, pp. 222–23, for another listing of perspectives on middle-class delinquency.

nouvelle bourgeoisie, that is, among persons who have recently acquired a comfortable income but who have yet to assume the values of middle-class society. He pointed out that the older situation in which persons had to develop certain personality and behavior patterns before they could attain upward mobility and middle-class status no longer holds. Among other things, labor union membership assures almost instantaneous elevation of one's income. Bohlke also contended that stratification inconsistency of another kind is implicated in delinquency; the situation in which individuals have suffered a decline in income while still retaining allegiance to middle-class values, or in which income level has not kept up with the demands of the person's position. Finally, Bohlke suggested that the spatial mobility which often accompanies a change in economic position may have a dislocating effect which contributes to delinquency. He argued that movement of a family from a working-class to a middle-class neighborhood, or from the city to a suburb, may create a situation of marginality in which the youngster is cut off from a rich network of peer group relationships and other community ties.[57] This argument lacks evidential backing, but Bohlke did suggest a number of lines of research testing which it might generate.

Lower-Class Value Diffusion and Delinquency

Another theory of middle-class delinquency has been proposed by William Kvaraceus and Walter Miller.[58] Their argument started off from a base which contended that the deferred gratification pattern among middle-class citizens has been weakened by such developments as installment buying, mandatory school attendance, and changes in the economy. One of the results of these trends, according to Kvaraceus and Miller, is that lower-class values have been diffused upward into middle-class society. These values tend in the direction of hedonistic pursuit of short run pleasures, so that they draw middle-class youths who follow them into delinquency. These writers based

---

[57] The concept of marginality has been applied to joyriding behavior by the author. See Don C. Gibbons, "Problems of Causal Analysis in Criminology: A Case Illustration," *Journal of Research in Crime and Delinquency,* III (January 1966), 47–52.

[58] William Kvaraceus and Walter B. Miller, *Delinquent Behavior: Culture and the Individual* (Washington, D.C.: National Education Association, 1959); Kvaraceus and Miller, "Norm-Violating Behavior in Middle-Class Culture," in Vaz, *Middle-Class Juvenile Delinquency,* pp. 233–41.

their case in considerable part upon an account of the spread of lower-class Negro jazz music, albeit in somewhat modified form, to middle-class groups. This argument is far from convincing, so that it remains to be shown that lower-class values are pursued by many middle income persons.

Subterranean Values and Delinquency

Another perspective which appears to have some relevance to middle-class delinquency is the subterranean values position of David Matza and Gresham Sykes.[59] They suggested that the values which are pursued by many juvenile offenders, centering around hedonistic pleasure-seeking, the pursuit of "kicks," disdain for work, and aggressive demonstrations of masculinity, are far less deviant than they are commonly portrayed. In their opinion, the search for adventure, excitement, and thrills is a subterranean value that exists in the adult world side by side with the values of security, routinization, and the rest. Although the latter are the publicly enunciated values of "respectable" people, unverbalized subterranean values are also pursued by these same individuals. If this is so, delinquent perspectives may simply be exaggerated and immature variants of these adult values. The Sykes and Matza argument does not require acceptance of the oppositional characterization that is contained in many statements about youth cultures. Here again, there is little evidence which can be focused upon the speculative formulation of Sykes and Matza.

RESEARCH ON MIDDLE-CLASS DELINQUENCY

We are currently at a stage in delinquency study regarding middle-class lawbreaking that has been passed in the area of working-class misconduct; the fact that we have only recently become interested in middle-class offenders has resulted in a flurry of theorizing based on hunches, bits of evidence, and speculative guesses. The next decade will probably be one in which empirical investigations will begin to fill in many of the gaps in our knowledge about middle-class delinquency. Yet there are some research studies now available which allow us to arrive at some tentative conclusions.

---

[59] David Matza and Gresham M. Sykes, "Delinquency and Subterranean Values," *American Sociological Review*, XXVI (October 1961), 712–19; see also Matza, *Delinquency and Drift* (New York: John Wiley & Sons, Inc., 1964).

Nye's Study[60]

F. Ivan Nye's investigation was an ambitious study of predominately middle-class offenders in three adjacent Washington cities of
modest size. Delinquents in this research were youths who confessed
to a number of relatively innocuous acts on a self-report delinquency
questionnaire.

One matter which Nye investigated centered about socioeconomic
variations among offenders and nondeviants. Nye found no correlation
between economic status and delinquency, but it should be noted that:
(a) serious, subcultural lawbreaking was not involved in this study, and
(b) the communities investigated did not show the extremes of socioeconomic position which would be observed in a large metropolitan community.[61]

In these communities it was found that those youngsters who at-
tended church were less involved in misbehavior than those who were
not churchgoers. Birth order was related to delinquency; oldest children were least involved in lawbreaking. Also, boys from large families
were more often involved in delinquency than those from small families.[62]

Nye reported that a slight relationship existed between broken
homes and delinquency, in that 19.7 percent of the homes of all the
boys in the study were broken ones, while 23.6 percent of the homes of
the delinquents were broken. However, the psychological climate of
the home, rather than the broken-unbroken status, was more important
in misconduct. Nye asserted that: "As to categories, less delinquent
behavior was found in broken homes than in unhappy unbroken homes.
The happiness of the marriage was found to be much more closely
related to delinquent behavior in children than whether the marriage
was an original marriage or a remarriage or one in which the child was
living with one parent only.[63] However, it ought to be pointed out that
these contentions about family life were based on questionnaire responses of the youths; it is possible that the perceptions of family life of
some of the subjects were out of sorts with evaluations that might have
been rendered by neutral observers.

Nye also found that delinquency was most common in families in
which mothers were employed. Juvenile offenders were also frequent in
families that had experienced spatial mobility.[64] Parental rejection

---

[60] Nye, *Family Relationships and Delinquent Behavior.*

[61] *Ibid.,* pp. 23–33.

[62] *Ibid.,* pp. 34–40.

[63] *Ibid.,* p. 50.

[64] *Ibid.,* pp. 53–59.

also appeared to be related to misconduct, as did unfair or inconsistent discipline by the father.[65] All in all, Nye's study bears most directly upon hypothesis that "under the roof" culture is related to middle-class delinquency.

Other Research

Gerald Pine has conducted a study in an urban New England community which dealt with middle-class youngsters.[66] About 700 students in grades nine through twelve were studied. These children were assigned to three social status levels: upper middle, lower middle, and lower-class. They were also placed into mobility groups on the basis of their parents' economic status, their educational plans, and so on. Upwardly mobile, downwardly mobile, and stable categories resulted from this process.

The children in the study were given a 120-item questionnaire dealing with delinquent acts. Some procedural details are lacking, but it appears that the subjects were mainly involved in petty delinquencies, for they confessed to less serious violations than did a group of training school wards.

The results of Pine's investigation showed no socioeconomic correlation with juvenile lawbreaking, but the study dealt with petty activities rather than serious misconduct. Middle-class youngsters did not receive preferential treatment from the police. The most significant finding was that downwardly mobile youths were more involved in misconduct than were the other youngsters. Upwardly mobile, college-oriented juveniles were the least delinquent.[67] These findings parallel the claims of Karacki and Toby concerning lack of commitment, and also the contentions of Bohlke dealing with stratification inconsistency.

Another inquiry into middle-class delinquency was the work of Andrew Greeley and James Casey, dealing with an upper middle-class gang.[68] The members of that gang were from backgrounds of academic failure, school discipline problems, and "father-absent" families that were upwardly mobile in a "socially disorganized" new suburb. These findings lend some credence to middle-class delinquency theories stressing stratification inconsistency and masculinity problems.

[65] *Ibid.*, pp. 69–91.
[66] Gerald J. Pine, "Social Class, Social Mobility, and Delinquent Behavior," *The Personnel and Guidance Journal*, XXXXIII (April 1965), 770–74.
[67] *Ibid.*, pp. 772–73.
[68] Andrew Greeley and James Casey, "An Upper Middle-Class Deviant Gang," *American Catholic Sociological Review*, XXIV (Spring 1963), 33–41.

The study by Herbert Herskovitz, Murray Levene, and George Spivak of institutionalized middle-class delinquents indicated that these children were characterized by psychological conflict.[69] These youths had experienced negative intra-family patterns; many of them had been exposed to inconsistent, indulgent, over-protective mothers and / or distant, hostile, and aggressive fathers.

Donald Carek, Willard Hendrickson, and Donald Holmes also reported on middle income deviant youths in an essay in which some clinical impressions were presented.[70] These persons argued that parents often derive vicarious satisfaction from the lawbreaking acts of their children, or that parents encourage the delinquencies of their children in other ways.

Automobile Theft—"Joyriding"

Automobile theft of the "joyriding" form is a frequent occurrence in the United States. "Joyriding" is that kind of car theft in which the offenders steal automobiles to use them for short-run recreational purposes rather than to deprive the owner permanently of his car. Joyriding is one form of deviance which spans juvenile delinquency and adult criminality, for it is often carried on by persons from about thirteen to twenty years of age. Many of these individuals are apprehended and sent off to juvenile courts so that they become "juvenile delinquents" in point of legal fact, while others are turned over to criminal courts and receive the legal status of "criminal."

Gibbons has offered a description of the average juvenile joyrider which suggests the following causal dynamics.[71] First, joyriders are relatively well-adjusted boys who are on good terms with most of their peers, particularly fellow joyriders with whom they steal cars. They are predominately middle-class youngsters who have grown up in a family setting which is relatively stable, but which creates problems of *masculine identity* for adolescent males. Further, boys who steal cars often show family backgrounds involving some mild degree of *parent-child tension.* However, out of all middle-class boys who show social-psychological problems surrounding masculinity, the ones most likely

---

[69] Herskovitz, Levene, and Spivak, "Anti-Social Behavior of Adolescents from Higher Socio-Economic Groups."

[70] Donald J. Carek, Willard J. Hendrickson, and Donald J. Holmes, "Delinquency Addiction in Parents," *Archives of General Psychiatry,* IV (April 1961), 357–62.

[71] Gibbons, *Society, Crime, and Criminal Careers,* pp. 299–308.

to get involved in car theft seem to be those who are involved in situations of *marginality* of one kind or another. Marginality is our term for a host of conditions which prevent the youth from working out his problems of masculinity in nondeviant ways. The pimply boys who have communication problems with girls, those who are too small to participate in high school athletics, or the ones who have difficulties in becoming socially integrated into school life because their families show residential mobility in the form of frequent moves within the community are the ones who are prospects for careers in joyriding. What is offered is a hypothesis stressing a multi-faceted process through which certain middle-class boys are drawn into car theft.[72]

This hypothesized etiological background in joyriding is an elaboration of the Parsons-Cohen line of analysis which dealt with masculine protest. We have added to this framework the two ingredients of parent-child tensions and marginality to form an overarching structure for a series of specific contingencies which some middle-class adolescents encounter. It should be noted that one British criminologist has offered this masculinity hypothesis to account for car thieves he studied, holding that these youths were from families in which the fathers failed to serve as adequate role-models.[73]

How well do these claims stand up in the face of empirical evidence? Unequivocal answers cannot be given to this question; the available data on car thieves is inadequate to the task. The major problem with the findings now available is that they were drawn from official records and do not contain information on matters such as masculinity anxiety, marginality, and the like.[74]

Detailed surveys of the existing information regarding car theft have been made by Leonard Savitz[75] and by Jerome Hall.[76] One of the salient facts about automobile theft presented by these authors was that about 90 percent of the vehicles reported stolen are ultimately recovered, usually undamaged, and frequently within a short time interval.[77] Reports of the San Francisco Police Department also show that of the cars stolen in the nine police districts in that com-

[72] *Ibid.*, pp. 299–301.

[73] T. C. N. Gibbens, "Car Thieves," *British Journal of Delinquency*, VIII, 4 (1958), 257–68.

[74] This issue is discussed more fully in Gibbons, *Society, Crime, and Criminal Careers*, p. 303, and in Gibbons, "Problems of Causal Analysis in Criminology: A Case Illustration."

[75] Leonard D. Savitz, "Automobile Theft," *Journal of Criminal Law, Criminology and Police Science*, L (July-August 1959), 132–43.

[76] Jerome Hall, *Theft, Law and Society*, 2nd ed. (Indianapolis: The Bobbs-Merrill Co., Inc., 1952), 233–88.

[77] Savitz, "Automobile Theft," p. 133; Hall, *Theft, Law and Society*, pp. 240–45.

166 DELINQUENT BEHAVIOR

munity, more than half were recovered within the same area in which they had been stolen.[78]

One of the major studies regarding joyriders was that of William Wattenberg and James Balistrieri.[79] These researchers examined the detailed case records of over 200 white boys apprehended for car theft in 1948 by the Detroit police, and compared them with several thousand other white youngsters who had been arrested for other delinquencies. Negro car thieves were not studied because they were infrequently encountered, at least by the police, even though Negroes constituted a sizable portion of the Detroit population.

The main impression which came out of the comparisions of car thieves with other offenders centered about the "favored group" status of the former. Auto thieves were from neighborhoods rated as "above average" by the police, from uncrowded single-family homes, from houses in good repair, and from racially homogeneous neighborhoods. They were also from families in which only one parent was employed. The car thieves were on good terms with their peers. Although the automobile thieves were rated as rambunctious gang members by the police, they were frequently evaluated by the officers as "responsive." Finally, the parents' involvement in their sons' recreation was judged to be "occasional" rather than "seldom" or "regular."[80] Wattenberg and Balistrieri interpreted this pattern of findings as an indication that automobile thieves are the product of a permissive upbringing which results in an "other-directed" personality pattern. These boys were thought to be easily drawn into peer-supported patterns of deviant conduct at the same time that they are unresponsive to larger social entities and their values.[81]

A second report on juvenile car thieves is contained in a study by Charles Browning.[82] He examined 56 car thieves, 63 truants, and 58 control group nondelinquent juveniles, all of whom were Los Angeles County probation wards. Greater numbers of both groups of delinquents were from broken homes than were the nondelinquents. The car thieves and controls were more commonly from middle income backgrounds than were the truants. Similarly, the car thieves and nonoffenders showed better community and personal adjustment than

[78] "An Analysis of Auto Thefts and Recoveries by Police District," mimeographed.
[79] William W. Wattenberg and James Balistrieri, "Automobile Theft: A 'Favored-Group' Delinquency," *American Journal of Sociology*, LVII (May 1952), 575–79.
[80] *Ibid.*, pp. 577–78.
[81] *Ibid.*, pp. 578–79.
[82] Charles J. Browning, "Differential Social Relations and Personality Factors of Parents and Boys in Two Delinquent Groups and One Nondelinquent Group," (Doctoral dissertation, University of Southern California, 1954).

did the truants. Considerably more automobile thieves had backgrounds of residential mobility than did the other two groups; about three-fourths of the car thieves had lived for less than five years at their present address. In the main, these results parallel those of Wattenberg and Balistrieri, particularly with respect to the "favored group" status of car thieves.

Another inquiry to be considered is one by Erwin Schepses involving wards in the New York state training school at Warwick.[83] He compared 22 boys who were "pure" car thieves, that is, who had records solely of car theft, with 59 "mixed" automobile thieves, who had been involved in other delinquencies as well, and 81 control group cases of training school boys who had engaged in offenses other than car theft. He observed that, in most cases, joyriding is a group form of deviance, in that most of the thieves had been apprehended in the company of at least one other offender or "fall partner."[84]

A number of other major results were uncovered in this study. First, car thieves were more frequently white boys, rather than Negro or Puerto Rican, than were the control cases, even though Negro car thieves were fairly common in the Warwick population. This finding varied from that of Wattenberg and Balistrieri, who identified few Negro joyriders in their sample. Automobile thieves were generally more intelligent and advanced in reading skills than were the other offenders. They were also more commonly from comfortable economic situations than were the control youngsters. The "pure" car thieves were principally from unbroken homes, while the "mixed" auto thieves and the control group cases were from broken homes in over half the cases.[85] According to Schepses, the car thieves exhibited a wide variety of family constellations; some had passive fathers, some had authoritarian parents, others showed various other family situations. In his opinion, theories which assert that a specific kind of nuclear, middle-class family pattern leads to joyriding are incorrect.[86]

One indicator of the differences between the social process which draws youths into car theft and that which leads youngsters into other forms of lawbreaking was found in Schepses' observation that the auto thieves were older at their first court appearance than were the other offenders. His materials also indicated some slight tendency for car thieves to make a poorer institutional adjustment than the other

---

[83] Erwin Schepses, "Boys Who Steal Cars," *Federal Probation*, XXV (March 1961), 56–62; Schepses, "The Young Car Thief," *Journal of Criminal Law, Criminology and Police Science*, L (March-April 1960), 569.

[84] Schepses, "Boys Who Steal Cars." pp. 58–59.

[85] *Ibid.*

[86] *Ibid.*, pp. 58–60.

wards; for example, more of them had records as runaways from the training school.[87] Finally, the three groups differed somewhat in post-release adjustment.[88]

Martin Dosick has offered some further evidence on car thieves, drawn from a study of federal Dyer Act offenders.[89] He hypothesized that car theft takes three general forms: joyriding by juveniles, along with "short history" and "long history" patterns of automobile theft among young adults (seventeen to twenty-one years old, predominately). "Long history" thieves had been involved in a variety of deviant acts, were criminally sophisticated, and were enmeshed in delinquent subcultures. "Short history" car thieves were youths who had been less involved in criminality. In Dosick's view, the young adult car thieves stole cars for instrumental reasons, but for motives which differed between "short history" and "long history" offenders. Among "long history" offenders, cars were stolen for various impulsive reasons which were usually illegitimate, but "short history" thieves stole cars as an illegitimate route to legitimate or conventional goals, such as a new job. What these findings seem to indicate is that car theft is quite complicated in form—not all of it is of the joyriding form.

Several other studies of violators of federal auto theft laws are available for perusal. In one of these, a group of auto thieves received in federal institutions in 1964 were examined.[90] The investigators found that 49 percent of these lawbreakers had previously been convicted for auto theft, and 20 percent had stolen two or more cars in their last offense. The reasons for auto theft seem varied, for 52 percent of the offenders had taken cars for transportation, 32 percent had stolen them for joyriding, and only 5 percent had stolen the car in order to sell or strip it. However, 71 percent of the offenders under the age of 17 had taken cars for joyriding purposes.

Larry Karacki examined a group of 632 federal offenders charged with car theft and compared them with 369 prisoners who had engaged in other offenses.[91] The car thieves showed more residential mobility than did the other offenders; 59.3 percent had moved three or more times in the previous five years. More auto thieves had been

[87] Ibid., pp. 60–61.

[88] Ibid., pp. 60–62.

[89] Martin L. Dosick, "Statement for Presentation to the Subcommittee to Investigate Juvenile Delinquency, United States Senate, January 17, 1967," mimeographed.

[90] Federal Bureau of Prisons, Auto Theft Offenders, 1964, mimeographed.

[91] Larry Karacki, "Youthful Auto Theft Offender Study," Federal Bureau of Prisons, 1966, unpublished.

in military service or confinement prior to their offense than was true of the other prisoners. More auto thieves had poor work records than did the other offenders. The institutional adjustments of car thieves were poorer, more of them having been involved in disciplinary problems, escapes, transfers to other correctional facilities or to close or maximum confinement. The car thieves showed poorer post-release records; 63.8 percent had violated parole in the two years after release, as contrasted to 46.3 percent of the other prisoners. Karacki was led to conclude that car thieves are from more unfavorable backgrounds than most other violators, a conclusion different from most of the claims made about car thieves.

The conclusion that emerges most consistently from these studies is that car thieves are from "favored group" backgrounds. But these reports are not entirely consistent in this regard, and are even less uniform on such matters as the ethnic backgrounds of car thieves. Most have little to say about specific contentions regarding family patterns in joyriding. Clearly, more research is in order which would collect firsthand information about dimensions of personality, family life, and other variables.

PSYCHOLOGICAL PATTERNS

Most of the theories and research studies considered in this chapter imply that the majority of middle-class delinquents are youths without markedly deviant personalities. There are several investigations of this question; for example, Leon Fannin and Marshall Clinard dealt with lower- and middle-class boys in a state training school in a midwestern state.[92] The subjects of this inquiry were sixteen and seventeen year old boys who had lived in urban areas of 300,000 or more population. The results of the study showed that the lower-class boys viewed themselves as tougher, more powerful, more fierce, fearless, and dangerous than did the middle-class youths. The latter regarded themselves as more loyal, clever, intelligent, smooth, and bad than did the working-class delinquents. Thus Fannin and Clinard concluded that the lower-class delinquents entertained self-perceptions as "tough guys," while the middle-class offenders regarded themselves as "daring and loyal comrades."[93] These variations in self conception were accompanied by differences of other kinds; the lower-class boys were

---

[92] Leon F. Fannin and Marshall B. Clinard, "Differences in the Conception of Self as a Male Among Lower and Middle Class Delinquents," in Vaz, *Middle-Class Juvenile Delinquency*, pp. 101–12.

[93] *Ibid.*, p. 106.

more involved in violence; they had different occupational aspirations than did the middle-class youths; their attitudes toward sexuality more often approved of coercion and violence toward girls.[94]

Another bit of evidence on personality patterns of offenders comes from a report by Reiss, dealing with male probationers in the Cook County, Illinois Juvenile Court.[95] The subjects of that study were sorted into three psychological types by the clinical personnel of the court: relatively integrated offenders, delinquents with defective superego controls (gang delinquents), and delinquents with markedly weak ego controls. The last category held the greatest number of disturbed youngsters. It also appeared to include more middle-class youths than did the other two; the weak ego offenders were more often from settled residential areas, but they showed the greatest degree of residential mobility. They were not well-integrated in peer groups; they had poor deportment in school and records of truancy; and they were from small families. But it should be pointed out that the percentage differences between the weak ego youths and the other types were frequently not marked. Thus, for example, open conflict between parents characterized 14.2 percent of the relatively integrated offenders, 26.5 percent of the defective superego cases, and 24.1 percent of the weak ego youngsters.[96] Also, while this study portrayed middle-class delinquents as possessed by personality pathology, it should be recognized that juvenile court probationers represent a distorted sample of all middle-class lawbreakers. Quite probably, the more psychologically deviant offenders have the greatest chance of being turned over to a juvenile court.

SUMMARY

This chapter has examined a sizable body of evidence showing that middle-class youngsters are involved in a considerable quantity of delinquent activities, much of which goes unreported. Although there are a number of theories which have been advanced to account for middle-class delinquency, relatively little research designed to test these formulations has been conducted. The heterogeneous character of middle-class delinquency demands that theories and hypotheses specific to particular forms of lawbreaking, such as joyriding, need to be subjected to test. Concerning the half dozen theories of middle-

[94] *Ibid.*, pp. 108–10.
[95] Albert J. Reiss, Jr., "Social Correlates of Psychological Types of Delinquency," *American Sociological Review*, XVII (December 1952), 710–18.
[96] *Ibid.*, pp. 712–13.

class misbehavior, the relatively little research evidence now at hand seems most congruent with arguments about lack of commitment to adult roles and about status inconsistency.

chapter seven

FEMALE DELINQUENCY

INTRODUCTION

Criminality and delinquency in modern societies appear to involve men and boys for the most part, judging from the statistics on law-breaking. As a case in point, Federal Bureau of Investigation data show that the arrest rate in 1965 for seven index offenses (serious crimes) plus larceny under $50 was 1097 per 100,000 males but only 164 per 100,000 females, so that men are arrested about ten times more frequently than are women.[1] Delinquency statistics show much the same thing, so that from one juvenile court to another, boys are four, five, or six times more frequent among referrals than are girls.

Crime and delinquency statistics are assumed by most observers to be relatively accurate indicators of real and substantial differences in criminality between the sexes. Most sociologists would argue that girls and women are markedly less deviant than are males, owing to such things as social restrictions imposed upon females which curtail their involvement in criminality, the nature of sex roles in modern societies, and other factors of that kind. Women are less inclined to lawbreaking due to the sex-role socialization they undergo from birth onward.

[1] Don C. Gibbons, *Society, Crime, and Criminal Careers* (Englewood Cliffs, N.J.: Prentice-Hall, Inc., 1968), pp. 104–5.

They also have relatively few opportunities to engage in criminal or delinquent acts.

Otto Pollak is the most well-known dissenter on this issue, arguing that females are actually as enmeshed in criminality as are men.[2] He contended that women are surreptitious and devious in their law-breaking, so that most of their criminality remains hidden and un-detected. However, most readers of Pollak's work have remained unimpressed by it, for he failed to marshal much convincing evidence in favor of his thesis. It is our view that Pollak is wrong, so that women and girls are less involved in criminalistic behavior than are males. Much of this chapter will be devoted to an exposition of this view.

The brevity of our discussion relates to the lesser involvement of girls in juvenile misconduct, but also to the fact that female delin-quency has received relatively little attention by social scientists, so that we cannot call upon a rich lode of theoretical or research work on female lawbreaking.[3] Relatively few studies have been carried out on delinquent girls, while a number of those that have been accom-plished were conceptually and methodologically weak and of doubtful significance.

THE EXTENT OF FEMALE DELINQUENCY

The correctional machinery can be likened to a series of sieves characterized by screening mesh of varied size. The police net scoops up a large number of offenders, many of whom have engaged in quite petty and inconsequential acts of deviance. Law enforcement agen-cies tend to sort out those persons who have committed petty pec-cadilloes, releasing them back into the community without further action. As a result, the courts receive a collection of more serious cases which they then sift through, diverting the most difficult ones to insti-tutions. The end result of these screening operations can be seen in the police cases, juvenile court referrals, and institutionalized offend-ers. Because of these sifting procedures, girls in state training schools are not a representative sample of all female offenders.

[2] Otto Pollak, *The Criminality of Women* (Philadelphia: University of Pennsyl-vania Press, 1950).

[3] Some useful sources of material on female criminality and delinquency are: "The Female Offender" issue, *N.P.P.A. Journal*, III (January 1957); Harry Manuel Shulman, *Juvenile Delinquency in American Society* (New York: Harper & Row, Publishers, 1961), pp. 468–94; Ruth Shonle Cavan, *Juvenile Delinquency* (Phila-delphia: J.B. Lippincott Co., 1962), pp.101–10.

Police Arrests

One indication of the extent of female delinquency can be obtained from a survey carried out in California. The report of this project indicated that of the 238,376 arrests of persons under eighteen years of age in California in 1957, 34,562, or 14 percent, were girls.[4] The authors of this survey also observed that sexual misconduct is the behavior of adolescent girls which provokes the most marked societal reaction, so that many of the girls were arrested for that reason.

William Wattenberg and Frank Saunders have provided a detailed portrait of female offenders based on Detroit police department youth bureau cases for 1952.[5] They observed that of 4553 juvenile complaints in that year, 3451 were boys and 1082 were girls. About one-fourth of the boys and one-fifth of the girls were subsequently referred to the juvenile court, so that most of these police cases were relatively minor instances of delinquency.

Comparisons between the boys and girls in the Detroit police complaint cases showed that most of the girls had been apprehended for incorrigibility, sexual delinquency, or truancy, while most of the boys were in trouble for burglary, assault, or malicious mischief. When the subjects were subdivided by age, the investigators found that the girls under thirteen years of age were principally involved in shoplifting, therefore the youngest females showed the most similarity to boys in terms of offenses. Boys in all of the age categories were involved in property offenses. Not surprisingly, the male delinquents were generally more engaged in recreational activities of one kind or another than were the girls. Broken or disrupted home conditions were more common among the female offenders; 22 percent of the girls and 16 percent of the boys lived with a stepfather, while 35 percent of the girls and 26 percent of the boys lived in a home in which no father was present. Marked quarreling in the home was reported for 32 percent of the girls but only 20 percent of the male delinquents.

Wattenberg and Saunders contended that delinquent girls are frequently subjected to tension in the home, along with relatively close, controlling relationships maintained over them by parents. This pattern produces hostility on the part of the girls; 14 percent of them

---

[4] Charlotte D. Elmott, Jane Criner, and Gertrude Hengerer, *Girls and Young Women in Conflict With the Law in California* (Sacramento: California Committee on the Older Girl and the Law, 1958), p. 6.

[5] William Wattenberg and Frank Saunders, "Sex Differences Among Juvenile Offenders," *Sociology and Social Research*, XXXIX (September-October 1954), 24–31.

(compared to 4 percent of the boys) said that someone picked on them at home. Similarly, 16 percent of the girls (compared to 5 percent of the boys) said they disliked their father, while twice as many girls (34 percent) than boys (17 percent) declared that they disliked their stepmother. The data also suggested that the parents frequently reciprocated the hostility shown toward them by their children.

The poorer social adjustment of girl delinquents was also indicated in the observation that more of them had poor relationships with their peers, as well as that more of them were known as lone wolves. Over one-fourth of the girls had hostile attitudes toward teachers, as compared to about 14 percent of the boys. The essence of these findings is captured by Wattenberg and Saunders:

> The most interesting differentials between the sexes relate to home situations. For girls we have the picture of closer ties to parents, but the closeness gives rise to bitter in-fighting. . . .Also, broken homes and parental fighting seem to be more significant for girls than for boys. . . .Another major factor is the relative weight of the peer group for the two sexes. For boys, gang membership is not only more frequent but also involves more contact with delinquent conduct. In all their relationships with people, the girls appear to be more emotionally disturbed than the boys.[6]

This interpretation of the mainsprings of female delinquency is one which is widely shared. The common view is that girls get involved in delinquency because of tension-ridden home situations in which they are on poor affectional terms with their parents. This perspective contends that the sexual misbehavior which is common to female offenders represents an attempt on their part to obtain affectional relationships outside the home. It also ought to be noted that a number of investigators have pointed out that charges such as incorrigibility or ungovernability under which many female offenders are dealt with in juvenile courts are merely euphemisms for sexual misconduct; sexual delinquency is by far the most common reason for girls falling into the hands of the police or courts.

One footnote to this discussion of police arrest cases is provided by Ruth Cavan. She discussed a study in Onondaga County, New York, during 1957–1958, which showed that boys outnumbered girls in all the offenses known to the police in that county. Female offenders tended to be almost exclusively involved in sexual misconduct or euphemistic charges, while boys more commonly engaged in theft, motor vehicle offenses, vandalism, and the like. But because males are much more frequently subjected to police arrest, boys were responsi-

[6] *Ibid.*, p. 31.

ble for 53 percent of the sex offenses known to the police and 58 percent of the ungovernability arrests.[7]

Juvenile Court Referrals

The character of male and female juvenile court referrals is shown in a study by Don Gibbons and Manzer Griswold of court cases in Washington state between 1953 and 1955.[8] Among other things, they noted that nonwhite youngsters were over-represented in the juvenile court (7 percent of the referrals were nonwhite, while only 2.5 percent of all ten to nineteen year old youths in the state were nonwhite in 1950). More girls were referred to courts from sources other than the police, in that 91.5 percent of the boys and only 78.6 percent of the girls were taken to the court by the police.

The juvenile court referrals in this study showed offense patterns parallel to those in the Detroit police cases. For boys, 46.1 percent were charged with running away or ungovernability, and 9.8 percent were referred as sex delinquents. On the other hand, 64.3 percent of the boys were charged with theft or malicious mischief. As in the Wattenberg and Saunders study, the youngest girls showed the most similarity to boys in offense terms; 35.4 percent of those under thirteen years of age had been involved in theft.

On the whole, the female court referrals appeared to be from less satisfactory social situations than the boys. More girls than boys were living in families which received some form of public support, and only 42.2 percent of the females and 57.3 percent of the boys were living with both parents. Fewer girls than boys were enrolled in school. Gibbons and Griswold indicated that nearly half of the boys and girls were released from court custody without formal action, but, of those retained by the court, twice as many girls as boys were sent to correctional institutions (25.8 percent and 11.3 percent).

Institutionalized Offenders

One indication of the characteristics of institutionalized male and female delinquents can be found in a California Youth Authority re-

---

[7] Cavan, *Juvenile Delinquency*, pp. 101–2.

[8] Don C. Gibbons and Manzer J. Griswold, "Sex Differences Among Juvenile Court Referrals," *Sociology and Social Research*, XXXXII (November-December 1957), 106–10.

port on first commitments during 1967.[9] Newly committed boys had been involved in auto theft, forgery, burglary, and robbery in 43.4 percent of the cases, while only 13.8 percent of the girls had engaged in these offenses. The female wards were involved in incorrigibility, running away, sex offenses, and kindred acts in 66.2 percent of the instances, while these activities involved only 14.8 percent of the boys. The Youth Authority report included a profile of the average first commitment female, in which it was noted that 69 percent of the girls were from below average economic circumstances, 66 percent were from homes characterized by divorce, separation, or death of one parent, 67 percent of the wards had been involved in serious school misbehavior, and 79 percent had indifferent or negative attitudes toward school. On the other hand, many of the female wards appeared to be relatively stable girls, for 64 percent were diagnosed as without serious psychological disorders, while 88 percent associated with peers who exhibited delinquent orientations. Nearly three-fourths of the girls had experienced at least three contacts with law enforcement agencies prior to Youth Authority commitment, 40 percent had been involved in misbehavior with delinquent companions, and 40 percent had used marijuana or dangerous drugs.[10] It is apparent from these findings that girls in training schools are from more disorganized backgrounds and are more involved in misconduct than are other samples of female offenders.

Evelyn Guttmann has provided a companion report on California Youth Authority wards. In comparing parolees from juvenile institutions, she reported that Youth Authority girls had more unfortunate histories and less desirable backgrounds than did the boys, more girls had displayed serious emotional disturbance, more had lived in more than one household, more were involved in persistent truancy, more disliked school, more were from broken homes, and more were from homes regarded as undesirable places for them to return to on parole.[11]

Somewhat similar observations came out of a comparison of boys and girls in Colorado training schools.[12] Most of the male wards had been involved in burglary, robbery, and car theft, while most of the

---

[9] Department of the Youth Authority. *Annual Statistical Report, 1967* (Sacramento: State of California, Youth and Adult Corrections Agency, 1968), p. 68.

[10] *Ibid.*, p. 19.

[11] Evelyn S. Guttmann, *A Comparison of Youth Authority Boys and Girls: Characteristics and their Relationship to Parole Violation* (Sacramento: State of California, Department of the Youth Authority, 1965), pp. 1–2.

[12] Gordon H. Barker and William T. Adams, "Comparison of the Delinquencies of Boys and Girls," *Journal of Criminal Law, Criminology and Police Science,* LIII (December 1962), 470–75.

females had been incarcerated for incorrigibility, sex offenses, or running away. The authors of this study speculated that the deviant acts of boys represent attempts to gain status by deviant means, so that many of them were efforts to demonstrate masculinity through acts of daring. The delinquencies of girls were thought to be expressions of hostility toward parents or efforts to obtain needed gratification such as affection.[13]

Broken homes were equally common among male and female delinquents; over 60 percent of each group were from broken homes. Then, too, other indicators of family disorganization were common in both groups—most of the boys and girls were from homes in which parents were alcoholic, criminalistic, or in other ways inadequate. However, more girls than boys were involved in school misbehavior or had become school dropouts.[14]

To this point, all of the data that we have examined suggest that delinquent girls are relatively uncommon compared to delinquent boys. Those misbehaving females who fall into the hands of the police are often dealt with informally, but the most delinquent are sent on to the court, and some of these girls eventually end up in training schools. But what of hidden delinquency among girls? Is it possible that large numbers of juvenile females are without official records but nonetheless involved in lawbreaking? Perhaps there is a sizable collection of females from middle-class backgrounds who commit serious delinquencies but who remain hidden and unknown to the police. If this is the case, the unfavorable social backgrounds observed among official delinquents may not be causally significant. Conceivably, girls from disadvantaged backgrounds may be more closely watched by the police, while females from favored backgrounds who commit serious deviant acts go unnoticed. What kind of information can be brought to bear on this issue?

Hidden Female Delinquency

In one revealing study of hidden delinquency, Short and Nye compared high school youths and training school wards in several parts of the country.[15] Their comparisons of self-reported delinquency among high school girls and training school girls in a western state showed

---

[13] *Ibid.*, pp. 470–72.

[14] *Ibid.*, pp. 472–75.

[15] James F. Short, Jr. and F. Ivan Nye, "Extent of Unrecorded Delinquency: Tentative Conclusions," *Journal of Criminal Law, Criminology and Police Science,* XXXXIX (November-December 1958), 296–302.

that large numbers of high school students admitted they had skipped school, defied parents, stolen items of small value, or engaged in similar acts at least once or twice. But much larger numbers of training school wards said they had done these things; at the same time many of them admitted involvement in more serious offenses as well. Thus 95.1 percent of the training school girls, but only 14.1 percent of the high school students, said they had engaged in sexual intercourse. This contrast was even more marked when girls were asked to note those offenses they had committed more than once or twice. Few of the high school girls acknowledged repetitive involvement in even the petty acts of misbehavior, while the incarcerated girls admitted frequent involvement in both petty and serious acts. For example, 81.5 percent of the training school girls confessed to repetitive acts of sexual intercourse, 80.5 percent acknowledged frequent drinking, and 32.1 percent confessed repeated acts of property damage.

Another investigation of female hidden delinquency was conducted by Nancy Wise and dealt with 1079 sophomore and junior students in a high school in a Connecticut suburban community.[16] These students were sorted into socioeconomic levels and asked to complete a self-report questionnaire on delinquent acts. The group of youths categorized as middle class included approximately equal numbers of boys and girls. However, the middle-class girls accounted for only 49.9 percent of the sex offenses, 49.2 percent of the alcohol cases, 36.2 percent of the ungovernability offenses, 34.9 percent of the thefts, and 21.4 percent of the assaults reported by the members of the group.[17] Thus the middle-class boys reported more delinquencies than did the females. The percentages of middle income girls and boys who admitted deviant acts are shown in Table 7-1.[18] The most commonly reported deviant act among girls (58.5 percent) in this study was participation in alcoholic parties. About 40 percent of the female subjects said they had skipped school, 34.9 percent said they had committed petty theft, while only 15.3 percent confessed to vandalism, 13.9 percent reported that they had run away, and none acknowledged involvement in drug use.[19] The major conclusion from this study was that middle-class girls participate in those acts of misbehavior which are not reflected in official statistics. But it is also readily apparent that these acts of lawbreaking were petty and in-

[16] Nancy Barton Wise, "Juvenile Delinquency Among Middle-Class Girls," in Edmund W. Vaz, ed., *Middle-Class Juvenile Delinquency* (New York: Harper & Row, Publishers, 1967), pp. 179–88.

[17] *Ibid.*, p. 183.

[18] *Ibid.*

[19] *Ibid.*, pp. 184–85.

TABLE 7-1   Self-Admitted Delinquency, Male and Female.

OFFENSE CATEGORY	FEMALES	MALES	TOTAL	FEMALE TO MALE DELINQUENCY RATIO
Sex	33.2%	36.6%	34.7%	1:1
Alcohol	54.7	63.7	58.8	9:10
Driving	27.1	46.9	36.0	3:5
Ungovernability	13.7	26.6	19.8	3:5
Theft	14.7	30.5	22.1	1:2
Vandalism	9.3	25.2	16.8	2:5
Assault	6.6	26.6	16.1	1:4

consequential ones for the most part, so that differential law enforcement does not account for hidden delinquency among middle-class girls. Quite probably, lower income females who engage in similar acts also go unreported. Most girls become identified as official delinquents as a result of participation in relatively serious acts of lawbreaking.

Several other bits of information on hidden delinquency among middle-class girls are contained in studies of shoplifting. Mary Cameron found in Chicago that juvenile female shoplifters, including middle-class ones, tended to steal relatively small amounts of merchandise, that the median value of merchandise recovered from adolescent thieves was $5 for girls and $3.71 for boys. Juvenile female shoplifters stole mainly small, inexpensive items of jewelry, leather goods, and the like. In addition, most of them engaged in *group stealing,* in contrast to adult thieves who carried out their law violations alone.[20] Gerald Robin has reported a parallel investigation in Philadelphia, involving three major department stores in that city.[21] He found that 58.1 percent of the detected shoplifters in these three stores in 1958 were juveniles, while 60.7 percent of the apprehended thieves were females. Juvenile shoplifters accounted for relatively small losses, for the median value of items stolen was $5.98. Very few of the youthful thieves were prosecuted, and 75.3 percent of the juvenile shoplifters were apprehended in the company of fellow thieves. These two studies suggest that shoplifting is a fairly common form of hidden delinquency among middle-class girls which is relatively innocuous in form.

[20] Mary Owen Cameron, *The Booster and the Snitch* (New York: The Free Press, 1964), pp. 101–4.
[21] Gerald D. Robin, "Patterns of Department Store Shoplifting," *Crime and Delinquency,* IX (April 1963), 163–72.

CAUSES OF FEMALE DELINQUENCY

One causal argument concerning female delinquency attributes this behavior to parent-child tensions within the home. This line of theorizing usually begins by noting that sex-role socialization in the United States is such as to restrict girls to forms of social behavior which emphasize unaggressive conduct, submissiveness, and "femininity." Girls are supposed to play with dolls rather than guns, to cook mud pies instead of building forts, and to be "nice" instead of "rough and tumble." In addition, girls at all ages are more closely supervised and managed by parents, so that their ties to them tend to be more intense than those of boys.

This male-female differentiation in parental control becomes particularly marked during adolescence, for most males are either released from parental surveillance or they emancipate themselves from parental supervision at this time. Teenage boys become heavily involved in peer activities and responsive to the values and norms of male peer groups. Among both adults and juveniles, adolescent boys are often expected to become engaged in aggressive demonstrations of toughness, "hell-raising," and sexual activities with girls. In short, they are supposed to begin to "grow up" by taking on some of the behavior of adults.

Although adolescent girls are also encouraged to begin to "grow up," they continue to be subjected to close parental attention. Girls are also held accountable to a double standard; they are expected to remain virginal, even though they become heavily caught up in dating behavior. The most frequent state of affairs among teenage girls involves "heavy petting with affection." Those adolescent girls who go beyond this point to involvement in sexual intercourse are vulnerable to marked social criticism by the adult community. In particular, those youthful females who appear to flaunt adult sexual mores by overt displays of promiscuity receive an especially hostile response from the standard bearers of adult morality.

This line of theorizing holds that most adolescent girls make their way into adulthood without major difficulties and manage to remain on relatively good terms with their parents. In some manner or another, they are able to balance the demands and values of the adult world against the pressures of peer culture. Most of them are able to refrain from involvement in sexual intercourse, as well as from participation in other deviant acts. Or, if they engage in sexual activity, they are able to do it in surreptitious ways so that they do not become identified by their parents or other adults as promiscuous persons.

However, some girls are not so fortunate. They experience a goodly amount of difficulty with their parents or substitute parents. Some females perceive that their parents are hostile toward them, they chafe under the restrictions of parental standards, or in other ways become caught up in situations of parent-child tension. Unlike boys, girls do not have a network of rich same-sex peer group ties to fall back upon for emotional support, so that the affectional deprivation they experience at home becomes particularly difficult to handle. One response to this situation is to become heavily involved with boys, so as to acquire substitute affectional gratification from that source. But according to this theory, affectional ties are purchased at considerable cost to the girl, for she must often offer sexual intercourse an an inducement to attract and keep the attention of boys. At some point, when her promiscuous conduct with males becomes noticeable, someone reports her to the police or court for sexual misconduct, ungovernability, or immorality. Another elaboration of this perspective contends that most of the nonsexual, delinquent activities of girls are also responses to "under the roof" problems of parental tension, so that teenage girls shoplift and carry out other acts of that kind in order to demonstrate defiance of parents. In one way or another, responsibility for most female delinquency is attributed to parental factors.

Some of the findings on official cases of female lawbreaking indicated that these girls are frequently from relatively lower income backgrounds and situations of social inadequacy. Sociological commentators often deal with this fact by adding these variables to the etiological argument about female delinquency. In this view, situations of social disorder operate as contingencies that divert girls in a delinquent direction. Females from middle-class backgrounds who are in situations of parental tension escape involvement in juvenile misbehavior because they are able to surmount their family patterns by their social ties to other relatives, by the intervention of private psychiatric counselors into their lives within the school or community, or by other advantages of that kind. The lower-class girl is more vulnerable to delinquency because she is less shielded by rich social ties and neighborhood stability.

Some Evidence

A number of studies, many of them old and of dubious significance, are available on the matter of causation of female delinquency. For example, Anne Bingham reported on the backgrounds of 500 female delinquents and described their cases as replete with all sorts of conditions of social inadequacy, including alcoholic or criminalistic parents, marginal economic status, and other deficiencies.[22] A study by Amy Hewes of girls in a state training school provided a parallel description of female delinquents in which all sorts of social liabilities were highlighted.[23] Other statements can be found in the work of F. Powdermaker and others,[24] Lauretta Bender and Samuel Paster,[25] and Mary Webb.[26] In the latter investigation, forty female sex delinquents in Seattle were studied. Webb indicated that nearly all of the homes of these girls were broken or disordered, while twenty-one of the girls had alcoholic, criminalistic, or mentally disordered parents. Some clinical, impressionistic observations of this kind are contained in a report by Irving Kaufman and others.[27] These authors claimed that female delinquency is a tension-management response to conditions of parent-child disharmony.

Markey has contributed an investigation of twenty-five girls and twenty-five boys charged with aggressive sex misbehavior in the Cuyahoga (Cleveland) County, Ohio, Juvenile Court, compared with control group court cases who were involved in other delinquencies.[28] The control group children of both sexes were less well-adjusted and from less adequate social backgrounds than the sex offenders.

Another report on female delinquency came from a study of 252 girls in the Wisconsin state training school.[29] Nearly three-fourths of these girls were from homes categorized as unfavorable. In addition,

[22] Anne T. Bingham, "Determinants of Sex Delinquency in Adolescent Girls Based on Intensive Studies of 500 Cases," *Journal of the American Institute of Criminal Law and Criminology*, XIII (February 1923), 494–586.

[23] Amy Hewes, "A Study of Delinquent Girls at Sleighton Farm," *Journal of the American Institute of Criminal Law and Criminology*, XV (February 1925), 598–619.

[24] F. Powdermaker, H. Turner Levis, and G. Touraine, "Psychopathology and Treatment of Delinquent Girls," *American Journal of Orthopsychiatry*, VII (January 1937), 58–66.

[25] Lauretta Bender and Samuel Paster, "Homosexual Trends in Children," *American Journal of Orthopsychiatry*, XI (October 1941), 730–43.

[26] Mary Louise Webb, "Delinquency in the Making: Patterns in the Development of Girl Sex Delinquency in the City of Seattle," *Journal of Social Hygiene*, XXIX (November 1943), 502–10.

[27] Irving Kaufman, Elizabeth S. Makkay, and Joan Zilbach, "The Impact of Adolescence on Girls with Delinquent Character Formation," *American Journal of Orthopsychiatry*, XXIX (January 1959), 130–43; somewhat similar impressions about girl delinquency appear in Gisela Konopka, *The Adolescent Girl in Conflict* (Englewood Cliffs, N.J.: Prentice-Hall, Inc., 1966).

[28] Oscar B. Markey, "A Study of Aggressive Sex Misbehavior in Adolescents Brought to Juvenile Court," *American Journal of Orthopsychiatry*, XX (October 1950), 719–31.

[29] Katherine DuPre Lumpkin, "Parental Conditions of Wisconsin Girl Delinquents," *American Journal of Sociology*, XXXVIII (September 1932), 232–39.

most of the wards were of below average intelligence; the modal IQ category among them was 66–75.

Some more recent studies have appeared on girl runaways. One of these by Ames Robey and others dealt with a sample of girls from a middle-class suburban juvenile court in Chelsea, Massachusetts.[30] The researchers argued that running away is not a childish escapade, instead, it is usually a last desperate attempt by the girl to deal with an intolerable home condition. Mary Diggs' study of runaway girls and other wards in the Maryland state training school also indicated that the runaways were from particularly disorganized homes.[31] The runaway girls were described as insecure, hostile youngsters as well.

Wattenberg's findings dealing with police complaint cases in Detroit also shed some light on female delinquency.[32] He found that girl repeaters were more likely to be involved in truancy and incorrigibility than were the first offenders, who were in the hands of the police for larceny or sex offenses. Recidivistic girls were on poorer terms with their parents, more of them were gang members, and their school adjustment was poorer than was true of nonrepeaters. However, recidivists were older girls as well, so that Wattenberg may have been looking at a collection of relatively similar girls who were at different stages of a common delinquency career. More girls than boys were reported to the police by their parents, and more females were from troubled homes than was true of the male offenders.

Some tangential support for the argument that female offenders are involved in affection-seeking by deviant means comes from a discussion of training school wards by Seymour Halleck and Marvin Hersko.[33] These observers noted that participation in "girl stuff" was admitted by 69 percent of the girls in the institution they studied. "Girl stuff" was the inmate argot label for homosexual-like activities of "going together," dancing, or other physical contact between the girls. However, only 11 percent of the wards said that they had engaged in fondling of other girls, and only 5 percent admitted genital stimulation of another girl.

---

[30] Ames Robey, Richard J. Rosenwald, John E. Snell, and Rita E. Lee, "The Runaway Girl: A Reaction to Family Stress," *American Journal of Orthopsychiatry*, XXXIV (July 1964), 762–67.

[31] Mary Huff Diggs, "The Girl Runaway," in National Probation and Parole Association, *Current Approaches to Delinquency* (New York: National Probation and Parole Association, 1950), pp. 65–75.

[32] William Wattenberg, "Girl Repeaters," *N.P.P.A. Journal*, III (January 1957), 48–53.

[33] Seymour L. Halleck and Marvin Hersko, "Homosexual Behavior in a Correctional Institution for Adolescent Girls," *American Journal of Orthopsychiatry*, XXXII (October 1962), 911–17.

Halleck and Hersko maintained that almost all of the girls they studied had been involved sexually with males prior to incarceration, but hardly any of them had achieved a mature sexual adjustment. These investigators contended that sexual intercourse was employed by the girls as a means by which to obtain an affectional relationship. The unsatisfactory feminine identification on the part of these girls grew out of their deprived family backgrounds, including alcoholic, mentally disordered, or inadequate parents. Halleck and Hersko argued that these youngsters were attempting to obtain gratification of dependency needs through involvement in "girl stuff," in much the same way that they had made parallel attempts with boys and men outside the institution.[34]

Other Contributions

Albert Reiss has provided some insights into female delinquency[35] and is of the view that sexual favors are frequently employed by girls who lack peer group status as a means for acquiring the attention of boys. He pointed out that adolescent girls at all social class levels derive much of their social standing among peers of both sexes in terms of their ability to attract boys. Those girls who are disadvantaged in this competitive struggle, due to physical unattractiveness, social clumsiness, or other liabilities, may have to offer more to boys in order to be able to depend upon their attention. However, once a girl becomes identified as "easy," she comes under even greater pressure from boys to interact sexually with them. Reiss identified a vicious cycle of status loss, promiscuity, further status loss, aggravated promiscuity, and so forth, in which adolescent girls become entangled. He also suggested that this activity receives a different response at different social class levels. Lower-class parents may be inclined to bring charges of rape against the boys they find dallying with their daughters in order to try to salvage the public reputation of the girls. Middle-class parents more commonly endeavor to cover up the misbehavior of their daughters in one way or another.[36]

George Grosser has developed a detailed exposition on sex role socialization and delinquency.[37] He suggested that the sexual mis-

---

[34] *Ibid.,* p. 914.

[35] Albert J. Reiss, "Sex Offenses: The Marginal Status of the Adolescent," *Law and Contemporary Problems,* XXV (Spring 1960), 309–33.

[36] *Ibid.,* pp. 314–15.

[37] George Grosser, *Juvenile Delinquency and Contemporary American Sex Roles,* doctoral dissertation, Harvard University, 1951.

behavior which gets adolescent girls into the juvenile court is usually fairly public and flamboyant in character and is difficult to ignore due to its visibility.[38] Much of his discussion involved a portrayal of the ways in which males and females are differentially socialized from birth onward to be "boys" or "girls." In particular, he contended that the gulf between socially approved patterns of male and female behavior becomes quite wide at adolescence, so that teenage boys are expected to deport themselves quite differently than juvenile females.[39] Grosser also observed that adolescent males are allowed more independence from parental control than are girls, so that the latter are encouraged to retain filial bonds to their parents, are accorded less freedom, and in other ways are treated differently than boys.

One major portion of Grosser's argument centered about the role-functions of delinquent acts. He suggested that boys are inordinately involved in stealing, in that theft may serve them in several ways. Much juvenile theft on the part of boys is *role-expressive;* they demonstrate masculinity through such behavior. Other boys are involved in *role-supportive* stealing, in which they steal in order to obtain money for clothing, dating, and the like. Finally, some males engage in *symptomatic* theft, which is related to personality problems. But, according to Grosser, girls are less often engaged in acts of larceny because thefts cannot be role-expressive for them. They are unable to demonstrate femininity in that way, so that most girls who steal do it for role-supportive reasons.

Grosser's interpretation of sexual misbehavior on the part of girls paralleled that of Reiss. He averred that erotic motives are not sufficient to explain the promiscuity of girl delinquents. Many of them claim they derive no marked satisfaction from intercourse, while some of them get involved in "wild" behavior and sexual activity before they are physically mature and capable of pronounced sexual gratification. It is for these reasons that Grosser suspected that the meaning of sexual misconduct to the female delinquent must be sought for in the parent-child relationship.

Grosser has also examined a collection of juvenile court cases in Boston, in which he claimed to have observed role-expressive theft in the activities of many of the male, but in few of the female cases. However, his research procedures were inadequate, so that it cannot be said that his data demonstrated the accuracy of the argument.

---

[38] *Ibid.*, pp. 27–28.
[39] *Ibid.*, pp. 78–118.

Another set of claims about female offenders has been advanced by Cohen and Short,[40] who speculated that there are several subcultures of female delinquency, including gangs organized around sexual activities. Other subcultures which they enumerated involve mixed male-female collectivities engaged in a versatile collection of deviant acts, girl gangs similar to male groups involved in aggression and hoodlum activities, and a female drug subculture.[41] It may be that female offenders, particularly lower-class ones, are members of subcultures, but Cohen and Short provide little evidence to support such a contention.

Cohen and Short also advanced a set of hypotheses about the motivational dynamics behind the subcultural patterns of delinquency they enumerated:

> In *Delinquent Boys* Cohen suggested the socially structured motivations to participation in what might be called a female parent delinquent subculture. He argues that a girl's status depends largely upon the status of the males with whom she is identified; that many girls, especially of lower socio-economic status, have not been trained in the arts and graces and lack the material means necessary for competing successfully for such attentions; that such girls, despairing of respectable marriage and social mobility, are inclined to seek reassurance of their sense of adequacy *as girls* by abandoning their reputation for chastity, which has proven, for them, an unrewarding virtue, and by making themselves sexually available; that they gain, thereby, the assurance of male attention and male favors, albeit within transitory and unstable relationships which further lower their value on the marriage market. Like its male counterpart, this pattern represents the rejection of conventional and respectable but unattainable status goals and the disciplines which lead to them, and the substitution therefore of the satisfactions to be obtained in the immediate present with the resources presently available.[42]

One piece of evidence upon which Cohen and Short drew for their claims about female subcultures was a study by Miriam Shypper.[43] That investigation concerned female drug users in Chicago, most of whom were Negro girls from lower income areas. Almost all of these females had experienced difficulties in establishing mature social relationships with members of the opposite sex. Most of the girls exhibited histories of isolation from normal, relaxed, boy-girl relationships,

[40] Albert K. Cohen and James F. Short, Jr., "Research in Delinquent Subcultures," *Journal of Social Issues*, XIV, 3 (1958), 20–37.

[41] *Ibid.*, p. 35.

[42] *Ibid.*, pp. 34–35.

[43] *Ibid.*, p. 35.

pronounced loneliness, depression, and pathetic yearnings for marriage to a stable, respectable, responsive male. Shypper reported that most of these female addicts had become entangled in a vicious cycle of addiction, prostitution, then further isolation from participation in respectable society, increased loneliness, and exacerbated psychological problems.

James Short and Fred Strodtbeck have also produced some material on lower-class, female gang delinquents in Chicago which supported some of the previous contentions about subcultures.[44] They claimed that their observations about these girls paralleled those of Rice, which dealt with gang girls in New York City.[45] The females whom Rice observed slouched about and wore downcast looks, indicating their feelings of social inadequacy. The girls studied by Short and Strodtbeck also appeared to be socially disadvantaged; many of them were unattractive and inarticulate. Concerning the dynamics of delinquency involvement, Short and Strodtbeck suggested: "Thus, both boys and girls are caught in a cycle of limited social abilities and other skills, and experiences which further limit opportunities to acquire these skills or to exercise them if acquired. These disabilities, in turn, contribute to the status dilemmas of these youngsters and in this way contribute to involvement in delinquency."[46] In short, they maintained that both lower-class male and female delinquents are handicapped by more than the usual number of problems, generally experienced by working-class youths, while their adjustment difficulties are further complicated when they engage in deviant conduct.

A final piece of evidence bearing upon lower-class female delinquency came from an inquiry by John Ball and Nell Logan.[47] These investigators, principally concerned with the sexual histories of these offenders, conducted interviews with forty-five delinquent girls at a southern state reformatory. Most of these girls were around fifteen years of age, most were white, the majority had lived in urban areas, most were from lower income backgrounds, and 80 percent were from broken homes.

According to Ball and Logan, most of these girls had begun intercourse in their early teens, about two-thirds of them had lost their virginity in a car, and most gave as their reason for submitting to

---

[44] James F. Short, Jr., and Fred L. Strodtbeck, *Group Process and Gang Delinquency* (Chicago: University of Chicago Press, 1965), pp. 242–43.

[45] Robert Rice, "The Persian Queens," *The New Yorker* (October 19, 1963), pp. 153ff.

[46] Short and Strodtbeck, *Group Process and Gang Delinquency*, p. 243.

[47] John C. Ball and Nell Logan, "Early Sexual Behavior of Lower-Class Delinquent Girls," *Journal of Criminal Law, Criminology and Police Science*, LI (July-August 1960), 209–14.

intercourse the initial time that they "liked the boy very much." Most of the girls had dated the boy with whom they first had intercourse several times prior to engaging in this activity. Most of the girls engaged in repeated acts of sexual intercourse in the next few months after their first sexual experience. By the time they were in the hands of the juvenile authorities, sexual intercourse had become a weekly or bimonthly occurrence for most of them. Finally, most of the girls reported they they perceived sexual intercourse to be an expected part of a dating relationship.

Ball and Logan failed to find support for the notion that girls engage in sex delinquency as a result of rejecting middle-class values concerning chastity. Instead, 69 percent of them said that premarital coitus was wrong in principle. The discrepancy between actual behavior and verbalized values was explained in the following manner by Ball and Logan: "The present findings most evidently support the differential association position. The delinquent girls were actively and continuously engaged in an adolescent subculture in which sexual intercourse was regarded as an expected part of the dating pattern.[48]

SUMMARY

The major points raised in this chapter can be briefly recapitulated:

1. Girls who have become the subject of attention by the police or juvenile courts tend to be involved in sexual delinquency or in activities which adults in the community suspect are indicators of budding sexual promiscuity on the part of the girls. Relatively few females are engaged in delinquency patterns similar to those of boys, although younger girls are most involved in theft behavior.

2. The screening processes of the police and courts operate so as to send the most serious offenders into probation caseloads or to correctional institutions. Institutionalized female delinquents show the most pronounced backgrounds of social inadequacy.

3. Some girls who are without official records as delinquents are nonetheless involved in hidden misbehavior. However, their deviant acts tend to be relatively petty ones, and, in addition, hidden female delinquents are generally less involved in misconduct than are hidden male offenders.

4. "Under the roof culture" in the form of family tensions of one kind or another appears to be a major factor in female delinquency, although it is apparently also the case that various social class factors and social liabilities conjoin with parent-child relationships to push youngsters in the direction of delinquency involvement.

[48] *Ibid.*, p. 214.

5. Hypotheses about the existence of delinquency subcultures among girls are of undetermined accuracy, owing to the paucity of research on such questions. It may be that female delinquency subcultures exist in some neighborhoods in large urban communities, while they may be nonexistent in smaller communities. Then, too, claims about the function and meaning of delinquent acts to the participants in them (such as Grosser's contentions) must be subjected to research scrutiny, for the data now available do not bear directly upon such hypotheses.

More research is in order regarding nearly any behavioral question which can be posed, however, this observation is particularly true of female delinquency. Our view is similar to that of Cohen and Short, who declared:

It is our position that the meaning and function for the persons concerned, of any form of delinquent behavior can only be inferred from rich and detailed descriptive data about the behavior itself, about its position in a larger context of interaction, and about how it is perceived and reacted to by the actor himself and by other participants in that interactive context. These data are largely lacking for female delinquency.[49]

[49] Cohen and Short, "Research in Delinquent Subcultures," p. 34.

chapter eight

"BEHAVIOR PROBLEM" FORMS OF DELINQUENCY

INTRODUCTION

The notion that deviant persons are also aberrant individuals, driven by compulsions, impulses, or repressed urges of one kind or another, is extremely pervasive. It turns up in most explanations of homosexuality, drug addiction, and kindred forms of deviance, and has also played a prominent part in interpretations of criminality and delinquency. A goodly number of psychiatric observers have over the years testified about the defective mental health of juvenile offenders, basing their theories largely on impressionistic observations from clinical settings. The writings of Lucien Bovet,[1] K. R. Eissler,[2] and Kate Friedlander[3] are representative cases of this line of argument. Hypotheses about psychological pathology on the part of juvenile lawbreakers have also been incorporated into the discussions of some sociologists, as illustrated in the work of Herbert Bloch and Frank Flynn.[4]

[1] Lucien Bovet, *Psychiatric Aspects of Juvenile Delinquency* (Geneva: World Health Organization, 1951).

[2] K. R. Eissler, ed., *Searchlights on Delinquency* (New York: International Universities Press, Inc., 1949).

[3] Kate Friedlander, *The Psycho-Analytic Approach to Juvenile Delinquency* (New York: International Universities Press, Inc., 1947).

[4] Herbert A. Bloch and Frank T. Flynn, *Delinquency: The Juvenile Offender in America Today* (New York: Random House, Inc., 1956).

The psychogenic interpretation of delinquency has also enjoyed great popularity in the area of correctional treatment; therapeutic endeavors have often been predicated upon the assumption that the offender is a psychologically disturbed person who is in need of psychic tinkering of one kind or another.[5] The treatment worker has often entertained an image of the juvenile offender as a defective electronic instrument which has been wired improperly or which has blown a tube. The therapy agent views his task as one of rewiring or repairing the person through some kind of psychiatric therapy.

The popularity of psychogenic orientations to criminality and delinquency is certainly not due to any hard evidence. The empirical data on the question of psychological maladjustment among criminals has been examined by Gibbons,[6] and Chapter Four dealt with psychogenic hypotheses applied to juvenile offenders. That discussion demonstrated that there is little convincing empirical support for the contention that delinquents are commonly plagued by emotional problems to which their deviant acts are a response. This conclusion seems warranted even when attention is restricted to juvenile offenders who have become the subjects of official handling; the majority of juvenile court referrals, probationers, or training school wards do not appear to differ much in psychological well-being from nonoffenders. When psychogenic claims are examined against broader samples of offenders, which include hidden delinquents, these assertions are weakened further. The studies of hidden lawbreaking show that many of the youths who are usually included as "nondelinquents" in the customary comparisons with official delinquents have actually been involved in petty misconduct. If these youngsters were counted as delinquents, their numbers would further inflate the group of normal, psychologically healthy offenders.

The theory that delinquents are often psychopathic individuals has often been tautological in form, so that involvement in lawbreaking has been the symptomatology on which the psychopath diagnosis has been based. William and Joan McCord, in a major exposition, attempted to apply the concept of psychopathy to juvenile lawbreaking.[7] However, their efforts were not very rewarding, for among other things, they utilized a variety of source material of dubious

[5] For an extended commentary upon psychiatric approaches to offender treatment, see Don C. Gibbons, *Changing the Lawbreaker* (Englewood Cliffs, N.J.: Prentice-Hall, Inc., 1965).

[6] Don C. Gibbons, *Society, Crime, and Criminal Careers* (Englewood Cliffs, N.J.: Prentice-Hall, Inc., 1968), pp. 139–70.

[7] William and Joan McCord, *Psychopathy and Delinquency* (New York: Grune & Stratton, Inc., 1956).

quality, such as some rather questionable clinical reports by Robert Lindner.[8] Our assessment of the McCords' efforts is similar to that of Michael Hakeem, who suggested that their review of the psychopathy literature demonstrated the worthlessness of the concept.[9]

Taken en masse, it is clear that while juvenile lawbreakers are sometimes hostile, defiant, and suspicious individuals, they are not markedly different from nonoffenders in terms of psychological adjustment. The psychiatrist's claim that most delinquents are motivated by aberrant psychological urges is unequivocally in error. Yet, at the same time, most of us are unwilling to completely reject the possibility that the population of youthful offenders does contain some psychologically disturbed individuals. Even though the broad psychogenic position that most juvenile lawbreakers are psychologically disturbed must be rejected, this does not necessarily mean that there are no atypical, emotionally troubled youths who become involved in juvenile misconduct.

Support for the view that some offenders are psychologically deviant actors can be assembled from a variety of sources. For example, youthful arsonists sometimes make their way into juvenile courts, even though firesetting is an uncommon form of delinquency, and the psychiatric observers who have examined small groups of these youngsters tend to be in general agreement that they are atypical children. Helen Yarnell studied a small number of firesetters and concluded that they were hostile children from backgrounds of parental rejection and emotional deprivation. According to Yarnell, firesetting is an aggressive response which involves fantasies of burning up hated persons and other elements of that kind.[10] Lee Macht and John Mack have also offered some clinical impressions about firesetters which paralleled those of Yarnell.[11] Unfortunately, these reports were not entirely

---

[8] Robert M. Lindner, *Rebel Without a Cause* (New York: Grune & Stratton, Inc., 1944). In his book, Lindner reports upon the hypnoanalysis of a patient he diagnosed as a psychopath. According to Lindner, the patient was able to remember the experience of witnessing sexual intercourse between his parents, even though the subject was less than one year old at the time of the alleged event. This view of childhood memory functions does not accord with the teachings of modern psychology. An alternative interpretation of Lindner's report is that he unwittingly furnished this "memory" to the patient during analysis, so that the patient subsequently reported it back to Lindner.

[9] Michael Hakeem, "A Critique of the Psychiatric Approach," in Joseph S. Roucek, ed., *Juvenile Delinquency* (New York: Philosophical Library, 1958), p. 111; see this entire article, pp. 79–112, for a devastatingly lucid and sharp critique of the psychogenic orientation to criminality.

[10] Helen Yarnell, "Firesetting in Children," *American Journal of Orthopsychiatry*, X (April 1940), 272–86.

[11] Lee B. Macht and John E. Mack, "The Firesetter Syndrome," *Psychiatry*, XXX (August 1968), 277–88.

convincing, for they were usually intuitive hunches derived from unsystematic observations upon a small number of cases. Yet, at the same time, enough of these essays have appeared that the general hypothesis cannot simply be discarded. Then, too, a number of students of delinquency have offered clinical descriptions of juvenile offenders who have been engaged in deviant sex behavior which suggest that these children differ from normal youngsters in psychological well-being. Raymond Waggoner and David Boyd examined one group of sexual delinquents and concluded that most of them were from abnormal family backgrounds.[12] Oscar Markey studied a collection of fifty sexually delinquent boys and girls in the Cuyahoga County (Cleveland), Ohio, Juvenile Court who had been involved in sodomy, fellatio, and other deviant acts. He arrived at the view that most of these offenders were psychologically maladjusted.[13]

These instances of delinquency involving apparently atypical children are infrequently encountered among juvenile court referrals for at least two reasons. The first and most important one is that garden variety thefts, vandalism, joyriding, and the like are exceedingly common among juveniles, so that, for that reason, they make up the bulk of court complaints. But, in addition, forms of misconduct such as firesetting and deviant sexual behavior are quite likely to be seen by citizens, policemen, court officials, and other adults as symptomatic of very serious psychological maladjustment. Those individuals who are implicated in these activities are likely to be absorbed by child guidance clinics, or to be placed into private psychiatric care. Those disturbed offenders who are from lower-class backgrounds or who live in communities lacking in clinical facilities are the ones who tend to end up in juvenile courts tagged as delinquents.

Juvenile aggression is the most commonly encountered pattern of delinquency involving psychologically deviant youngsters turning up in juvenile courts. In addition, this "behavior problem" form of lawbreaking has been carefully examined by a number of skilled researchers, so that unlike the other kinds of conduct, there is a relatively rich research literature dealing with youthful aggression.

[12] Raymond W. Waggoner and David A. Boyd, "Juvenile Aberrant Sexual Behavior," *American Journal of Orthopsychiatry*, XI (April 1941), 275–91.
[13] Oscar B. Markey, "A Study of Aggressive Sex Misbehavior in Adolescents Brought to Juvenile Court," *American Journal of Orthopsychiatry*, XX (October 1950), 719–31.

JUVENILE AGGRESSION

The Nature of Aggression

Aggressive conduct takes two general forms: group or gang violence, and individualistic aggression. Chapter Five observed that conflict activities among juvenile gangs, in the form of "bopping," "rumbling," and gang fighting are quite common among youthful gangs. These actions should not be viewed as stemming from problem personalities. Norms which require involvement in physical combat against rival gangs are central to the behavioral standards of many juvenile gangs. Boys who engage in "bopping" against enemy groups can be said to be demonstrating normal behavior in the eyes of their peers. This kind of aggression might be likened to the combative activities which soldiers direct at enemy troops, which are viewed as commendable in the eyes of fellow soldiers and the citizens of the nation employing them.

However, there is another form of aggression—individualistic aggression. This behavior, which has been called "unsocialized aggression" by some observers, involves acts of violence, physical assault, and extreme cruelty directed at persons, animals, or other objects, carried on by persons acting alone. Aggression of this form is viewed as deviant by all except the actor himself.

This behavior can be arranged on a continuum. One end of the assaultive scale involves persons of exceedingly meek disposition, some of whom are probably regarded as deviant by others because of their timidity. Most "normal" persons would be placed further along on the gradation of aggression, since they are occasionally hostile and assertive. However, at some point, combativeness exceeds the tolerance of others, so that the actor's behavior arouses the concern of others. Youths who are quick to engage in fist fights with peers or who periodically assault others might be placed at that point upon the continuum. Finally, there are some "unsocialized aggressive" individuals who engage in markedly violent and dangerous acts, who exhibit gross cruelty to animals, and who show aggression in other ways. Some delinquents who were studied were involved in relatively mild or benign forms of aggression, while others exhibit more untrammeled kinds of behavior. Finally, it appears that the background conditions which produce aggression also vary in intensity. Parental rejection which looms large in the causation of this behavior can be observed in mild form in some cases and in extreme severity in other instances.[14]

[14] An excellent survey and assessment of the literature on human aggression can be found in Leonard Berkowitz, *Aggression* (New York: McGraw-Hill Book Company, Inc. 1962).

Aggressive Delinquency

Ruth Topping's account of aggressive delinquents in the New York State Training School at Warwick was one of the early reports on these youths.[15] Her impressions, based upon case studies, led her to enumerate a list of characteristics of these wards. She declared that they had suffered early rejection by their parents or guardians; they showed an evident and verbalized sense that "nobody cares"; and they showed childhood experiences in neighborhoods of low standards. The personality characteristics of these boys included an acute desire for acceptance and affection, aggressive speech flavored with threats to kill people, and a sense of having a hard life and being faced with unequal odds. Topping also noted that the youths were indifferent to the consequences of their actions, lacking in insight and humor, and often showed an overprominent sex drive.[16]

Another report on aggressive children has been provided by psychiatrist Sidney Berman, based on clinical observations.[17] He claimed that youngsters who show antisocial character disorder also exhibit hostile, aggressive, uncontrollable acts toward the property or persons of others as an attempt to get rid of tension or anxiety. These children show no feelings of guilt or remorse about their antisocial behavior. They engage in truancy, defiance of teachers, stealing and firesetting, and fights with other children.[18] Further, Berman averred that these youngsters develop out of disordered families in which defective mother-child relationships predominate; the mothers of the children reject them, while the youths exhibit hostility toward their mothers.[19]

One of the most well-known and influential pieces of research on aggressive offenders, by Richard Jenkins and Lester Hewitt, concerned 500 children who had been referred to a Michigan child guidance clinic.[20] That study was particularly impressive, not only because

[15] Ruth Topping, "Case Studies of Aggressive Delinquents," *American Journal of Orthopsychiatry*, XI (July 1941), 485–92.

[16] *Ibid.*, p. 486.

[17] Sidney Berman, "Antisocial Character Disorder," in Ruth Shonle Cavan, ed., *Readings in Juvenile Delinquency* (Philadelphia: J. B. Lippincott Co., 1964), pp. 141–52.

[18] *Ibid.*, p. 143.

[19] *Ibid.*, pp. 145 ff.

[20] Richard L. Jenkins and Lester Hewitt, "Types of Personality Structure Encountered in Child Guidance Clinics," *American Journal of Orthopsychiatry*, XIV (January 1944), 84–94; see also Jenkins, *Breaking Patterns of Defeat* (Philadelphia: J. B. Lippincott Co., 1954), pp. 9–28; Jenkins, "Motivation and Frustration in Delinquency," *American Journal of Orthopsychiatry*, XXVII (July 1957), 528–37.

of the large numbers of cases included in it, but also because it followed a theory of delinquency and because careful methods of research were employed by the investigators.

The findings of Jenkins and Hewitt included the discovery that there were three basic patterns of child maladjustment among the clinic referrals: pseudosocial offenders (gang delinquents), unsocialized aggressive youths, and overinhibited children (nondelinquents). About two-fifths of the youngsters fell into one of these three categories, while the remainder were unclassified. But these children were quite young and had been referred for a variety of reasons, so that the categorized referrals represented only the most serious cases.

The unsocialized aggressive children identified by Jenkins and Hewitt had been involved in an assortment of violent and cruel acts directed at children, adults, and animals. In turn, the major background experience which turned up in the cases of these children was early and severe parental rejection. Many were illegitimate children, while others had experienced psychological rejection by their parents. The unsocialized aggressives were markedly different from the pseudosocial youngsters who were relatively normal children from low income backgrounds and situations of parental neglect.

The research results of Jenkins and Hewitt concerning aggressive youths were replicated in later studies by Richard Jenkins and Sylvia Glickman.[21] In addition, Hilda Lewis found that unsocialized aggressive children at an experimental reception center at Mersham, England, were commonly the products of situations of parental rejection.[22]

The findings of this group of investigations led Jenkins to conclude that juvenile delinquency takes two basic forms. In his opinion, unsocialized aggression is a frustration response on the part of individuals who have experienced situations of frustration and deprivation, while pseudosocial delinquency is a goal-motivated response exhibited by those who have been exposed to schooling in delinquent techniques.[23] The pseudosocial offender is formed by parental neglect and exposure to criminogenic influences, while the aggressive lawbreaker is the product of parental rejection.[24]

The work of Fritz Redl and David Wineman with aggressive young-

[21] Richard L. Jenkins and Sylvia Glickman, "Common Syndromes in Child Psychiatry," *American Journal of Orthopsychiatry*, XVI (April 1946), 244–61; Jenkins and Glickman, "Patterns of Personality Organization Among Delinquents," *Nervous Child*, VI (July 1947), 329–39.

[22] Hilda Lewis, *Deprived Children* (London: Oxford University Press, 1954).

[23] Jenkins, "Motivation and Frustration in Delinquency," p. 528.

[24] *Ibid.*, p. 529.

sters stands as a modern classic in terms of their rich, detailed observations of these children.[25] They studied a group of hostile youngsters who were undergoing treatment in Pioneer House, a small group home in Detroit. The subjects were between eight and eleven years of age, had normal IQ's, and apparently exhibited relatively mild patterns of aggression. In order to be accepted for treatment, the subjects had to be manageable in the residential center and able to attend school.[26]

Redl and Wineman make it abundantly clear that aggressive children are the products of atypical and deficient family backgrounds. They state: "Aside from continuity, the quality of the tie between child and adult world was marred by rejection ranging from open brutality, cruelty, and neglect to affect barrenness on the part of some parents and narcissistic absorption in their own interests which exiled the child emotionally from them."[27] Continuing this analysis, Redl and Wineman indicated that in addition to parental rejection, open, naked sibling rivalry was found in the backgrounds of many of the children. They also exhibited poor school and community adjustment, and most of them had also been exposed to some traumatic experience, such as the death of a parent.[28] Indeed, these youngsters were from inadequate family and social situations, for Redl and Wineman enumerated some other "missing links" in their lives; many of them were deprived of gratifying recreational outlets, opportunities for adequate peer relationships, satisfactory community ties, and other personal resources.

In the opinion of Redl and Wineman, the aggressive subjects showed deficient ego controls, and had low frustration tolerance, an inability to cope with insecurity, anxiety, and fear, and other shortcomings in the area of impulse control.[29] Redl and Wineman also presented a rich description of the ego mechanisms of aggressive children.[30] These mechanisms are defense techniques through which the actor endeavors to follow out his antisocial impulses in the face of threats and persuasion from others. These defense techniques include assertions that "We were all in on it," "He had it coming to him," and other rationalizations by which the person tries to exculpate himself from blame.

One more investigation of aggressive children has been reported by Albert Bandura and Richard Walters.[31] This study was a model of

[25] Fritz Redl and David Wineman, *The Aggressive Child* (New York: The Free Press, 1957).

[26] *Ibid.*, pp.29–57.

[27] *Ibid.*, p. 50.

[28] *Ibid.*, pp. 50–57

[29] *Ibid.*, pp. 74–140.

[30] *Ibid.*, pp. 141–96.

[31] Albert Bandura and Richard H. Walters, *Adolescent Aggression* (New York:

careful, painstaking, empirical inquiry structured by a clear, explicit, theoretical framework. The investigation involved twenty-six aggressive boys and their parents, who were compared with twenty-six control group youngsters and their parents. Most of the aggressive youths were from a probation department in the San Francisco Bay area. The delinquent and control subjects were of average or above average IQ, from intact homes, and from relatively comfortable backgrounds. Most of the fathers of the boys were skilled laborers or minor white collar workers. Apparently, the aggressive children in this study were near the mild end of the hostility scale, in that most of them had been involved in truancy and disruptive school behavior.[32] The benign character of this aggression was also revealed in interview material which indicated that some of the boys had exhibited verbal hostility toward their parents but none of them had physically assaulted their parents. In fact, the parents were horrified by the suggestion that their child might have struck them. Then, too, the aggressive boys showed hostility toward teachers and peers, but incidents of physical attack upon these persons were relatively uncommon. Interestingly, the boys' parents often appeared to have encouraged their aggressive activities outside the home.[33]

The Bandura and Walters investigation was structured around a detailed socialization theory that adequate socialization which produces normal, well-adjusted children requires the development of a dependency motive whereby the child learns to want the interest, attention, and approval of others. In addition, once a dependency need has been established, socialization demands and restrictions must be imposed upon the child so that he learns the pattern of deferred gratification. The youth who is allowed to avoid socialization pressures in the form of demands and restrictions tends to seek immediate and unconditional impulse gratification and to behave in other socially unacceptable ways. Finally, the Bandura and Walters formulation contended that consistent discipline is a prerequisite of adequate socialization.[34] Applied to aggressive delinquency, the theory holds that this pattern of deviance arises out of the disruption of a child's dependency relationship to his parents.

Bandura and Walters hypothesized that the aggressive boys and the normal, control youths would both show satisfactory early life experi-

---

The Ronald Press Company, 1959).

[32] *Ibid.*, pp. 6–31.

[33] *Ibid.*, pp. 88–140.

[34] *Ibid.*, pp. 29–31.

ences with parents, in which both groups acquired dependency needs through the nurturing experiences of infancy. But they expected to find that the aggressive boys had subsequently been subjected to some degree of rejection and had been frustrated in their dependency strivings. Then, too, it was hypothesized that the aggressive delinquents had been inconsistently or insufficiently disciplined by their parents.

The hypotheses of this study were tested through lengthy, focused interviews with the boys and their parents; rating scales were compiled from the interviews; and thematic personality tests were given to the boys. On the whole, most of the findings were consistent with the guiding hypotheses of the research.

The interview materials showed that all of the boys, whether aggressives or controls, had received a good deal of parental affection and warm interaction in infancy. However, as they grew older, the control group boys experienced closer and warmer relationships with their fathers than did the aggressive youths. Both the aggressives and controls were on relatively warm terms with their mothers. The aggressive boys showed less emotional dependency on their parents than did the controls, while they also had more anxiety about relating to their parents in a dependent manner. A number of the aggressive youths had been rebuffed and sometimes punished when they had endeavored to secure dependency gratification from their parents. They had been admonished to stop being a "baby" or had been encouraged to "stand on their own two feet." The interviews with the aggressive youths also showed them to be less dependent upon teachers and peers than the control boys. For example, the aggressive youngsters were less likely to seek help with their school work from parents, teachers, or peers than were the controls. Finally, the aggressive boys felt more rejected by their parents than did the controls, although the degree of perceived rejection was quite mild.[35]

In the area of sexual socialization and sexual behavior, the findings indicated that the early sexual training of the two groups of boys was quite similar. However, the parents of the aggressive boys were more permissive regarding adolescent sexual experimentation with members of the other sex than were the parents of the control youths. That is, the parents of the aggressive boys tended to assume that their sons would become involved in sexual intercourse with teenage girls. Not surprisingly, the aggressive boys had actually experienced more sexual activity than the control youngsters. But it should be noted that in all these cases, the differences between the aggressives and the control subjects were relatively slight.[36]

[35] *Ibid.*, pp. 48–87.
[36] *Ibid.*, pp. 141–87.

Consistent with the hypotheses of the study, the aggressive boys had been subjected to fewer disciplinary pressures by their parents than had the control youngsters. Fewer behavioral limits had been placed upon them, and their parents had lower expectations regarding their school performance than was true of the controls. Although fewer restrictions were imposed upon the aggressive boys by their parents, the aggressives were more inclined to resist and resent these parental controls than were the nonaggressive boys.[37] The social-psychological concomitants of these parent-child patterns were that the aggressive boys showed less identification with their fathers than did the control group youths. In addition, the aggressive children exhibited weaker guilt feelings about violations of conduct standards than was true of the normal youths.[38]

The overall flavor of the Bandura and Walters findings is captured in their summary:

> The fathers of the aggressive boys were typically hostile to, and rejecting of their sons, expressed little warmth for them, and had spent little time in effective interaction with them during the boy's childhood. Although the mothers' greater warmth had apparently sufficed to establish dependency needs during the boys' infancy, their tendency to punish and discourage dependency behavior reduced the boys' striving for secondary rewards in the form of dependency gratification, thus reducing the effectiveness of important sources of control. Because of the fathers' rejection and the mothers' inconsistent handling of dependency behavior, the boys become anxious and conflicted in dependency situations. This dependency conflict generalized to other authority figures and even to peers, so reducing their effectiveness as possible socializing agents. The parents' use of punitive methods of discipline not only further alienated their sons but fostered the hostility and aggression with which the boys had responded to emotional deprivations. The absence of consistent socialization demands, and the failure of the parents to follow through on the demands that they made, provided some reinforcement of defiance and resistance and left the boys without any clear guides for controlling and directing their behavior.
>
> Although there was no evidence that any of the parents in study had displayed consistently blatant antisocial behavior, many of the fathers of the aggressive boys undoubtedly provided hostile and aggressive models for imitation. There was also evidence that many of the parents had subtly, if not openly, instigated and encouraged their sons' aggressive behavior outside the home and in some cases even toward the other parent.[39]

[37] *Ibid.*, pp. 188–246.

[38] *Ibid.*, pp. 247–311.

[39] Albert Bandura and Richard H. Walters, *Adolescent Aggression* (New York: The Ronald Press Company, 1959), pp. 354–55.

SUMMARY

It is not uncommon to find sociologist-criminologists heaping scorn upon the assertions of psychiatrists and psychologists which hold that criminalistic persons are also characterized by personality maladjustment. Harsh judgments about psychogenic claims have been based upon several grounds. For one, it has often been argued, not without merit, that many of the writings of psychiatrists are hopelessly ambiguous, tautological, and in other ways so vague as to be unamenable to research test. Then, too, much of the empirical work of psychogenic students of deviance has been flawed, so that fuzzy, intuitive, subjective procedures have been employed, exceedingly small numbers of cases have been examined, and other critical defects have marred much of this work.

However, the theorizing and research on aggressive delinquents cannot be easily dismissed as faulty or worthless. In particular, the studies of Jenkins and Hewitt and of Bandura and Walters are models of careful, thoughtful scientific investigation. We venture to claim that these investigators have established the existence of aggressive offenders and they have demonstrated that parental rejection is a factor of major importance in this behavior. If we were to judge most of the research of sociologists in the area of delinquency against the methodological standard set by these inquiries on aggression, many of the former would have to be evaluated as inadequate. In short, scientific candor compels us to conclude that the link between parental rejection and aggressive conduct is one of the more firmly established generalizations concerning delinquency.

The major conclusions of this chapter are few in number and can be stated in the following generalizations:

1. Offenders who are engaged in bizarre forms of misconduct and/or who exhibit pathological patterns of personality structure are relatively uncommon among the total population of juvenile offenders and are even relatively infrequently encountered within the group of officially handled lawbreakers. "Behavior problem" kinds of delinquency include firesetting and deviant sex behavior, but the most common form of behavior problem lawbreaking is individualistic aggression. In turn, aggressive behavior comes in various gradations, so that unsocialized aggressive offenders are markedly deviant individuals, while other delinquents exhibit aggression and personality problems of a milder form.

2. Overly aggressive offenders are the product of situations of parental rejection, with the most severe forms of aggression stemming from conditions of early and marked rejection and milder patterns from less marked instances of parental rejection.

Chapters Five through Eight have been concerned primarily with American delinquency. Our attention has been directed at various patterns of juvenile lawbreaking which are common in this nation. However, juvenile misconduct is not restricted to the United States. We might well ask whether any of the patterns identified in preceding chapters have counterparts in other lands. Accordingly, in Chapter Nine, our interest shifts to the question of international patterns of juvenile delinquency.

chapter nine

INTERNATIONAL PERSPECTIVES ON DELINQUENCY

INTRODUCTION

The suspicion that juvenile delinquency is largely an American phenomenon is widely shared among laymen and social scientists alike. The common view is that those features of American society which produce juvenile misconduct and adult criminality are relatively lacking in other nations. Thus the assumed higher level of lawbreaking in the United States is seen as due to the disrespect for law and order, widespread social disorganization, and other characteristics of this country.

Whatever the true level of juvenile delinquency in various nations, the fact is that theorizing and research studies concerning youthful misconduct have been largely restricted to the United States until relatively recently. In short, most of our knowledge of youthful lawbreaking has been restricted to *American* delinquency. Generalizations about youthful misconduct have been restricted to American juvenile deviance. However, the past several decades have witnessed a growth of interest and attention directed at cross-cultural aspects of delinquency. We will examine those general formulations which identify such factors as societal complexity and affluence as the major ones which lie behind the delinquency rates which vary from one nation to another. Then we will turn our interest to a series of studies of juvenile misconduct in various parts of the world.

DELINQUENCY, SOCIAL CHANGE, AND AFFLUENCE[1]

According to various authorities, delinquency has increased markedly in many countries throughout the world in the period since World War Two. For example, T. C. N. Gibbens and R. H. Ahrenfeldt contended that youthful lawbreaking has become more common in Belgium, Canada, Japan, Russia, and a number of other nations, in addition to the United States.[2] One major proposition relative to this world-wide upsurge in delinquency claims as its cause the growing complexity of these nations and the breakdown of traditional patterns of social organization in them. In brief, this argument holds that the greater the degree of industrialization, modernization, urbanization, and the like, the higher the rates of delinquency and criminality.

Ruth and Jordan Cavan have collected a large mass of material which bears upon the social complexity thesis.[3] They have assembled data on delinquency among Eskimos, as well as upon youthful lawbreaking in Mexico, India, Russia, England, and eight other European countries. Their report on juvenile misconduct among Eskimos is indicative of the cultural complexity view. Cavan and Cavan asserted that delinquency was nonexistent among Eskimos until recently, due to the social control exerted by their extended family pattern, harmonious folk culture, lack of social class differences, and other factors of that sort. However, with the increase of social contacts with non-Eskimos, movement to towns, and breakdown of traditional social structure, delinquency and crime among Eskimos have become prominent. Much of this behavior takes the form of loitering, drunkenness, and sexual deviance.[4] In the same way, Cavan and Cavan indicated that juvenile and adult lawbreaking are least frequent in Mexican villages, while they increase as we move from villages, to small towns, to Mexico City.[5] In India, delinquency and crime are most common in the cities (although less often encountered than in Western societies). Also, lawbreaking is apparently on the increase in India.[6] According to Cavan and Cavan; "At present, city delinquency, like much of city life itself, is in a rudimentary stage of development. It grows

---

[1] One useful, general discussion of cultural factors in delinquency is T. C. N. Gibbens and R. H. Ahrenfeldt, *Cultural Factors in Delinquency* (Philadelphia: J. B. Lippincott Co., 1966).

[2] *Ibid.*, pp. 111–60.

[3] Ruth Shonle Cavan and Jordan T. Cavan, *Delinquency and Crime: Cross-Cultural Perspectives* (Philadelphia: J. B. Lippincott Co., 1968).

[4] *Ibid.*, pp. 13–41.

[5] *Ibid.*, pp. 42–70.

[6] *Ibid.*, pp. 71–103.

out of poverty, dire need, and lack of social organization in the slums."[7]

In our view, the most incisive discussion of the ingredients of social change which produce an upsurge of delinquency is to be found in the work of Jackson Toby.[8] He asserted that in industrialized (and industrializing) societies, the sociocultural gulf between adolescents and adults tends to increase, due to changes in the economic order and certain other factors. Then, too, the traditional agencies of socialization and social control which contain the behavior of juveniles within socially approved limits tend to break down under the influence of modernization. Finally, the "sting" of economic deprivation increases with the rise of affluence, so that the "have nots" grow more resentful of their place at the bottom of the economic heap. Their sense of being unjustly deprived grows as they compare themselves to others who are not so unfortunate.[9] In Toby's words: "People steal, not because they are starving, but because they are envious, and they are more likely to be envious of the possessions of others in countries with rising standards of living."[10]

Toby found evidence for the relationship between affluence and delinquency in the case of post World War II Japan. He indicated that the crime rate rose most rapidly from 1955 to 1964 among persons under eighteen years of age, while it did not change markedly for persons over eighteen years old.[11] These trends were also revealed in a report by Hideo Fujiki.[12] The total number of persons arrested for crimes in Japan did not increase in the years 1948–1958, but the subgroup of arrested juveniles did increase in size, particularly from 1953 to 1958. The increment in juvenile arrests was out of proportion to the growth of the youthful population segment. According to Fujiki, this upsurge of adolescent lawbreaking took place in a period of growing prosperity and rapid economic growth.[13]

Toby found further evidence of the upturn in delinquency in statistics for Sweden, which showed that the most pronounced increases in

---

[7] *Ibid.*, pp. 100–101.

[8] Jackson Toby, "The Prospects for Reducing Delinquency Rates in Industrial Societies," *Federal Probation*, XXVII (December 1963), 23–25: Toby, "Affluence and Adolescent Crime," in The President's Commission on Law Enforcement and Administration of Justice, *Task Force Report: Juvenile Delinquency and Youth Crime* (Washington: U. S. Govenment Printing Office, 1967), pp. 132–44.

[9] Toby, "The Prospects for Reducing Delinquency Rates in Industrial Societies."

[10] Toby, "Affluence and Adolescent Crime," p. 132.

[11] *Ibid.*, pp. 134–35.

[12] Hideo Fujiki, "Recent Trends of Juvenile Crime in Japan," *Journal of Criminal Law, Criminology and Police Science*, LIII (June 1962), 219–21.

[13] *Ibid.*, p. 220.

rates of criminality for individuals under the age of twenty.[14] Some parallel material for Europe was contained in E. Jackson Baur's report on juvenile offenses in the Netherlands.[15] According to Baur, juvenile court cases increased by 108 percent in that nation between 1954 and 1961. He also averred that parallel increases occurred in Belgium, Norway, and Denmark in this period.[16] Interestingly, nearly all of the change in delinquency in the Netherlands was due to an increase in traffic cases centering about offenses having to do with motorbikes.[17] From 1949 to 1961, motorbikes grew in number from under 5,000 to over one million. Traffic offenses made up 67 percent of all juvenile offenses in 1954 and 81 percent of all youthful violations in 1960.[18]

Baur's interpretation of the changes in juvenile misconduct in Holland centered about the hypothesis of growing affluence. He showed that both in the United States and in the Netherlands, the gross national product, the level of wages and salaries, and the value of personal consumption expenditures increased significantly between 1954 and 1960. Baur maintained that affluence makes its impact upon juvenile behavior in several ways. It works directly through leading persons to entertain new desires for property, leisure pursuits, and the like, and it operates indirectly through the deterioration of family solidarity which accompanies modernization.[19] Baur echoed Toby's hypothesis about affluence when he concluded: "Spreading prosperity may increase delinquency both among those whose money enables them to do things that bring them into conflict with the law, and among those who resort to stealing to satisfy wants raised above their means by the affluence of others."[20]

Returning to Toby's perspective, he observed that no single, inevitable outcome of economic deprivation always produces criminality. Instead, he noted: "Feelings of deprivation do not inevitably lead to crime. On the contrary, they are rarely acted upon. Under what conditions does the impulse to steal lead to theft? If affluence not only

[14] Toby, "Affluence and Adolescent Crime," pp. 137–40.

[15] E. Jackson Baur, "The Trend of Juvenile Offenses in the Netherlands and the United States," *Journal of Criminal Law, Criminology and Police Science,* LV (September 1964), 359–69. This article stands as a good indicator of the problems which are involved in studying delinquency cross-culturally. The laws in the Netherlands are different from those in the United States, and, in addition, the court systems of these two countries differ. Thus children who would appear in the juvenile court in this country turn up in several different courts in Holland.

[16] *Ibid.,* p. 359.

[17] *Ibid.,* p. 371.

[18] *Ibid.,* p. 367.

[19] *Ibid.,* pp. 365–69.

[20] *Ibid.,* p. 369.

arouses predatory motives but gives the potential predator some prospect for 'getting away with it,' it greatly increases the probability that motives will find expression in action. As the next section will show, urban, industrial societies do precisely that for adolescents: They loosen social controls and thus provide the opportunity for delinquency."[21] Continuing this line of argument, Toby asserted that industrial societies tend to nuclearize family structures and to deemphasize generational ties among family members. These changes in family structure loosen the social control exerted over adolescents. Thus, freed from adult control, juveniles are in a position to form teenage subcultures which may encourage acts of deviance on the part of members.[22] The product is heightened delinquency in the countries in which these alterations occur.

Our remarks to this point have been general in character, with relatively little concern being paid to variations in juvenile misconduct in specific countries. Indeed, relatively diffuse remarks are in part a reflection of the delinquency literature which shows a paucity of good evidence concerning youthful lawbreaking in particular nations. Yet there is some excellent evidence about juvenile crime in certain countries. In particular, delinquency has been studied by a number of investigators in England.[23] As a result, it is possible to examine the question of differences and similarities between juvenile lawbreaking in England and the United States.

DELINQUENCY IN ENGLAND

The gross outlines of delinquency in Great Britain have been presented by the Cavans. Among other things, they noted that, as in the United States, rates of juvenile misconduct increased markedly during both the first and second World Wars. In addition, they reported that delinquency has continued to grow in the period since World War II, so that currently about 3 percent of English youths are involved in indictable (serious) offenses per year. Delinquency is most common among older youths and the most serious acts of lawbreaking are accomplished by these juveniles. Boys outnumber girls by an even greater ratio than in the United States. Finally, clear-cut delinquent gangs are relatively uncommon in England, although loosely-structured antisocial groups are to be found in London and other large

[21] Toby, "Affluence and Adolescent Crime," p. 140.

[22] *Ibid.*, pp. 140–41.

[23] An excellent summary of this research can be found in David M. Downes, *The Delinquent Solution* (New York: The Free Press, 1966), pp. 100–136.

cities.[24] The Cavans also enumerated a number of theories which have been put forth regarding British delinquency, mostly centered about the alleged pernicious effects of social-structural factors. These arguments represent English variants upon causal theories which have been produced regarding American delinquency.[25]

Another indication that British delinquency is relatively similar to the American brand is to be found in an ecological study by C. P. Wallis and R. Maliphant.[26] These researchers studied 914 London boys who were incarcerated in detention centers, Borstal institutions, and prisons. In general, they found that these youths were predominately from low income slum areas which ranked high on various measures of social breakdown. In other words, they were from the same sections of urban communities which produce large numbers of juvenile offenders in the United States.

John Barron Mays also has contributed material which bears out the parallels between British and American delinquency.[27] Mays, as superintendent of a settlement house in a Liverpool slum area, studied a group of eighty neighborhood boys and concluded that they were the products of the widespread criminogenic influences of the area. His interpretation closely paralleled the "delinquency tradition" argument which was favored by Thrasher, Shaw and McKay, and a number of other American students of juvenile lawbreaking. Regarding English delinquency, Mays asserted: "Delinquency (in underprivileged neighborhoods) has become almost a social tradition and it is only a very few youngsters who are able to grow up in these areas without at some time or another committing illegal acts."[28]

T. R. Fyvel has discussed post-war delinquency in Great Britain at length in a journalistic but nonetheless valuable essay.[29] He was particularly concerned with the "Teddy Boy" phenomenon among working-class youths in the late 1950's. "Teddy Boys" were youths who affected Victorian clothing styles, other exaggerated mannerisms, and who were also involved in lawbreaking. In support of the claim that

[24] Cavan and Cavan, *Delinquency and Crime*, pp. 152–89; Peter Scott, "Gangs and Delinquent Groups in London," in Rose Giallombardo, ed., *Juvenile Delinquency* (New York: John Wiley & Sons, Inc., 1966), pp. 319–34.

[25] *Ibid.*, pp. 180–87.

[26] C. P. Wallis and R. Maliphant, "Delinquent Areas in the County of London: Ecological Factors," *British Journal of Criminology*, VII (July 1967), 250–84.

[27] John Barron Mays, *Growing Up in the City* (Liverpool: University Press of Liverpool, 1954); see also Mays, *On the Threshold of Delinquency* (Liverpool: Liverpool University Press, 1959); Mays, *The Young Pretenders* (New York: Schocken Books, 1965).

[28] Mays, *Growing Up in the City*, p. 82.

[29] T. R. Fyvel, *Troublemakers* (New York: Schocken Books, 1962).

youthful misconduct has grown, Fyvel offered some statistics on the number of male offenders convicted of indictable offenses in past years. These showed that fourteen to seventeen year old youths were convicted of 13,517 serious crimes in 1955, while the number had increased to 23,059 by 1959. Similarly, 11,269 youths aged seventeen to twenty-one were dealt with for serious offenses in 1955, but 30,068 crimes were charged to them in 1959.[30] Fyvel also reviewed a collection of largely impressionistic evidence suggesting that troublemaking and "hooliganism" among the young have become common in other European nations as well. Thus he reports that while England had its "Teddy Boys" in the period of the late 1950's, West Germany and Austria were plagued with the *Halbstarken* ("Half Strong"), Sweden by the *Skinnknute* ("Leather Jackets"), and France by the rise of *Blousons Noirs* ("Black Jackets").[31]

Fyvel's general thesis was that postwar affluence in England and other European nations was responsible for the increase of juvenile lawbreaking.[32] In particular, affluence was singled out as heavily involved in the rise of "Teddy Boys" in England and their counterparts in other European countries. Fyvel's analysis of the dynamics of the "Teddy Boy" phenomenon bears a good deal of resemblance to the arguments about American delinquency which center about lack of commitment to adult roles. For example, Karacki and Toby identified a group of middle-class boys who were involved in gang delinquency. They held that these youths were caught up in juvenile misconduct because they had failed to develop an interest in mobility striving and preparation for adult roles.[33]

The nature of Fyvel's theory is captured in the following passage:

> British society in the 'fifties produced an increased number of young delinquents of a distinct social and psychological type. They were boys and girls (many more of them boys) from the more disorganized sections of working-class life. They tended to come from broken homes or to have inadequate parents, toward whom they often felt violently antagonistic; many of them could be described as neurotic or maladjusted; they tended to have indifferent school and bad employment records. They were concentrated in so-called bad areas, but there were in general enough of them about to create a new style of gang life which provided a collective sanction for their defiant outlook. The delinquency of the boys was usually expressed by larceny and breaking and entering —

---

30 *Ibid.*, p. 18.

31 *Ibid.*, pp. 27–34.

32 *Ibid.*, pp. 191–332.

33 Larry Karacki and Jackson Toby, "The Uncommitted Adolescent: Candidate for Gang Socialization," *Sociological Inquiry*, XXXII (Spring 1962), 203–15.

here the figures went up sharply. The trend of the girls was toward some shoplifting, but more often towards easy sexual promiscuity and prostitution — this is not so easy to measure, but the number of illegitimate births among teenage girls did go up quite noticeably. Lastly, the rise of delinquency during the period was so marked that it must have had its special causes.[34]

The essence of this argument is that "Teddy Boys" (and girls) were working-class youths who were drawn to the "Teddy Boy" subculture because they felt themselves to be outcasts from the mainstream of contemporary English society. The alienation of these youngsters was exacerbated by the educational patterns of postwar Britain, centered about a system of "tracking." The most able lower-class youths are skimmed off and placed in an educational path leading to improved chances of achieving a middle-class life style. However, those who are judged to be average or unexceptional in ability are diverted into an uninspiring school experience designed to prepare them for mundane jobs. These "also rans," particularly the ones who are burdened by the family situations and other personal characteristics enumerated by Fyvel, are the candidates for the "Teddy Boy" subculture. Fyvel suggested that the "Teddy Boy" phenomenon was a minority movement among working-class boys, drawing members from "a concentration of the insecure, of unstable adolescents, those with weak family ties and the fewest special interests, who are drawn to this nightly café life like as to a drug, to hold back their anxieties."[35]

The "Teddy Boy" subculture offered its members hedonistic pleasures of the moment, centered about cars, clothing, and aimless interaction in cafés. This kind of behavior system depends upon a level of relative affluence, even among working-class persons, in order to draw support. In addition, this hedonistic, consumption-oriented subculture owes much of its existence to modern mass media influences which have led to the exaggeration of consumption-oriented themes. In other words, these uncommitted youths have been encouraged by mass media models to entertain the view that the meaning of life is to be found in money and the purchase of fleeting pleasures.

We should recall that Fyvel's arguments about rebellious youth and affluence were meant to apply to most of the Western, industrialized, modernized world, rather than solely to England. Fyvel claimed: "From *avant garde* Sweden in the North to traditional Italy in the South, the basic trend was the same: the slow superimposition upon the old bourgeois class order of the less class-ridden and more fluid

[34] Fyvel, *Troublemakers*, p. 191.
[35] *Ibid.*, p. 122.

affluent society. With this, as in Britain and the United States, went the economic emancipation of youth on a large scale, and with this, in turn, a spread of commercial youth culture—and a rise in the delinquency figures."[36]

David Downes' recent essay and research report concerning subcultural delinquency in England is one of the most significant contributions to an understanding of British delinquency.[37] His contentions had a good deal in common with those of Fyvel. Downes began his exposition with a detailed and incisive review and critique of the gang subcultural theories which have been put forth by Cohen, Cloward and Ohlin, and others, all of which center about variables such as feelings of social or economic status deprivation which are presumed to impel working-class youths toward organized, group misconduct.[38] In Downes' view, these American formulations do not seem to apply to working-class lawbreaking in England. He suggested that British délinquent youths are not motivated by feelings of economic deprivation or failure in the economic world, nor are they concerned about attaining middle-class social status. They are not ambitious and do not aspire to middle-class social positions. Instead, they are interested in achieving the leisure goals of enjoyment and excitement.

Downes suggested that the English school system has much to do with the creation of uncommitted, alienated working-class youngsters, some of whom fall into delinquency. This system early in life begins to prepare the less advantaged persons for routine jobs in semiskilled and unskilled occupations. The majority of working-class boys have restricted social horizons, so that they are reconciled to a lifetime of dull, unrewarding unemployment.[39] But instead of being deeply resentful of their place in the social scheme, most of them become relatively fatalistic; they place a low value on work and turn to hedonistic pleasure-seeking for relief from the monotony of employment. The similarity of all this to Miller's characterization of lower-class culture in the United States is obvious.[40] Downes' views are nicely indicated in the following passage:

> The gradual erosion of 'working class culture,' especially those standards relating to the socialization of the child, is throwing into increasingly sharp relief the unplanned, squalid and violent version of it which persists among the unskilled, slum dwelling or slum-clearance sector of

[36] *Ibid.,* p. 123.
[37] Downes, *The Delinquent Solution.*
[38] *Ibid.,* pp. 1–99.
[39] *Ibid.,* pp. 230–36.
[40] Walter B. Miller, "Lower Class Culture as a Generating Milieu of Gang Delinquency," *Journal of Social Issues,* 14, 3 (1958), 5–19.

the working class. The encouragement of spontaneity and autonomy from an early age leads the working-class boy to resist the assertion of middle-class authority he is bound to encounter via school and the law. Working-class culture is at once rigourously defined and sufficiently at odds with the controlling middle-class culture to make a head-on clash almost inevitable.[41]

This image of the alienated but apathetic working-class individual was drawn by Downes from a statistical and observational study in two dockside, working-class areas of London, the Stepney and Poplar districts.[42] Adult criminality was much more frequent in Stepney than in Poplar. However, in neither district was it organized and career-oriented. The delinquency which developed in these areas consisted of informal gangs involved in non-utilitarian acts characterized by versatility and short-run hedonism. The juvenile offenders apparently did not graduate into careers in adult lawbreaking, so adult crime was not an alternative avenue for the materially oriented, upwardly mobile youngsters there. Instead, most of the delinquents drifted out of law-breaking in early adulthood. Apparently the kinds of neighborhoods identified by Cloward and Ohlin as existing in American cities do not exist in London. Downes did not find Stepney to be an area in which criminality was integrated with noncriminal patterns so as to provide an "opportunity structure" for upwardly mobile working-class youths.[43]

Downes' observations about London working-class delinquency were paralleled in a study by Peter Willmott.[44] In his investigation of youths in East London, he found that the probability of a boy getting into court before the age of twenty-one was about one in three. Willmott found a delinquency cycle among boys similar to that reported by Downes, in which most of them began with petty thievery which reached a peak at about age fourteen, followed by "hooliganism" which reached a peak at about seventeen years of age. Most of the boys studied by Willmott showed no marked sense of resentment or frustration concerning their position in the social or economic order.

All of the material considered points consistently in the same direction. English delinquency and criminality have a good deal in common with American lawbreaking in that property offenses and group forms of law violation are the mode in both nations. In both countries,

[41] Downes, *The Delinquent Situation,* pp. 110–11.

[42] *Ibid.,* pp. 137–254.

[43] Richard A. Cloward and Lloyd E. Ohlin, *Delinquency and Opportunity* (New York: The Free Press, 1960).

[44] Peter Willmott, *Adolescent Boys in East London* (London: Routledge and Kegan Paul, 1966).

run-of-the-mill offenders often derive out of working-class back-grounds. But, on the other hand, British delinquency appears to differ in some ways from the American version. In particular, the latter more often is the training ground for careers in adult criminality. Conversely, Britain is lacking in opportunity structures in organized crime, gangsterism, and the like. As a consequence, English delinquency seems more benign in form, less frequently culminating in adult deviance.

DELINQUENCY IN OTHER COUNTRIES

We have already observed that delinquency has been more heavily studied in England than in any other nation than the United States. Reliable information about youthful misconduct is relatively scarce for most other areas, but some data is at hand for some countries. Available cross-cultural evidence on juvenile offenders is, however, of varying quality. Much of this data must be regarded with some skepticism and caution.

European Nations

Cavan and Cavan have pulled together a variety of reports on juvenile delinquency in eight European nations.[45] They claimed that this information showed group delinquency to have become quite common in these eight countries since the second World War. This same contention has been advanced by Toby, as we have already seen.[46] Then, too, the study by Baur of delinquency in the Netherlands averred that juvenile lawbreaking increased markedly in that country in the postwar period.[47]

Other reports on European delinquency include one by Mark Field, dealing with the Soviet Union.[48] Field, after culling through a body of mass media comments on criminality in Russia, claimed that these showed that juvenile delinquency has become a problem of major proportions in that country in recent years, particularly in the form of

---

[45] Cavan and Cavan, *Delinquency and Crime*, pp. 190–216.

[46] Toby, "Affluence and Adolescent Crime."

[47] Baur, "The Trend of Juvenile Offenses in The Netherlands and The United States."

[48] Mark G. Field, "Alcoholism, Crime, and Delinquency in Soviet Society," *Social Problems*, III (October 1955), 100–109.

drunkenness and the occasional formation of juvenile gangs. He also asserted that juvenile lawbreaking is often encouraged by the indifference shown toward it by Russian adults.[49] Field also discussed the recent emergence of the *juenesse doree* group of offenders, consisting principally of the children of powerful officials and successful intellectuals. These youngsters were said to engage in debauchery, crime, and dissipation.[50]

The Cavans also provided some information on Russian delinquency.[51] They claimed that since World War II, juvenile lawbreaking has become frequent in all the strata of Soviet society. Working-class youths from slum areas sometimes become *Stilyagi*, or "hooligans," dressing in American-style clothing, listening to jazz music, and engaging in antisocial conduct in the form of public drunkenness and rebelliousness. Among the children of the socially elite, some become "gilded youths" and get caught up in drinking, wild parties, and carousing. A general cause which runs throughout these forms of juvenile deviance, according to the Cavans, is a desire on the part of youths to escape from the repressive features of Soviet life.

Gang delinquents in Paris have been studied by Edmund Vaz, who found them to be similar to British offenders in many respects.[52] His investigation involved several weeks of interviewing social scientists, educators, and correctional authorities in Paris. Vaz found that gang boys in Paris engage in a wide variety of offenses, including sex violations, assaults, robbery, drinking, and vandalism. However, many of the delinquent acts center about property violations; fighting gangs and drug addiction are nonexistent among Parisian gangs. In addition, no recognized community of adolescent gangs was observed, rather, the Paris gangs were loosely organized and small. Finally, the absence of large criminal or gambling syndicates in Paris meant that the American form of structural connections between juvenile and adult criminal groups was not found in Paris. As a consequence, most Parisian delinquents do not aspire to careers as adult offenders.[53]

As in the United States and England, gang delinquency in Paris occurs mainly in areas of low socioeconomic status, characterized by economic deprivation, inadequate housing, family disorganization, lack of recreational facilities, and the like. In both the United States and Paris, gangs flourish in older, deteriorated slums and in newly

---

[49] *Ibid.*, p. 100.

[50] *Ibid.*, p. 101.

[51] Cavan and Cavan, *Delinquency and Crime*, pp. 104–131.

[52] Edmund W. Vaz, "Juvenile Gang Delinquency in Paris," *Social Problems*, X, (Summer 1962), 23–31.

[53] *Ibid.*, pp. 25–27.

developed, low-rent housing blocks where traditional patterns of social organization have been disrupted. Juvenile offenders are often from multiproblem families within these neighborhoods.[54]

Other Countries

Our knowledge about delinquency in the world becomes very skimpy once we dispose of American and European studies. Reports on juvenile lawbreaking in Asia, Africa, and elsewhere are few and scattered in character.[55] Moreover, these bits and pieces are impressionistic and sketchy in many instances. A case in point is the essay on youthful offenders in Formosa (Taiwan) by Tsung-Yi Lin.[56] Although the author titled his report as a statement on Chinese society, it does not deal with mainland Communist China.

According to Lin, there are two kinds of juvenile offenders in Formosa, the *Tai-pau* and *Liu-mang.* The latter term is an old one which, roughly translated, means "vagrant" or "lawbreaker," while the term *Tai-pau* is a new one designating a form of delinquency which has recently arisen.

A number of contrasts exist between the old-style offenders and the newer *Tai-pau.* The *Tai-pau* are concentrated in large cities, while the *Liu-mang* are found in the older sections of cities and towns. The *Tai-pau* are noted for their Western dress, conspicuous appearance, and attention-getting mannerisms, and they hang around theaters, cafes, ping-pong houses, and parks. The *Liu-mang* are indistinguishable from other youths in appearance; they dress in native costume, live mainly with their parents, and much of their social activity takes place in their homes, the market place, or the temple. The *Tai-pau* are middle- or upper-class youngsters who are involved in hedonistic activities, who engage in truancy, and who steal in order to support their fun-seeking. The *Liu-mang,* on the other hand, are lower-class youths who are involved in drug trafficking, prostitution, and other racketeering. They are the closest approximation to American-style delinquents. According to Lin, these two patterns reflect the two subcultures which now coexist in Formosan Chinese society. The *Liu-mang* are the delinquent representatives of the illiterate, tradition-

---

[54] *Ibid.,* pp. 23–24.

[55] One Japanese study already noted is Fujiki, "Recent Trends of Juvenile Crime in Japan."

[56] Tsung-Yi Lin, "Two Types of Delinquent Youth in Chinese Society," in S. N. Eisenstadt, ed., *Comparative Social Problems* (New York: The Free Press, 1964), pp. 169–76.

oriented part of Chinese society, while the *Tai-pau* are the products of recent social changes in Formosa. They are one manifestation of the westernization of this society and they derive out of the literate, affluent, cosmopolitan subculture of Formosa. Lin summarized the major characteristics of the *Tai-pau* and *Liu-mang* forms of delinquency in Table 9-1.[57]

Lois DeFleur has provided a description of delinquency in Cordoba, Argentina, a large, rapidly industrializing city of over 500,000 population.[58] She contrasted a sample of juvenile court cases in that city with findings on American delinquents contained in Children's Bureau reports. In general, she found a good many points of similarity between offenders in the two countries.

In both Argentina and the United States, court referrals averaged about fifteen or sixteen years of age. In both places, boys outnumbered girls in a ratio of about five to one. Offense patterns were roughly comparable in both countries, so that very few serious offenses such as murder or manslaughter occurred. Crimes of theft were numerically most common in both sets of data.

On the other hand, cultural differences between the United States and Argentina do have some effect upon youthful misconduct. For one thing, female sexual offenders were rare in Argentina, and reflected a tolerant view of sexual experimentation in that nation. Most of the sex delinquencies were the work of boys and centered about child molesting.

Although theft was common among delinquents in both countries, it apparently takes a more violent form in the United States than in Argentina. Also, female theft in the United States is frequently comprised of shoplifting, while girls in Cordoba were more often charged with stealing from an employer. Vandalism and auto theft were infrequent or virtually absent in Cordoba, as was drug use. Finally, the assaultive acts reported to the Cordoba court were of a relatively petty form which tends to be handled informally in this country.

A final bit of cross-cultural data on delinquency is to be found in S. Kirson Weinberg's investigation in Ghana.[59] He studied 107 male offenders incarcerated in an institution in Accra, Ghana, as well as 67 training school girls in the same city. These youths were then compared with a collection of nondelinquent high school students.

[57] *Ibid.*, p. 172.

[58] Lois B. DeFleur, "A Cross-Cultural Comparison of Juvenile Offenders and Offenses: Cordoba, Argentina, and the United States," *Social Problems*, XIV (Spring 1967), 483–92.

[59] S. Kirson Weinberg, "Juvenile Delinquency in Ghana: A Comparative Analysis of Delinquents and Non-Delinquents," *Journal of Criminal Law, Criminology and Police Science*, LV (December 1964), 471–81.

TABLE 9-1 Delinquency Study in Formosa, by Class

SOCIOCULTURAL BACKGROUND AND BEHAVIOR	LIU—MANG	TAI—PAU
Historical	Traditional	New
Geographical	Old sections in cities and small towns	Modern theater and amusement
Age	Wider range from 10 or 12 to early adult; high concentration in 14 to 18 age group	Predominately between 14 and 18 years
Living	Residents of same district	Of same of differing districts
Education	Not beyond primary level	Middle School and the unsuccessful student
Occupational	Unemployed or taking odd jobs to earn a living	Not working; many still in school
Social class	Lower and lower middle	Middle and upper
Appearance	Indistinguishable from traditional dress	Student style with frequent western emphasis, i.e., blue jeans, aloha shirts, etc.
Participation in community affairs	Interest in temple and festival activities	No interest in traditional affairs
Favorite activities	Native games, drinking, gambling	Modern recreation: cars, movies, dances, etc.
Antisocial behavior	More organized, persistent and skillful	Sporadic, playful
Variability	Less variable, behavior transmitted to next generation	Variable with outside circumstances
Organization Size	Large: range from 10 or 20 to 100, infrequently over 100	Small: 3 or 4 up to 10
Membership structure	Boys only, stable membership	Both boys and girls, rapid turnover
Structure	Highly structured for long periods	Vaguely defined and of short duration
Loyalty	Absolute loyalty	Loyalty relative in time and degree
Group discipline	Severe beating, ostracism	Less severe
Community relations	Infiltration into community affairs	Isolated

Weinberg's evidence showed that the offenders were from disrupted homes more frequently than were the nondelinquents. More of them resided with guardians or distant kin, more had been shifted from one home to another, more had been runaways, and more had been traumatized by these breaches in family life. In addition, the offenders were alienated from school, having completed fewer grades and being more truant than the nonoffenders. The offenders were also more involved with deviant peers than were the nondelinquents. All of this led Weinberg to conclude that delinquents in Ghana have a number of experiences in common with American lawbreakers. He asserted:

> These indicators point to the transcultural influences of the family, school, and peers in both Ghanaian and American societies. In both societies, delinquents seemingly experienced more frustrating, less controlling, and less secure relationships with their parents than did the nondelinquents. In both societies, delinquents seemed relatively less able than nondelinquents to adapt and to discipline themselves to the norms of the school. And in both societies, the delinquents were thrust into marginal social roles and were predisposed or coerced to accept the deviant norms and practices of their delinquent peers amidst the rapidly changing context of the urban community.[60]

SUMMARY

This aspect of juvenile delinquency is unsatisfactory because of the thinness of the theoretical and research literature available. The indications seem to be that what "everybody already knows" is true, namely that delinquency is more widespread, more organized, and more serious in form in the United States than any place else in the world. Gangsters and juvenile delinquents are not found very often elsewhere. But, at the same time, a fair amount of evidence seems to indicate that the spread of modernization, industrialization, and affluence to other countries has begun to generate juvenile misconduct on a sizable scale in them. In particular, England and certain other European countries are well on the road toward patterns of youthful lawbreaking which duplicate those in the United States.

The major generalizations from the material in this chapter are these:

1. Although the United States apparently has the highest delinquency rates of nations of the world, juvenile misconduct has increased markedly in many other nations since World War II. The most pronounced increases in delinquency rates have been in European countries. Although the reasons for the upsurge of juvenile lawbreaking are numerous and complex, they center about recent industrialization, the growing complexity of societies and the breakdown of the old social order, and the increasing affluence of European countries.

[60] *Ibid.*, p. 481.

2. In a number of ways, delinquency in England is similar to juvenile law-breaking in the United States: boys are much more frequently involved in misconduct than are girls, juvenile lawbreaking occurs in loosely structured gangs, and it is most common in deteriorated, working-class neighborhoods similar to American "delinquency areas." Juvenile delinquency has apparently increased markedly in England since World War II. Juvenile offenders in that country are frequently drawn from the group of alienated, uncommitted working-class youths who are involved in the pursuit of short-run, hedonistic pleasures. Unlike American offenders, most of them do not show a marked sense of status frustration.

One thing is clear, namely that more research concerning youthful offenders around the world is needed. For example, almost no investigation has been carried out on hidden delinquency outside of the United States. A number of other lines of empirical inquiry need to be pursued. We can safely predict that an increased amount of this sort of research probably will be conducted in the decade to come.

Chapters One to Nine have dealt with questions of delinquency causation. However, one major facet of the etiological issue still remains to be addressed. What are the causal consequences of putting offenders into probation supervision, training schools, or some other kind of "treatment"? Do these experiences actually divert them from criminal careers? Perhaps the correctional actions directed at juvenile offenders have a benign effect upon them, so that their subsequent deviant careers are unaffected by such experiences. Still another possibility which has received all too little attention is that youthful lawbreakers may be pushed further into criminal careers by the stigmatizing effects of correctional handling. Quite probably, various treatment efforts affect different juvenile offenders in varied ways, so that no single result is produced. This matter is complex and demands detailed attention.

chapter ten

CORRECTIONAL PROCESSES AND DELINQUENT CAREERS

INTRODUCTION

What about the correctional handling of offenders in agencies such as probation services, training schools, and parole organizations? Many laymen see these activities and experiences as sharply marked off from the processes of causation, for correctional events are seen as things which happen *after* delinquent behavior has been caused. In short, correctional actions are undertaken to correct or reverse the effects of causal factors so as to change the offender back to a non-deviant.

However, the events of the real world may not be as simple as the common man thinks. For one thing, there are many persons, laymen and criminologists alike, who question the therapeutic efficacy of correctional processes. As a case in point, although training schools are supposed to turn out wards who refrain from further deviance upon release, it is well-known that many training school graduates continue on in criminality, eventually ending up in adult penal institutions. In these instances, the correctional institution has failed to achieve its aims. The usual interpretation of these failures is that the offenders are so enmeshed in lawbreaking and antisocial perspectives by the time they get to the institution that there is little that can be done with them there. In this view, although the training school failed to accomplish the goal of rehabilitation, it cannot be held directly accountable for the offender's reinvolvement in delinquency. The training school is presumed to have neither a positive nor negative effect upon the deviant. In short, the institution is said to "have done the best it could" with the intractable raw material with which it must work.

But another complication in the real world is that correctional organizations may sometimes have direct effects upon deviant careers. In particular, it may be that the experience of being placed on probation or in an institution has identifiable, negative consequences upon the deviant career of the offender. This possibility is captured in the common sense contention that training schools are "crime schools." According to this hypothesis, youths who are processed through these places come out with hardened attitudes, the resolve to go forth and commit more delinquent acts, and the intention to avoid getting caught. This argument suggests that correctional institutions (and other correctional activities) are not simply benign in character, having no important impact upon offenders, instead, these organizations function in ways which are at cross purposes with their official aims. These agencies may involve delinquents and criminals in experiences which stigmatize them as "bad guys" or which operate in other ways to foreclose upon their possibilities to extricate themselves from long-term careers in deviance.

We shall begin with some statistical source material regarding the size of the juvenile correctional workload in the United States. We will also examine some data concerning correctional outcomes in that section, particularly that regarding the rates of parole violation from institutions.

We must devote some detailed attention to the line of sociological theorizing concerning deviant behavior which identifies various "labeling" experiences as critical in the development of deviant careers. This point of view hypothesizes that correctional experiences may have harmful social-psychological effects upon persons who are subjected to them. One important part of this task centers about the study of training school social organization. There is a growing body of sociological evidence on the social structure of juvenile institutions which we need to inspect in order to get some sense of what these places are like and to get some feeling for how they may be perceived by those youths who live a part of their lives in them. Just what are the effects of training schools upon persons who are incarcerated in them? Although statistics dealing with parole success or failure are not too hard to come by, relatively little evidence identifies the particular social-psychological effects of the training school experience upon wards. Finally, how can correctional experiences be redesigned so as to have greater positive impact upon offenders than is now the case?

THE FLOW OF CASES IN THE
CORRECTIONAL MACHINERY

Delinquent conduct of at least a mild form is characteristic of nearly all youths as they pass through the adolescent years. There is a wealth of evidence on hidden delinquency which makes it clear that the correctional nets scoop up only a fraction of the lawbreaking youths in the nation. Law enforcement and correctional agents sift through the cases that come to their attention so as to screen out from official processing many of the youngsters who have been observed in misconduct. The police deal with many "contacts" by admonishing the youngsters or some other informal action, while probation agencies dismiss or place on unofficial probation some of the cases brought to them by the police. Doubtless some of these children who have been informally disposed of by correctional agents commit further acts of lawbreaking. In turn, some of these juveniles ultimately get officially processed and appear in correctional caseloads. At the same time, many of the youths who have been dealt with in an unofficial fashion refrain from further involvement in misconduct.

What happens to those children who are diverted into the official channels of the juvenile court? One indication of outcomes is found in the average daily number of juveniles in institutions or under probation or parole supervision in the community. In the United States in 1965, an average of 62,773 youths were to be found in custodial institutions for delinquents, while 285,431 were in community supervision.[1] Some of the latter were on parole from training schools, but most of them were under probation supervision. These statistics indicated that institutionalization is used as a last resort for youthful offenders, only a small fraction of all known delinquents end up in these places. The flow of cases through the major points of the correctional process is shown graphically in Figure 10-1.

The same general processes are identified in statistics for California, one of a small number of states which collect detailed data on the flow of cases through the correctional apparatus. In 1967, the police made 323,427 arrests of juveniles out of a population of about 2,925,000 in the age span of delinquency. Over one-half of these arrests were for relatively petty forms of misconduct: 198,013 of them were for "delinquent tendencies," while 125,414 were for law viola-

[1] Don C. Gibbons, *Society, Crime, and Criminal Careers* (Englewood Cliffs, N.J.: Prentice-Hall, Inc., 1968), p. 443.

FIGURE 10-1

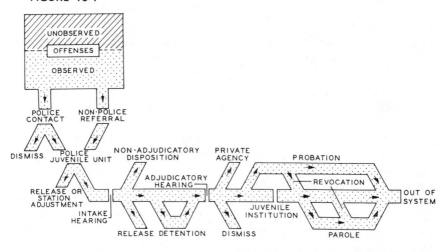

tions included in the criminal statutes.[2] The police settled most of the 323,427 cases informally, for only 123,653 of them resulted in initial referrals to the juvenile court. In turn, the courts sifted out well over half of the referrals from the official correctional machinery, closing them at intake. In 1967, 35 percent of the referrals to the court had petitions filed against them, 28,311 of the cases were placed on probation, and less than 4,000 youths were committed to the California Youth Authority for the first time.[3]

Another set of California statistics for 1967 showed that out of all the juvenile offenders who came to the attention of the authorities in that year, 9240 wards entered state training schools, while 8940 were released from these places.[4] There is a good deal of movement of former wards into and out of training schools, for of the 9240 commitments, 4246 were parole violators who were readmitted to institutions, while the remainder were youths who were institutionalized for the first time. The rate of first commitments of youths to the Youth Authority was 130 children out of 100,000 youngsters in the delinquency-aged population.

One of the most interesting observations in the 1967 California report concerned the variations in the yearly rates of first commitments to the Youth Authority. From 1960 to 1967, these rates varied

[2] Bureau of Criminal Statistics, State of California, *Crime and Delinquency in California, 1967* (Sacramento: Department of Justice, 1968), p. 208.

[3] *Ibid.*, p. 215.

[4] Department of the Youth Authority, *Annual Statistical Report, 1967* (Sacramento: State of California, Youth and Adult Corrections Agency, 1968), pp. 4–5.

from a high of 188.3 commitments per 100,000 youths in 1961 to a low of 129.6 in 1967. The number of first commitments also declined from 6190 in 1965 to 4998 in 1967. These fluctuations in the number of juveniles sent to the state youth agency were related to alterations in county correctional services, changes in court referral policies, and a number of other influences which have only been dimly identified so far.[5] Along the same line, the 1967 report indicated that the rates of first commitments that year from the 58 counties in the state ranged from 254 per 100,000 youths in one county to zero in another. The latter county, San Luis Obispo, is not sparsely populated, so that the lack of commitments was not the result of an absence of delinquents.[6] These rate variations surely point to marked differences in the way in which identified delinquent offenders are handled in different jurisdictions.

LABELING THEORY AND DELINQUENCY

What consequences flow from the decision to put offenders through one part or another of the correctional machinery? The possibility that the effects may be deleterious to the lawbreaker, pushing him further into deviance, was recognized many years ago by Frank Tannenbaum, although his insights were generally ignored until recently.[7] He contended that the effects of official dealings with deviants, ostensibly therapeutic in nature, instead constitute a process of "dramatization of evil." He argued that the result of official handling in the courts, training schools, and related places was frequently the reverse of the announced purposes of such actions. Instead of diverting the person from a deviant career, such experiences alert citizens in the community to the presence of an "evil" person in their midst. Once an individual becomes singled out as "bad," he is likely to be consistently thought of as "evil" in the future, quite apart from how he actually behaves. A lack of deportment change confirms the original diagnosis

---

[5] *Ibid.*, p. 8.

[6] *Ibid.*, pp. 16–17.

[7] Frank Tannenbaum, *Crime and the Community* (New York: Ginn and Company, 1938), pp. 19–21; considerable use has recently been made of Tannebaum's argument by Cloward and Ohlin. See Richard A. Cloward and Lloyd E. Ohlin, *Delinquency and Opportunity* (New York: The Free Press, 1960), pp. 124–43. Other general statements that parallel the views of Tannenbaum are Harold Garfinkel, "Conditions of Successful Degradation Ceremonies," *American Journal of Sociology*, LXI (March 1956), 420–24; John I. Kitsuse, "Societal Reaction to Deviant Behavior: Problems of Theory and Method," *Social Problems*, IX (Winter 1962), 247–56.

in the eyes of the community, and a behavior modification appears to be a clever attempt to hide the true nature. Either way, the offender cannot win, so his possibilities for action become narrowly circumscribed. In many instances, he develops sentiments of being unjustly dealt with and these operate as rationalizations for his misconduct. As a result, the end product of treatment is to reinforce the very behavior which the correctional agents are attempting to reduce.

During the past several decades, the perspective which holds that reactions to deviants represent an important area for study has become prominent in sociology. This point of view is often designated as the "labeling" orientation to deviance, for it places great emphasis upon the reaction and labeling processes directed at deviants of one kind or another.[8] As a case in point, Becker said about the drug addict career:

> When the deviant is caught, he is treated in accordance with the popular diagnosis of why he is that way, and the treatment itself may likewise produce increased deviance. The drug addict, popularly considered to be a weak-willed individual who cannot forgo the indecent pleasures afforded him by opiates, is treated repressively. He is forbidden to use drugs. Since he cannot get drugs legally, he must get them illegally. This forces the market underground and pushes the price of drugs up far beyond the current legitimate market price into a bracket that few can afford on an ordinary salary. Hence the treatment of the addict's deviance places him in a position where it will be necessary to resort to deceit and crime in order to support his habit. The behavior is a consequence of the public reaction to the deviance rather than a consequence of the inherent qualities of the deviant act.[9]

The labeling orientation applied to delinquency and criminality results in a number of hypotheses. Perhaps the initial contacts offenders have with the police and courts have stigmatizing effects upon them, they become identified as "bad" persons, and their opportunities for disengaging themselves from deviance become constricted. By contrast, lawbreakers who remain hidden more easily drift out of mis-

---

[8] Labeling notions in criminology are discussed in Gibbons, *Society, Crime, and Criminal Careers,* pp. 194–200; Some of the major statements of this perspective are Edwin M. Lemert, *Social Pathology* (New York: McGraw-Hill Book Company, 1951); Lemert, *Human Deviance, Social Problems, and Social Control* (Englewood Cliffs, N.J.: Prentice-Hall, Inc., 1967); Howard S. Becker, *Outsiders* (New York: The Free Press, 1963); Thomas J. Scheff, *Being Mentally Ill* (Chicago: Aldine Publishing Co., 1966); several important critiques of this approach are Jack P. Gibbs, "Conceptions of Deviant Behavior: The Old and the New," *Pacific Sociological Review,* IX (Spring 1966), 9–14; David J. Bordua, "Recent Trends: Deviant Behavior and Social Control," *Annals of the American Academy of Political and Social Science,* CCCLXIX (January 1967), 149–63.

[9] Becker, *Outsiders,* pp. 34–35.

conduct. Additionally, the experience of being on probation may be harmful to some offenders, so that they encounter difficulties in holding a job, remaining in good standing in school, and so forth. Finally, incarceration in an institution may be a criminogenic influence which produces antisocial attitudes. Most of the stress in labeling formulations has been upon alleged harmful influences of these experiences, although it ought to be noted that they could conceivably work in a different fashion to drive persons out of deviance.

In our opinion, there is much merit to the labeling and societal reaction orientation to deviance and criminality. At the same time, it ought to be acknowledged that this view is not yet a coherent theory supported by an abundance of research evidence. Instead, it is a general orientation, largely speculative in form, with little data in support of it.[10] The various ways in which different social reactions and correctional processes might effect delinquents and adult lawbreakers have not been spelled out, nor has much empirical investigation been devoted to these processes.

A number of variables have to be considered in a full-blown exposition of the effects of correctional experiences upon offenders. To begin with, these experiences conceivably could have any one of three effects: *positive*, in which they propel persons out of deviance; *neutral* or *benign*, in which they have no effect upon offenders; and *negative*, in which they contribute to the reinvolvement of the actor in additional lawbreaking. Quite probably, some correctional encounters have more positive or negative repercussions upon deviant careers than do others. For example, the first appearance of the delinquent in the juvenile court may have a markedly traumatic impact upon him, but later occurrences, such as being placed in a forestry camp, may contribute little to his subsequent behavior. In short, to acknowledge that correctional agencies have deleterious effects does not mean that all such organizations are equally criminogenic in their workings.

We ought not to lump all training schools, all probation agencies, or other correctional structures together when we look at the question of labeling processes. Quite probably those wards who are processed through a state training school in a progressive correctional system are influenced by institutionalization in ways that are quite different from those that play upon wards in a punitive, harsh training school. The same point holds for probation agencies and parole services, for some of them are staffed by professional correctional workers and others are simply quasi-police agencies.

---

[10] Gibbs has discussed a number of the ambiguities of this thesis. See Gibbs, "Conceptions of Deviant Behavior." Some evidence on labeling processes and criminality can be found in Gibbons, *Society, Crime, and Criminal Careers*, pp. 236–40.

Neither should offenders be lumped together as though correctional organizations have the same impact upon all of them. Instead, incarceration in a training school might have very different meanings for first offenders as opposed to urban, gang delinquents who are wise in the ways of institutions.

MEASURING CORRECTIONAL OUTCOMES

Two problems confront us as we attempt to identify the effects of correctional experiences upon lawbreakers. The first of these is that the full range of possible consequences of different forms of correctional treatment and handling upon the various kinds of offenders who are subjected to these processes has not yet been identified in a theoretical structure. The second problem revolves about the research problems which lie in the path of anyone who would accumulate evidence on these matters.

To begin with, there is a paucity of data of any kind on correctional outcomes. Correctional agencies have infrequently engaged in even the most routine forms of statistical record keeping; they have rarely been equipped with funds for this sort of activity. But, in addition, many correctional services have a stake in *not* knowing about their impact upon their charges. In a great many instances, existing agencies have a low success rate with the wards they handle, often for reasons over which they have little control, such as inadequate financing. But if they were to publicize systematically gathered statistics showing their inefficiency, they might find their financial resources further reduced by the political figures who control economic resources.

However, there are other obstacles to the development of adequate data on correctional outcomes. Consider first the broad problem of measuring the effects of defining processes on deviants. Research investigations on a heroic scale would be called for in order to examine fully the kinds of hypotheses advanced by the labeling school of thought. For example, in order to determine whether the process of being identified by the police as an offender has career consequences for deviants, the ideal research design would be one in which samples of criminal deviants were somehow randomly subjected to either police apprehension or nonapprehension. In this way, we might be able to discover whether police contact per se has identifiable effects upon lawbreaker careers. Carrying this program a step further, apprehended offenders might be randomly indicted and placed through

a trial or dismissed by the authorities, in order to study the stigmatizing effects of court handling. In the same way, randomly assigned
groups of adjudicated offenders might be placed on probation or
turned loose, while other samples might be sent off to institutions or
ignored. In addition, some way would have to be found to control the
effects of other experiences which occur to deviants additional to the
labeling ones under study. This kind of investigation has a strange
sound to it, for it is obvious that experimentation on this scale is not
likely to be encouraged by the general public. In addition, if we were
somehow able to obtain a mandate to pursue this sort of inquiry, this
commentary should make it abundantly clear that such research would
be exceedingly difficult to prosecute.

Research obstacles and pitfalls are also common in instances of
correctional outcome research on a more modest scale, such as investigations concerning the *relative* effectiveness of two or more training
schools. It is possible to examine several institutions and to find that
one produces fewer parole violators than the other, without being able
to separate out the precise contribution which these places make to
parole success or failure from the influences of other variables.

Paul Lerman has indicated a number of cases in which correctional
outcome studies of this kind have been flawed by logical or methodological deficiencies.[11] To take one instance, Lerman discussed a comparison between Wiltwyck School, a private training school, and a
state training school, by William and Joan McCord. These researchers
claimed that Wiltwyck was considerably more successful than the
other institution, in that it showed complete success in 43 percent of
the cases and partial success in 28 percent of the instances, for a total
of 71 percent of the cases. The figures on success for the state school
were 48 percent complete success and 5 percent partial success, or a
total of 53 percent. But in both schools those youngsters who were
recorded as partial successes had been in court for law violations
following release from incarceration. The critic of this study might
suggest that these youths would be more properly classified as failures,
rather than as successes.[12] In that event, it could hardly be contended
that the private institution was more successful than the public one.

When we discuss the available evidence on correctional outcomes
in the pages to follow, we will need to raise the question of the logical
and methodological adequacy of the research studies which produced
this material. Most of these investigations are centered upon training
schools, rather than on probation agencies and kindred structures.

[11] Paul Lerman, "Evaluative Studies of Institutions for Delinquents: Implications
for Research and Social Policy," *Social Work*, XIII (July 1968), 55–64.
[12] *Ibid.*, pp. 62–63.

Unfortunately, little data is at hand concerning the success or failure rates of probation organizations. Several time-and-motion studies of probation do exist and show that probation agents are overburdened with huge caseloads.[13] Inferentially at least, these investigations suggest that probation agencies are not directly responsible for either the successful or unsuccessful cases they produce, for the correctional agents have not devoted much time to them.

Before we take up the issue of training school outcomes, we need to look at the structure of training schools, in order to get the flavor of these places.

TRAINING SCHOOL SOCIAL ORGANIZATION[14]

Training Schools: An Overview

Most training schools are relatively small compared with adult prisons; in many states, the boys' schools handle a few hundred boys or less, and the girls' schools handle even fewer. Training schools usually involve a relatively "open" architecture; they are unwalled institutions made up of a number of dormitory buildings euphemistically called "cottages." Groups of several dozen or more juveniles, or "wards" as they are often called, inhabit these dormitories, and much of the social

[13] Gertrude M. Hengerer, "Organizing Probation Services," *National Probation and Parole Association Yearbook, 1953* (New York: National Probation and Parole Association, 1954) pp. 45–59; Lewis Diana, "Is Casework in Probation Necessary?" *Focus*, XXXIV (January 1955), 1–8; one study dealing with the effectiveness of juvenile probation is Frank R. Scarpitti and Richard M. Stephenson, "A Study of Probation Effectiveness," *Journal of Criminal Law, Criminology and Police Science*, LIX (September 1968), 361–69. These investigators studied the results of probation, non-residential group interaction programs, and institutional commitment upon male delinquents in Essex County, New Jersey. They found that the probation agency received the least delinquent, "easier" cases. In addition, a significant number of probationers were "in-program failures" who were sent back to court before completing their program. The boys who did not complete their probation program were more delinquent and less tractable than those who finished the probation period. In this sense, they resembled the youths who were in the other programs. Among those boys who complete one or another program (probation, non-residential treatment, institutionalization), the probationers had the highest post-release success rate. What all of this adds up to is a picture of probation working with youths with relatively favorable social backgrounds and short delinquency histories. The high success rate for these boys is probably an indicator that they are "self-correctors" who need minimal treatment, and not that probation *per se* is responsible for their favorable behavior.

[14] Don C. Gibbons, *Society, Crime, and Criminal Careers: An Introduction to Criminology* © 1968, Reprinted by permission of Prentice-Hall, Inc., Englewood Cliffs, N. J.

life of the institution goes on within these structures. Training schools also include an assortment of other buildings, such as a school, trade training shops, barns and other farm buildings, and so on. Juvenile institutions often resemble residential academies or schools, although many of them are more rundown and deteriorated. Escapes, or "rambles," are frequent from training schools, partly because of the ease of escape from such places.

The superintendent of the training school traditionally has been the product of the political "spoils" system, such as an ex-county sheriff or similar person to whom a political debt is owed. It goes without saying that he has often been a singularly unimpressive figure, ill-trained for the job of maintaining and managing a custodial institution. The rest of the staff tends to be divided into two general groups. The first includes work supervisors, teachers, and sometimes social case workers, who deal with the inmates in one capacity or another during the day. Also included in this group are the kitchen personnel, clerks, and similar workers. The second general group of employees in the school is made up of cottage supervisors or cottage parents who have the major responsibility of managing the wards at night and during those times of the day when the inmates are not involved in some formal program. The cottage workers have the greatest amount of interaction with the wards and the most difficult experiences with them. Prevention of runaways and other disturbances of the institutional routine is usually their responsibility.

Training schools in the past have usually operated a minimal kind of treatment program. Most inmates have been placed in a school program or some kind of vocational or other work experience. Occasionally they receive some kind of individual therapy from a social case worker, but this tends to be a relatively infrequent event.

The overriding concern in juvenile institutions has revolved around prevention of escapes and large-scale disturbances. Staff members regard runaway behavior as serious indeed, for even though most fugitives are quickly apprehended and normally do not create any incidents in the surrounding community, the community reacts negatively to escapes. Consequently, the juvenile institution which acquires a reputation for frequent escapes usually receives a good deal of hostile and highly vocal criticism. In turn, runaways come to be defined as extremely serious by the employees.

Juvenile facilities share certain structural shortcomings with their adult counterparts,—prisons. In both places, uncooperative individuals must be restrained in some way, but a number of potentially effective control techniques are not available to the authorities. Wards cannot be controlled by constant physical beatings or by starvation. Although the training school personnel can keep their charges "in line" by occasional beatings and other kinds of physical coercion, they must be circumspect in the use of force. This is not to say that corporal punishment is never used in juvenile institutions. Coercion which transcends the official rules is employed, but tends to be relatively mild in form and used as a supplement to other control devices.[15] There is a very real danger that the word will get out to the community if beatings become a regular part of the disciplinary program of the school. Cottage parents who utilize physical aggression as a main technique of control are also in some danger of reprisals. The worker may be physically able to intimidate any individual ward, but may not emerge the victor in a fight with a half-dozen or more inmates.

The tactic commonly employed to deal with uncooperative boys parallels the arrangements in adult prisons. The institutional staff enters into tacit bargains with certain inmate leaders in the dormitories. These older, physically mature, sophisticated juveniles operate "kangaroo courts" in which they coerce other, weaker youths into docile behavior. In addition to keeping order and preventing "rambles," these toughs use their power to force other inmates into homosexual practices, obtain money from them, and victimize them in other ways.

As these remarks suggest, there is a prisoner system in juvenile institutions; a kind of inmate code characterizes training schools, a juvenile parallel of that found in prisons, centering around the same kinds of antisocial norms as the adult counterpart, and antiadministration and antitreatment in content. It prescribes "playing it cool" as model behavior for wards, they are expected to do their time as pleasantly as possible, without entering into meaningful relationships with staff members.

A pattern of role-types or social roles also exists in juvenile institutions. The system tends to be relatively simple, based on differences in physical prowess and criminal sophistication. Two major role types emerge in training schools, "toughs" or "dukes," and "punks." The former are juveniles who have been in the institution for a relatively long time, have extensive delinquency records, and are physically superior to other inmates. The second group is made up of boys who are physically immature and are often less sophisticated offenders.

---

[15] Sethard Fisher, "Social Organization in a Correctional Residence," *Pacific Sociological Review*, IV (Fall 1961), 88.

Research on Training School Organization

Some years ago Albert Deutsch presented a body of impressions about state training schools.[16] He travelled about the country looking at a large sample of these institutions, then reported that ten "deadly sins" characterize most of them: regimentation, institutional monotony in the form of unvaried diets and the like, mass handling of inmates without regard to individual needs, and partisan political domination, and other such faults. Additionally, he listed public penury, isolation, complacency, excessive physical and mental punishment, Babelism, and enforced idleness as other deficiencies. Babelism was his term for various semantic reforms that are common in corrections, in which "the hole" is renamed the "adjustment center" but the character of the punishment program is not changed, the recreation program is retitled "mass treatment," or the name of the institution is changed from Boys' Industrial School to Brown Mountain School for Boys.

Ohlin and Lawrence recently discussed the treatment problems which arise in such training schools where interaction occurs among hostile "clients" and group norms define the model inmate as one who is "playing it cool," that is, who is refraining from significant involvement with therapeutic agents.[17] Their remarks paralleled the earlier ones of Ruth Topping, who noted that treatment of "pseudosocial" delinquents (gang offenders) is complicated by the group interaction which develops among these offenders in institutions.[18] She reported that many of them exhibit a classical "crime-punishment" orientation in which they see themselves as serving time to pay their societal debt. Many of these same youngsters disavow any conceptions of themselves as having problems or in need of therapy. In both of these investigations, some procedural tactics which might circumvent some of these difficulties were suggested, including development of treatment efforts centered within cottage units in order to utilize the inmate social organization in therapy.

The social structure of a boys' training school in Colorado has been described by Gordon Barker and W. Thomas Adams.[19] Rigid interac-

[16] Albert Deutsch, "A Journalist's Impressions of State Training Schools," *Focus*, XXVIII (March 1949), 33–40.

[17] Lloyd E. Ohlin and William C. Lawrence, "Social Interaction Among Clients as a Treatment Problem," *Social Work*, IV (April 1959), 3–13.

[18] Ruth Topping, "Treatment of the Pseudo-Social Boy," *American Journal of Orthopsychiatry*, XIII (April 1943), 353–60.

[19] Gordon W. Barker and W. Thomas Adams, "The Social Structure of a Correctional Institution," *Journal of Criminal Law, Criminology and Police Science*, XLIX (January-February 1959), 417–22.

tion and communication barriers between inmates and staff members were reported, along with a pervasive spirit of authoritarianism in which the offenders did not identify with the values and goals of the staff. The authors also noted the existence of a status order among the inmates, heavily centered around displays of physical toughness and victimization of peers. They speculated that this system may be the result, at least in part, of widespread insecurities among delinquent boys regarding masculinity.[20]

Howard Polsky has provided a detailed description of the social structure among inmates through a study of the boys residing in a cottage within a private correctional institution.[21] He reported a diamond-shaped status system in which a few boys had very high or low rank among their peers, with the largest group falling into a middle range. Polsky claimed that this system was independent of the particular youths who filled it at any particular period, for it persisted relatively unaltered over time, even though cottage residents entered and left the system. Departure of a leader, for example, produced competition, conflict, and jockeying among inmate aspirants for the position, followed by reestablishment of equilibrium. According to Polsky, the status types in the cottage included "toughs" and "con artists" at the apex of the order, "quiet types" in the middle range, and "bushboys" and "scapegoats" at the bottom of the system. The latter were subjected to unrelenting physical and psychological attacks by those higher in the pecking order. Probably the most significant of Polsky's observations was that the inmate system was abetted by the institutional staff. He noted: "Thus, the theme of aggression with all of its authoritarian overtones is structurally configured in the cottage. Under the roof the cottage parents join the older boys in scapegoating the defenseless low-status boys—the sneaks, punks, and the sick. The latter 'deserve' the beatings because of *their* provocativeness and 'unfitness.' The unwritten compact of cottage parents and toughs makes it unbearable for the 'deviants' because they are blamed for everything."[22]

In a recent examination of a training school in California, Fisher observed the social structure among inmates.[23] He found that both the wards and supervisors rank and victimize certain boys and, moreover, the low-ranked boys in the eyes of the officials were also the low-

[20] *Ibid.*

[21] Howard W. Polsky, "Changing Delinquent Subcultures: A Social-Psychological Approach," *Social Work*, IV (October 1959), 3–15; Polsky, *Cottage Six* (New York: Russell Sage Foundation, 1962).

[22] *Ibid.*, p. 133.

[23] Fisher, "Social Organization in a Correctional Residence," pp. 87–93.

status inmates in the ward hierarchy. Staff workers often interpreted disruptive behavior by low-status boys as evidence of psychological maladjustment rather than as a result of the social structure and interactional patterns among offenders. Low-ranked, victimized inmates were defined as "mess-ups," implying that they willfully engaged in disapproved behavior out of psychological tensions. Instead of attempting to undermine the inmate system, the authorities reacted to boys in its terms, so that institutional rewards were differentially accorded to boys who had high status among their peers.

Some attention has been given to organizational problems which develop in training schools upon introduction of rehabilitation as a major goal. One of the earlier warnings of the potential problems was sounded by R. L. Jenkins,[24] who indicated that treatment clinics are likely to become mere institutional window-dressing if they are simply grafted on to a custodial program and not connected to the rest of the institution. They become reduced to making diagnostic and treatment recommendations which are diverted to custodial ends or are systematically ignored. To be effective, clinical operations must be heavily centered around the cottage groups and cottage personnel.

More recently, George Weber had identified a number of areas in which conflict arises between professional and nonprofessional personnel in institutions where treatment is introduced.[25] One major problem which he identified and which was also noted by Ohlin,[26] centers around the role-difficulties which develop for cottage workers. Their authority position is often reduced or undermined with the introduction of treatment goals. They are likely to feel that their prestige has been lowered with the entry of professional personnel into the program. Redefinition of the role of the cottage worker also occurs, and he is expected to run a quiet and well-disciplined dormitory and to contribute to therapy. But because he is not given clear instructions as to how to accomplish these ends, he experiences much the same role-dilemma as the prison guard. Weber and others have suggested that a number of negative consequences develop from introduction of "rehabilitation" into previously custodial institutions.[27] Staff cooperation is reduced

[24] R. L. Jenkins, "Treatment in an Institution," *American Journal of Orthopsychiatry*, XI (January 1941), 85–91.

[25] George H. Weber, "Conflicts Between Professional and Non-Professional Personnel in Institutional Delinquency Treatment," *Journal of Criminal Law, Criminology and Police Science*, XLVIII (May-June 1957), 26–43; see also Weber, "Emotional and Defensive Reactions of Cottage Parents," in Donald R. Cressey, ed., *The Prison* (New York: Holt, Rinehart & Winston, Inc., 1961), pp. 189–228.

[26] Lloyd E. Ohlin, "The Reduction of Role-Conflict in Institutional Staff," *Children*, V (March-April 1958), 65–69.

[27] Weber, "Emotional and Defensive Reactions of Cottage Parents"; Mayer N.

and replaced by conflicts between professional and custodial personnel, defensive reactions develop among cottage workers, and other difficulties arise. Inmates manipulate these conflicts to their own ends by playing competing groups against each other.

The most ambitious research on training schools to date compared six juvenile institutions.[28] These training schools varied in size, several were very small institutions while others had inmate populations of well over 100 boys. Some of the schools were private institutions, others were state schools. These facilities also varied in terms of program, ranging from institutions favoring obedience and strict conformity by boys, to treatment-oriented milieu operations. The researchers supposed that variations in size might influence the social structure of the schools, as would the different auspices under which these places operated. State facilities should be under greater pressure from the general public. Finally, the investigators hypothesized that the treatment-oriented schools would be more conflict-ridden than the strictly custodial plants.

In general, the findings supported these contentions. Among other things, the institutions varied in terms of the leadership "styles" of their executives. The staff members exhibited different perspectives on delinquents; the workers in custodial institutions viewed boys as more willful than did employees in treatment schools. Rather marked variations in the level of staff conflict existed from school to school, with greatest staff conflict in the rehabilitation-oriented institution in which a high degree of staff *interdependence* existed; in the milieu treatment school, staff members representing different segments of the school program were in frequent communication with each other and were involved in much joint decision-making.

FRICOT RANCH SCHOOL FOR BOYS: A "TREATMENT" INSTITUTION

What is life like in a state training school? A detailed appreciation of the character of institutional life can be obtained from a recent report from the state of California, which dealt with the Fricot Ranch School for Boys, a California Youth Authority facility. Fricot Ranch is a relatively new institution in the state which is noted for having the most progressive, treatment-oriented correctional system of any state

---

Zald, "Power Balance and Staff Conflict in Correctional Institutions," *Administrative Science Quarterly*, VII (June 1962), 22–49.

28 David Street, Robert D. Vinter, and Charles Perrow, *Organization for Treatment* (New York: The Free Press, 1966).

in this nation. Accordingly, we should expect to find this place to be more therapeutically structured than many state training schools in other states. Yet the characterization found in the Fricot Ranch report portrays that institution in relatively uncomplimentary terms. It is difficult to conclude from this report that Fricot Ranch has many very positive effects upon its wards. The passages which follow are taken from the Fricot Ranch report:[29]

Administrative Structure

The formal Fricot organization, headed by the superintendent includes a staff of approximately 110 persons who care for and treat an average population of slightly over 220 boys, in five living units. Under the superintendent and his assistant, on the organization chart, are four major division heads—Business Manager, Supervisor of Special Treatment (social work staff), Supervisor of Academic Instruction, and Head Group Supervisor. The Home Life division, under the Head Group Supervisor, is the direct descendant of the traditional custodial department of penal institutions. It is this staff, by far the largest division of the institution, which has responsibility for the daily care and treatment of the boys.

The relationship between the social work staff headed by the Supervisor of Special Treatment and the staff of the Home Life section is imprecisely defined and has been in a state of evolution for several years. Fricot has been a leader in integrating the services of social work and psychological staff into the entire program rather than having them function in isolated settings in individualized therapy. During most of the last two years of this study, after the small staff had been increased, one social worker was assigned to each of the five lodges, where he worked closely with the supervisors on all aspects of the program. As individual therapy is not an important aspect of the program, the social worker has had to develop new approaches to treatment. Such a change of role necessarily takes time, and there is still conflict to be resolved in defining areas of responsibility.

The role of the academic school teacher is akin to the traditional one, and seemed to present fewer difficulties in definition. One major problem noted appeared to hinge on the reluctance of teachers, who have often had considerable formal training in the treatment of children, to give over the responsibility for treatment to the Home Life staff. Their role as "treaters" remains ambiguous. Another problem faced by the teachers was the sustaining of enthusiasm and high productivity goals in the face of the lack of feedback from community and parents, the limited time invested in each boy's development, and the indifferent, sometimes hostile attitudes of many of the wards.

[29] Carl F. Jesness, *The Fricot Ranch Study* (Sacramento: State of California, Department of the Youth Authority, 1965), pp. 8–34.

It is the group supervisor around whom the daily program revolves: with him a boy deals most often outside school hours. The supervisor's job embodies an enormous variety of skills and responsibilities. His role combines the tasks of friend, counselor, group manager, and lodge administrator. Each boy entering Fricot is assigned a "Fricot Dad" from among the supervisors in his lodge. This special counselor will follow the boy's case closely, recommend referral to parole when he judges the boy ready for release, and will give him individual attention and advice wherever possible. Thus, the supervisor is a most important person, not only in determining the milieu of the living unit, but also in deciding the fate of the ward. Almost any Fricot staff member, asked to define the Fricot treatment program and how it differs from that of other institutions, is likely to mention the assignment of "Fricot Dads" as a key concept, and it is on the supervisor that our attention will be focused.

The daily program at Fricot is a busy one, with planned activity filling almost every hour of the day. The routine for a boy in any one of the lodges would run much as follows:

Lights are turned on at 6:05 A.M. The group is on silence during dressing and washing up, then the boys line up in the hallway, where quiet talking is allowed until they leave for the dining room at 6:35. On the dining hall ramp the boys stand silent at attention until the "At ease, quiet talking" order is given. In the dining room low talking is allowed, but no horseplay or trading of food. After breakfast the group is moved to the lodge yard, where the supervisor takes a count and runs a bathroom call. He selects crews to sweep and mop the lodge washroom, locker room, day room, dormitory, honor room hall and office, and supervises the work. At 8:25 the boys are ordered into formation, the supervisor takes another count and then accompanies the group to the academic school building. When classes are let out at 11:30 A.M., boys go directly to the dining hall ramp, met by their supervisor, who takes a count before the group enters. After lunch the boys go to the lodge, usually for a quiet period in the day room or on their beds, sometimes going on a short hike or playing outdoors. At 1:05 P.M., they are ordered into formation for a count, then move again to the school building, followed by the supervisor. School is dismissed for the day at 4:15, and the boys go directly to their lodge yard, met by their supervisor, who takes a count, then usually allows free play. By 4:30 P.M., the boys are moved into the lodge to wash up before dinner, and they leave the lodge about 5:05 P.M. to march to the dining hall. After the meal the group moves back to the lodge for a count, a bathroom call, and a brief period of free play outdoors or in the lodge. At 6:15 P.M., the group is split, following the preferences of the boys, for the evening activities, which may include a hike, organized games, or supervised crafts. Activities end at 8:00 P.M., when the boys are returned to the lodge. They brush their teeth, undress, put their shorts, socks and tee shirts into laundry bags, and take showers by groups. As soon as they have showered, the boys go to their beds, and there is "package call"—which means that those who have received from home packages of cookies, candy, and toys, may enjoy these treats until 9:30, when all boys must be in their beds. No boy is allowed out of bed after 10:30 unless it is to go to the bathroom, and during the night the supervisor quietly moves through the lodge to take a count of the boys three times every hour.

While the routine activities, or "program," provides the vehicle for the interpersonal relationships which are the basis of treatment, the nature of these interactions are shaped as much by the assumptions and preoccupations of staff as by the officially stated goals. Officially, the program is meant to provide a basis for warm, meaningful relationships through which the children can mature. Unofficially, the problems of managing large groups often seem to interfere. At Fricot, as at other institutions, control is a major concern of administration and staff. The supervisor who achieves quick, certain response from a group, with a minimum of disorderliness, often is designated by staff as a "strong" supervisor; whereas one who has difficulty in obtaining obedience is considered a "weak" supervisor. Group supervisors are more often known by their control techniques and effectiveness than their counseling abilities.

The achievement of control leads to a conspicuous smoothness of operation; on the surface the school seems to be run with great efficiency. However, there is a cost in the methods by which firm control is achieved. It is when discussing the use of punishment and the other effects of the emphasis on control that the researcher must rely on direct observation for generalizations rather than depend upon the consensus of the custody staff, for many of the influences which impinge upon the wards are unverbalized, unrecognized and unlabeled, and to some extent denied by staff. The staff's need for self-deception begins mildly at this point but often reaches to where staff members lose sight of control as a necessary concomitant of orderly management, and see it as an end in itself.

The emphasis on control is not difficult to understand. In addition to the ancient precept that punishment must follow transgression, there is the penology tradition which assumes that without punishment, misbehavior will recur. There is also the community pressure which shows itself in the preoccupation with prevention of escape, even though at Fricot the possibility of dangerous behavior by an escaped ward is not great due to age of youth and geographic isolation. Once these concerns gain priority, a "tone" is established which tends to place emphasis on control. At Fricot, for instance, "sight supervision" is required at all times; a boy must always be in the direct line of vision of the person supervising him.

Even without historical precedents and tradition, a very realistic reason for emphasis on control is the fact that when one man supervises 50 impulsive, aggressive, emotionally disturbed children, the simplest routines such as getting to meals, going to and from school, washing hands, and making beds, become major problems in logistics and technique.

Staff pressures add another reason for firmness. There can be painful embarrassment of a supervisor when boys in his charge are disorderly or out of control. The wards themselves seem to understand this, and it may be by more than chance that such incidents happen more often when the supervisor is not well liked by the boys, and occur, moreover, in public places such as the dining room or the playfield.

Obtaining obedience so dominates the thinking of staff that a new supervisor coming on duty is instructed primarily in control techniques, with his role as counselor and friend to the wards relegated to a minor position. Because it is assumed that a new supervisor must gain control solely by inspiring fear, the door is open for such extremes as the advice given to new supervisors by some superiors that they should not smile at the boys for at least the first six weeks.

The need to enforce conformity leads to the second major unverbalized treatment variable, common to both experimental and control lodges, and that is the ever-present threat of punishment. In a research interview, an experienced supervisor bluntly stated, "You have to be mean as hell to get control." Because of the official policy against the use of corporal punishment, techniques are valued which enable punishment to be executed as inconspicuously as possible. Nevertheless, punishment is a constantly observable part of the daily scene. In the Gremlin control lodge, over the periods observed, group punishment was commonplace, occurring almost every day. It took the form of standing at attention for long periods, or strenuous group calisthenics, or sitting in silence, or "suffer hikes" over difficult terrain, or retiring early to bed. Physical violence, never condoned, occurs fairly routinely, although supervisors learn to make rather mild physical punishment inspire fear and seem much worse than it is by their accompanying gestures, threats, and noise.

There are other attitudes, largely unverbalized, which seem to characterize the Fricot approach. Among them are the following:

1. There is a feeling that a boy should be tough and self-sufficient, and should not show dependency on an adult. Such independence is encouraged in part because of the apparent necessity for self-sufficient behavior in a 50-boy unit where staff attention cannot be given to every minor demand. The dilemma is that, with many of these boys, part of their problem may be precisely that they have been neglected and have never been involved in any close or dependent relationship with an admired adult.

2. There is a belief by many that the ideal boy is one who does not hesitate to be aggressive. Physical aggression is felt necessary for a boy to take care of himself among peers, and therefore a good fighter is admired so long as he "fights fair." (It should be noted that this is a totally masculine environment except for the addition of one female training intern to each lodge during the summers. Staff resistance to and resentment toward these women interns is sometimes clear enough to be felt by the interns, as the research staff learned through interviews.)

3. An assumption is made that a boy learns primarily by being told. The learning-through-lecture theme pervades the "counseling" relationships as well as other verbal exchanges. More often than not, a "counseling" session might be better described as a "chewing-out." 4. The question of whether or not a boy has respect for authority, and whether or not he is "sincere," are major points on which his rehabilitation is rated. Staff feel they can judge earnestness of intent, and one of the highest compliments they pay a boy is to say he is "really trying." 5. An important element often unverbalized or even denied is the need to form alliances with those boys who have the most peer influence. These are not consciously made "deals" but the arrangements that all persons running large groups apparently need to make work in cooperation with existing group leadership. The research team, after many hours of observation, became convinced that it would be almost impossible for a supervisor to maintain control solely through coercive, punitive methods. Often, however, the arrangement results in partiality toward wards whose influence is sought. Boys are extremely sensitive to this and often mentioned to the research staff the lack of fairness of certain supervisors. On the other hand, boys understood that almost all supervisors tended to favor their own "Fricot Sons" and were less perturbed by this favoritism. Although some supervisors tried to be scrupulously fair, they often had trouble because of it, since punishment of a member of the leadership clique could lead to disruption of group functioning—at times even reprisals.

Associated with the strict control required by authoritarian leadership is the rigid "structuring." A boy at Fricot has little need for thought, initiative, or decision-making during his entire day—a lack of responsibility clearly enjoyed by many. When, as at Fricot, the staff assumes the entire burden and responsibility for operations, it leads to cumbersome and laborious details such as in the following excerpt from procedure instructions to supervisors for leaving the Fricot gymnasium after the showing of movies:

"Boys put on shoes when the movie is over. The Gremlins leave last, following the movie, and it usually is done as follows: first group stand and move out to the door, each row making a right face, until the entire group is there and formed in a column of twos. Take a count. The boys are then moved to the top of the stairs and from there to the lodge door and on into the lodge, single file to the washroom doorway. Take a count. Move the honor room boys into the washroom for brushing of teeth and getting drink, and then move them into the hall where they will sit down. Move in half of the dormitory boys for the same procedure, and finally the remainder of the group."

The Peer Subculture

For the inmates, life at Fricot is clearly peer-centered. Aside from the boys' interactions with their own teacher, and with less frequency, their Fricot Dad, contacts with staff on an individual basis are limited. However, the boys are constantly interacting with one another, and as is the case with young people generally, there is developed a set of values and understandings—a subculture with distinct characteristics.

The functional value of testing reality through peer interaction and play must not be underestimated; at Fricot the general maturing or socializing process is speeded up for many boys who have not had friends prior to their stay at the school. Sociometrics taken by the research team demonstrate that with few exceptions the boys are able to improve their ability to develop friendships and get along with peers by the time they leave.

It would be unwise, however, to assume that all peer influences are helpful and healthy. Without objective measures, which the research staff had neither the time nor ingenuity to devise, evaluation of the impact of the peer culture is difficult, for interpretation is particularly susceptible to coloration by the subjective views of the observer. One of the research staff placed great emphasis on the negative impact of the group.

An early observation made by this member of the research team was as follows: "Two of the more salient behavioral practices among inmates are victimization and patronage. Several varieties of these practices are observable among inmates. Victimization is a predatory practice whereby inmates of superior strength and knowledge of inmate lore prey on weaker and less knowledgeable inmates. The ends sought by aggressors range from 'getting even' for some capricious grudge to acquisition of commodities such as toys and candy. Three of the common forms of victimization on Lodge G are physical attack, agitation, and exploitation" (Fisher, 1961).

An observer can, indeed, make such an interpretation of what occurred. But over time and hundreds of hours of observation the research staff learned to evaluate its observations using a wider frame of reference. For example, the staff had noticed that the game of Foursquare offered an unusually clear picture of the functioning of the power clique. The strong boys could maintain themselves in squares as long as they wished, and there was tacit understanding that lower-status boys were not to put them out. Clique boys could establish their own rules, which appeared on the surface to be cheating, especially to boys very new to the institution. The blatant exploitation of the weak by the strong at first seemed clearly a function of the institutional setting and a manifestation of the delinquent subculture. However, the following quotation will illustrate why this was soon seen in a different perspective:

"In Foursquare there are things called Friendsies, when you don't try to get any of your friends out. An then there's Homesteading where nobody else can play except the people you want. If there's two, that's all there is, and if there's four, then there's four. Sometimes the kids standing in line quit and go to another square. Sometimes if you accidentally put out one of your friends the other kids might come running back and say, 'That was my place, so I'm in D now,' and then sort of get into a fight. The ones you don't like are put out by giving them fast balls, and also they never get 'overs,' and the popular kids keep getting 'overs.' "

The quotation above did not come from one of our subjects, but from the eight-year old daughter of one of the research team members, describing the game as played in the local public school. The similarity of structuring by the power clique suggested we go slow in attributing their behavior to the existence of a special "deviant subculture." Whether they are deviant or "normal," of course, the peer values are influential and must be understood before any judgment can be made as to whether the subculture of the adolescent tends to facilitate or to subvert treatment. It is clear that many of the practices were not sanctioned by official policy or viewed as desirable.

The most conspicuous fact of the boys' world is the existence of a power structure. Despite periodic staff efforts to eliminate his role, the duke is the one person in every lodge who is well known and easily identified. Surrounding the duke is a clique of "strong boys" who form the most influential social body within the unit. The strong clique, ordinarily aggressive and domineering, sets the informal rules and establishes precedent. With boys of this age, the structure may be unverbalized and understood at only a subconscious level, but nevertheless its presence is understood by all.

For example, at a time when a particularly "strong" clique was functioning in one unit, it became apparent that a certain part of the recreation area was the clique's "territory." Boys who did not understand this, or who were indifferent to it, were punished by the clique for infringing on its ground. But actually most of the weaker boys not in the group or on a friendly basis with it, appeared to find this convenient, since at least during the time when the clique boys were playing within their own territory, they could play uninterrupted elsewhere.

How influential is a duke on the lodge? How conscious of his power is the duke himself, and the other boys, and the supervisors? We can allow them to answer in their own words from recorded interviews selected to illustrate the point.

Speaking of his relationship with a duke who had just been paroled, a boy recalls, "Sometimes I was afraid that we'd have an argument or something, and he would get me. Sometimes in the afternoon when we'd fall in, he wouldn't want those guys to mess up, so he wouldn't have to suffer for it. So he would tell them to quit messing around, and they would do it."

A lodge duke, speaking of a supervisor who once gave him trouble, concludes: "But he doesn't mess with me no more. I got mad one day and told some boys I was going to kill him, and we was up at at summer camp, and we stole some knives off the kitchen. We was waiting for him to come back to the tent. Then after a little boy had told on us we threw the knives away, but he ain't messed with me no more since then."

When asked how the strong boys keep their names off the demerit lists at times, a duke explains, "We talk. We say to the supervisor, 'Oh, you just take my name for nothing!' We start talking real loud, and a lot of guys say this together with you. We get with each other and saying it, and then he would erase your name."

A boy describes how group punishment increases when a duke is paroled and the hierarchy is upset, and compares the present duke with his predecessors: "When Mike leaves for home, it will be just the same as after Harry and Cliff left. Everybody will be suffering, all the time. A lot of boys act like they are afraid of Mike, but Mike does not really fight very often."

A low-status boy reports: "I tell you, sometimes a supervisor is afraid to get on the big dukes of the lodge. Cause they're afraid they're going to get them. That's when I get scared, sometimes."

Another boy describes what happens when he gets a package from home and the duke sees it. "Sometimes he would press you for candy, but sometimes he wouldn't, and you were afraid if you didn't give it to him he would beat you up."

The supervisors are not unaware of the duke's influence. In emphasizing the power of a particular duke, a supervisor states, "Then if he turns around and says, 'Okay, make noise on Mr. S' and these other kids don't —watch out! Because they know all his friends will get them. Then you've got hell on your hands."

A second supervisor relates, of another duke, "The duke is leading this bunch, and oh boy—what he says goes. If I say 'Shut up,' and he says, 'Talk,' they talk. It makes no difference whether I'm standing taking names or not. If the duke says 'Talk,' they'd better talk, or the duke will kick the—out of them."

A duke explains how he protects his friends: "If somebody mess with them, they run over and tell me, and I just say, 'Stop hitting on him,' and they stop."

The power hierarchy in the lodge extends from the duke and the strong clique at the top through the middle boys to the "messups" at the very bottom of the heap. The few lowest-status boys tend to cause friction and problems for themselves and, as we shall point out, for everyone else in the lodge as well.

In addition to the dukes and messups are other types which tend to be characteristic. Among the most conspicuous at Fricot are the following:

a. "Finks" or tale-bearers, are unpopular and scorned. Because they are not to be trusted, they are left out of intimate groups. There is considerable accuracy in the group in being able to pick out the finks, except for the finks themselves, who are so closely identified with the official program that they do not apply the label to themselves. Boys with high peer status, particularly those in the strong clique learn who not to trust and can describe and identify the lodge finks with accuracy and consensus. Other boys trusted none of their peers when they came, and none when they left.

b. The "kissy" who may sometimes also be a fink, ingratiates himself with supervisors and is despised here as elsewhere. This may be partly because he seems too close to the adults, to whom all the boys would probably like to relate if they were not prevented by their reluctance to show emotion and their repression of dependency feelings. The kissies rarely achieve high standing as measured by sociometrics.

c. A "messup" is scorned because his inappropriate behavior brings group punishment upon all members of the lodge. The messup can also cause concern because he arouses in the group feelings which must be repressed or denied. In addition, a messup is often socially unaware, insensitive, and may embarrass others and cause arguments or problems among his peers even when the ultimate result is not group punishment. Some of these boys were extremely slow in learning the fundamentals of group membership despite enormous peer and staff pressure.

d. A "chicken" is a boy unwilling to fight or accept challenges. Because part of lodge social prestige comes from daring and aggressive behavior, a chicken is not respected. One of the first steps toward gaining status is to show willingness to stand up and fight, and this is particularly approved if the opponent is an established scapegoat. While an occasional fight was condoned by staff, they were usually stopped as quickly as possible.

e. In this subculture, as in most nondelinquent societies, a person who cheats—except under certain sanctified situations—or who fails to pay off obligations, or who lies—particularly at the wrong time—is not respected. There is a time and a place for cheating, and for lying; and it is particularly against protocol to lie so as to get another boy in trouble if the other boy has some social status.

As numerous examples would indicate, the staff to some extent adopts, or brings into the setting, many of these values, using the same terms to describe the boys as the boys themselves. Many practices maintain themselves because they function to introduce some organization of the group and facilities management. As has been amply shown by several investigators, staff here as elsewhere tends to enable the peer power structure to function. Equally important in the establishment of norms, however, is the resourcefulness and aggressiveness of the peer leadership.

As in settings with nondelinquents, social power among the delinquent boys is associated with a variety of talents. The lodge leaders at Fricot seem to exemplify the skills and daring which most boys of this age idealize. Dukes have qualities of leadership, of social sensitivity, and of being likeable. Race did not seem important, although on occasion was obviously a factor in the formation of certain cliques. Physical strength was necessary but not sufficient. A boy who attempted to duke his way on the basis of physical power alone was never known to establish stable leadership status. The strong clique which developed sometimes excluded him altogether, although more often he was taken in later as a lieutenant under the clique control. The true duke who sets the standard often shows positive qualities—or at least qualities the other boys would like to see in themselves.

However, at least a part of the power of the duke and his strong clique comes about through their use of physical aggression. The threat to "get" somebody is commonplace as a strong-arm method of gaining control over peers, who are in further jeopardy if they fink. This puts lower-status boys in an uncomfortable position, wanting revenge but at the same time wishing to avoid further trouble from their stronger peers. As boys become socially tuned-in they learn to conform and "take low," refusing to fink to staff about the punishment meted out by the strong clique.

The use of agitation, in exerting pressure on boys to conform to peer standards, is a rather clever means by which official punishment can be brought onto those who do not fall into line. As examples, "sex talk," "mother talk," and "race talk" are common methods of causing a boy to become angry enough to blow up. The victim "fires at"—hits—someone, and a member of the clique will report his behavior or it will be noticed by the supervisor, who then punishes the boy for his apparent aggression. Successful use of agitation requires a social sensitivity and adeptness not possessed by many of the low-status boys.

Perhaps the most powerful means of getting boys into line is through excluding them from high-status social groups. In the ultimate—the "stone-out" situation seen in older boys' institutions—no one will speak to the boy at all, and anyone who might speak to him is also stoned out. At Fricot the exclusion is less refined; the boy who breaks taboos and does not learn his position in the hierarchy is merely told to get out of a group, and is not allowed to join in desirable activities. It is the very lowest boys in the hierarchy who seem to have the most difficulty in learning protocol, and the group has the poorest control over them. Many of these boys are mentally disturbed and are not aware of protocol, are socially immature, and have little control over their own feelings or actions which they express immediately and directly as they experience them.

As implied above, the simplest way for a boy to deal with the strong clique is to conform to its requirements. Taking low, and playing the part of the obedient follower, is a convenient way to gain some acceptance. In learning his place, the new boy perceives that this group is powerful, that he cannot successfully fight them, and had better join them. This means he must follow the rules they set down—not putting them out in Warball games, not finking on them, not getting ahead of them in chow line, giving them help when they require it, and so on.

Not only obedience, but material possessions also, may be demanded by the duke and his lieutenants, or by more aggressive individuals. The low-status boy must learn to share his package from home without too much protest, and must not fink when he is pressured for candy and other treats. These tributes do not buy him permanent status, however; even a boy with a steady supply of boxes from home does not improve his position unless he can gain prestige through other means as well and loses whatever status he has when his supply is cut off.

THE IMPACT OF TRAINING SCHOOLS

What impact does the training school experience have upon the youth who is processed through it? Certainly the foregoing discussion has made it abundantly clear that juvenile institutions are not warm, friendly places in which wards are surrounded by therapeutic influences. Instead, even the best of them seem to be schools in which few offenders look forward to residing. The preceding accounts of these harsh organizations easily lead to the hypothesis that their effects are harmful upon delinquents, driving them further into deviance as a consequence of the bitterness and hostility they develop out of institutional experience. Yet the training school may have only a benign effect upon offenders. Perhaps they enter these places with a bleak outlook on life and antisocial attitudes, but these perspectives may not worsen as a result of incarceration. Accordingly, we need to examine the evidence that can be brought to bear upon the question of training school impact.

What if we should find statistics which show that most wards released from training schools became reinvolved in misconduct? Would this demonstrate that these institutions are directly responsible for recidivism? Not necessarily, for it is possible that the juveniles who are paroled from training schools would continue in criminality even if they had been dealt with in some form of community treatment. In other words, parole failures may be attributable to characteristics and experiences which wards bring with them to the training school, rather than to the effects of the institution itself.

Unfortunately, the kind of evidence which is required in order to probe this issue in depth is not available in quantity. However, one bit of data can be found in the Community Treatment Project in California.[30] In that experimental effort, being conducted in Sacramento, Stockton, and San Francisco, youths who would normally be sent to Youth Authority training schools are instead being dealt with in the community. Two kinds of intervention are involved; in one, differential treatment units consisting of a supervisor, treatment agents, and a work supervisor counsel wards who have been sorted into diagnostic types. Guided group interaction units are administering group treatment to offenders in the second kind of intervention. Youths in the community treatment experimental groups have been matched with control group subjects who have been institutionalized. In the manner of conventional experimental design, wards have been randomly assigned either to community treatment or to a training school.

The findings on this project initially seemed to indicate that community treatment is more effective than institutionalization, or, stated differently, that training schools are harmful to many wards. Experimental subjects from Stockton and Sacramento who had been exposed to parole for fifteen months showed a parole violation rate of 29 percent, while the control group cases had a violation rate of 48 percent.

However, we should not be too quick to accept the community treatment results as an indictment of training schools. Lerman has observed that the parole violation figures suggest that the experimental subjects were less delinquent in post-release behavior than the controls (institutionalized wards). But in fact, the community-treated youths had committed an average of 2.81 offenses in the parole period as compared to an average of 1.61 for the control subjects. He indicated that the parole officers of the experimental cases were more likely to know about delinquencies on the part of their parolees than were the agents of the controls, so that the total incidence of post-release misconduct was probably similar for the two groups.

While the agents observed more lawbreaking on the part of the experimental parolees than the control cases, they took action more frequently against the control subjects. When the parole offenses of the subjects are classified in terms of seriousness, some interesting results turn up. The percentages of offenders who had their paroles revoked for offenses of low or medium seriousness were considerably higher for the control subjects than the experimentals, so that only in the case of parolees committing high seriousness acts did the parole agents revoke similar proportions of them.[31] Lerman concluded that:

[30] Department of the Youth Authority, *The Status of Current Research in the California Youth Authority* (Sacramento: State of California, 1966), pp. 22–27.
[31] Lerman, "Evaluative Studies of Institutions for Delinquents," pp. 57–58.

Instead of the misleading conclusion derived from using only parole violation differences, it appears that the potential rates of failure of the two programs are similar (at this point in time). The behavioral outputs of the experimentals and controls are probably the same; however, the experimentals' parole agents notice more of this behavior and therefore give the impression that the experimentals are more delinquent. But even though the behavior of the experimentals attracts more notice, it is not evaluated in the same way as the behavior of the controls. This important study may have exercised excellent control over the random selection of boys; unfortunately, the ideology of treating boys in the community spilled over into the post experimental phase. The experimental and control groups appear to differ in the behavior of the parole agents with respect to the revocation of parole—not in the delinquent behavior of the boys.[32]

These observations on community treatment are not to be taken as an argument for the incarceration of juveniles in training schools. To argue that institutions may be benign in effect is not to recommend them. Our suspicion is that these places do not usually contribute much to rehabilitation, so that there is a sense of irrelevancy to them. But we ought to be cautious about indicting them for parole failures in the absence of evidence which shows them to be at fault.

One other observation from the Community Treatment Project is in order. In that experiment, 75 percent of all wards processed through state reception centers met the eligibility criteria for inclusion in the community project, even though many were not assigned to it. Thus training school commitment may be employed too often as a disposition made of offenders.

Let us return to the matter of training school outcomes. What does the evidence show regarding post-release behavior of parolees from different training schools? What data are at hand concerning social-psychological dimensions of the training school experience as it impinges upon wards?

Parole Violations

Several reports are available concerning parole violation behavior of wards released from California state training schools. In one of these, Robert Beverly and Evelyn Guttmann dealt with the parole performance of wards paroled between 1956 and 1960 during the

[32] *Ibid.*, p. 58.

first fifteen months of release from institutions.[33] Parole violation rates varied quite markedly from one institution to another, so that while the rate for all releasees was 47 percent, reception center parolees had a rate of 39 percent, while the figures were 36 percent for camps, 43 percent for Fricot Ranch, 57 percent for Paso Robles School, 60 percent for Fred C. Nelles School, 50 percent for Preston School of Industry, 45 percent for Deuel Vocational Institution, and 41 percent for Soledad Prison (the latter two institutions also hold adult criminals). The investigators contended that these parole violation differences were due to (a) selection factors at commitment, which send the least tractable persons to the high violation rate institutions, and (b) variations in training school influences upon wards. One other point worth noting from this report is that there was considerable variation in parole violation rates for a single institution from year to year. Thus the 1956 cohort of parolees from Fricot Ranch had a violation rate of 53 percent, while the rate for the 1960 parolees was 43 percent.

What happens to paroled wards over a longer period of time? Another report from California indicated that of those parolees released during 1962 and 1963, 61.9 percent had become violators by December 31, 1967, while 36.9 percent had been discharged from supervision without a violation and 1.2 percent were still on parole. The violation rate over this longer period was 64.1 percent for boys, but only 47.7 percent for girls.[34] These are not very encouraging figures, but we might go on to ask what happens to the juveniles who are discharged. Do they stay out of trouble permanently? Apparently not, judging from a California study by Carolyn Jamison, Bertram Johnson, and Evelyn Guttmann.[35] In this research, 4000 delinquent wards discharged from the Youth Authority in 1953 and 1958 were examined. Less than 20 percent of the female wards acquired any sort of criminal record in the five-year follow up period after discharge, so that girls most commonly became "successes." Quite different paths were followed by boys. About 22 percent of the male wards had been discharged from Youth Authority custody as a result of being sent to prison. Another 22 percent were sent to prison within five years after discharge, while another 26 percent received one or more nonprison sentences (fines, jail, and/or

[33] Robert F. Beverly and Evelyn S. Guttmann, *An Analysis of Parole Performance by Institution of Release, 1956–1960* (Sacramento: State of California, Department of the Youth Authority, 1962), p. 7.

[34] Department of the Youth Authority, "The Status of Current Research," p. 5.

[35] Carolyn B. Jamison, Bertram M. Johnson, and Evelyn S. Guttmann, *An Analysis of Post-Discharge Criminal Behavior* (Sacramento: State of California, Department of the Youth Authority, 1966).

probation). Thus only 30 percent of the boys managed to remain free from detected criminality.

Training schools do not seem to be directly responsible for the production of these careers of failure and ruined lives reflected in these dismal figures. Some complex concatenation of factors involving social liabilities stemming from faulty social experiences within the family and community, along with negative effects of correctional handling at earlier stages of the offender's delinquent career, probably lie behind them. By the time these lawbreakers get to training schools, their social opportunities to disengage themselves from misconduct have become severely constricted.

Social-Psychological Effects of Training Schools

There is a group of studies of training school experiences which seems to bear out this argument about their effects on youths. One of these by Martha Baum and Stanton Wheeler dealt with youths committed for the first time to a Boston Reception Center, in which youths normally stay for six to eight weeks prior to being sent to a regular institution.[36] They interviewed 100 boys who had been in the center for two weeks.

Baum and Wheeler found that most of the youngsters did not have a clear idea of the center and its operations before being admitted there. Most of the offenders were shocked and upset when informed by the court that they were going to be committed to the center. Most of the delinquents arrived there with negative opinions of the staff members and of the other boys in the institution. Baum and Wheeler concluded that most of the delinquents perceived the center as a deprivational experience and expected to receive punishment there, rather than treatment.[37]

Although the center wards brought some negative attitudes about the place with them, these were balanced by other more positive sentiments which developed on their part. Most of the youths saw their commitment to the place as a fair decision. Over 80 percent of the boys acknowledged that they were mainly to blame for their present predicament. Most of the youngsters continued to have strong, positive feelings about their families and about their eventual return

[36] Martha Baum and Stanton Wheeler, "Becoming an Inmate," in Stanton Wheeler, ed., *Controlling Delinquents* (New York: John Wiley & Sons, Inc., 1968), pp. 153–85.
[37] *Ibid.*, pp. 159–70.

to the parental situation. While most of the youths had developed more negative views of the center after having been there for several weeks, and complained about the dull routine, bland food, and so on, their opinions of staff members had become more positive. Most of the boys thought their stay at the center would help them, although many of them were uncertain as to precisely how it would effect them. Parenthetically, most of those who thought the center would help them took a short-run deterrent view of the place, holding that it would "teach me a lesson."[38]

Another investigation of a reception center was conducted in California, involving interviews with twelve "Preston potentials" (youths likely to be sent to Preston School of Industry).[39] These boys were interviewed at the end of their first week in the center, at the midpoint of their stay there, and at the end of the fifth week in the place. Most of these youths came to the center thoroughly briefed by other delinquents as to what to expect there. During their first weeks in the center, they were preoccupied with "beating the system" and with figuring out how to obtain a parole. Apparently the center developed negative attitudes on the part of the boys toward custodial personnel and positive views toward the dentists and doctors.

Thomas Eynon and Jon Simpson conducted research on inmate perceptions in Boy's Industrial School, Lancaster, Ohio, and two open camps operated by the school.[40] The training school was large and had an average daily population in 1960–1961 of 887 boys, while the camps averaged 65 boys. In Lancaster, 485 first admission wards were given a detailed, multi-faceted questionnaire at the point of admission and just before release. The results of this study indicated that the camp boys developed feelings of adjustment to the camp social structure, while the training school wards were more bewildered by life in that place. The reason for this difference can be found in the gross disparity in size of these places. The most significant finding was that both the training school boys and camp wards developed more positive attitudes, value orientations, and social outlooks during their stay in the institutions. Both groups of boys saw themselves as "delinquents" at intake and this self-perception did not change over the institutional stay. The camp boys thought they received some benefit from the experience, while the training school youths said they got

---

[38] *Ibid.*, pp. 170–80.

[39] Stuart Adams, *Impact of the Reception Center Clinic on California Youth Authority Wards: II* (Sacramento: State of California, Department of the Youth Authority, 1959).

[40] Thomas G. Eynon and Jon E. Simpson, "The Boy's Perception of Himself in a State Training School for Delinquents," *Social Service Review*, XXXIX (March 1965), 31–37.

less than they anticipated from their stay. In response to the question as to whether they would want a friend who was in trouble to be sent to the institution, 31 percent of the Lancaster boys and 87 percent of the camp inmates responded affirmatively. Also of some major significance is the fact that the boys most often chose cottage supervisors or work supervisors as the persons they knew best, with whom they would share good news, and so on.

Some evidence on the social-psychological effects of training schools is also found in the study of David Street, Robert Vinter, and Charles Perrow,[41] who conducted a comparative investigation dealing with six public and private institutions which ranged in size from 35 to 400 boys. Part of that research dealt with staff-inmate relationships in these schools.[42] Another part of the inquiry concerned inmate perspectives.[43] The researchers reported that wards had the most positive perspectives in the treatment-oriented institutions, but the wards of these schools also saw the staff members as unfair and given to playing favorites. The investigators also indicated that the perspectives of boys in custodially oriented schools deteriorated somewhat further over the period of incarceration. In the treatment-oriented plants, group behavior and inmate leadership was structured around more positive attitudes than was true of custodial schools. The boys in the custodial schools were concerned about demonstrating overt behavioral conformity, while the wards in treatment-focused institutions showed more internalized concerns.

The Fricot Ranch study from which the earlier account of training school life was taken also provided information on attitudinal changes on the part of wards in institutions.[44] Part of that experimental study involved psychological measures of various kinds administered to the subjects. The differences between the treatment subjects in the special program and the control wards in the regular Fricot Ranch program were not great, but apparently in the latter, the offenders learned impulse control and repression, while in the experimental milieu programs, greater self-awareness, spontaneity, and internal anxiety were produced. More important, both the treatment and control subjects seemed to get no worse in psychological adjustment over their stay in the school.

Jerome Beker also studied this subject in the Berkshire Farm for Boys, a private training school holding about 150 boys.[45] Beker re-

[41] Street, Vinter, and Perrow, *Organization for Treatment.*

[42] *Ibid.*, pp. 151–91.

[43] *Ibid.*, pp. 195–221.

[44] Jesness, *The Fricot Ranch Study*, pp. 99–118.

[45] Jerome Beker, "Male Adolescent Inmates' Perceptions of Helping Persons,"

ported that the wards there claimed that they would go to case-workers for *succorance needs,* that is, to talk over problems with them and for other help of that kind, although the boys did not have very positive attitudes toward the social workers on other items. The main thrust of this data was to suggest that inmates are perhaps less hostile toward staff members than some of the training school literature would have us believe.

IMPROVING THE IMPACT
OF CORRECTIONAL PROCESSES

This book is not concerned with a detailed exposition of theories and tactics of correctional treatment, nor is it designed to deal with experimental and innovative approaches to the prevention or correction of juvenile lawbreaking. These matters ought to be dealt with separately at length.[46] Our attention in this text is directed to the question of what happens, in fact, to offenders as they develop delinquent careers and as they are processed through the conventional law enforcement-correctional machinery. We are less interested in examining the nature of various innovative, experimental, or demonstration efforts in corrections. Similarly, we have not devoted much space to various community-oriented, preventive ventures that have been tried out in recent years in the United States because they fall outside our focus.

The kinds of endeavors which we have passed over quickly include street worker or detached worker programs that have been contrived in many large American cities.[47] These efforts, directed at urban gangs, involve social workers who work in specific neighborhoods, who attempt to "reach out" to deviant groups, and who try to become affiliates of a particular delinquent group in order to encourage it to develop nondeviant norms and behavior patterns. On a grander scale, there have been a number of massive preventive efforts in large cities in recent years in which a multi-faceted approach has been taken to community reorganization in order to reduce delinquency and criminality. These projects, such as Mobilization for Youth in New York City and the Midcity Project in Boston, have grown out of subcultural theories of gang delinquency.[48] In brief, they attempt to alter community so-

---

Social Work, X (April 1965), 18–26.

[46] One detailed exposition on treatment theories and tactics is Don C. Gibbons, *Changing the Lawbreaker* (Englewood Cliffs, N.J.: Prentice-Hall, Inc., 1965): see also Gibbons, *Society, Crime, and Criminal Careers,* pp. 493–512.

[47] Gibbons, *Changing the Lawbreaker,* pp. 236–41.

[48] These programs are described in *Ibid.,* pp. 177–82.

cial structure in order to increase the opportunities for area residents to engage in nondeviant behavior.

Let us examine some pieces of research investigation which have made an effort to maximize the impact of regular correctional programs, particularly in training schools.[49]

Psychiatric Treatment

One of the most enduring notions in the field of delinquency correction is that offenders can be led to improved behavior through psychiatric intervention which alters the psychological tensions from which their behavior is presumed to be a result. An early effort to deal intensively with delinquents through psychiatric therapy has been reported by LaMay Adamson and H. Warren Dunham.[50] They examined the history of the Wayne County (Detroit) Clinic for Child Study in Michigan. From 1924 to 1948, the clinic staff was heavily augmented with additional psychiatric professionals, thus its effects upon wards should have become more prominent if psychotherapy is effective. But follow-up study of boys who had been in court in 1930, 1935, 1940, and 1948 showed almost no reduction in the proportions of treated youths who got into further trouble. In 1930, 45 percent of the boys were later arrested by the police, as contrasted to 39 percent of those who had been in the clinic in 1948. Adamson and Dunham concluded that the therapy apparently failed because it probably was inappropriate for the working class delinquents to whom it was applied.

More recently, Guttmann has presented findings from a short-term psychiatric treatment experiment in California at Fred C. Nelles School and at Preston School of Industry.[51] In both these institutions, boys were placed in a psychiatric treatment unit in which they received psychotherapy from a psychiatrist, a psychiatric social worker, and psychologists. The parole violation rate of the youths who received psychiatric treatment was compared to that for other control boys who had been processed through the regular school program.

---

[49] For a summary of these programs being conducted in California, see Department of the Youth Authority, *The Status of Current Research in the California Youth Authority* (Sacramento: State of California, 1968).

[50] LaMay Adamson and H. Warren Dunham, "Clinical Treatment of Male Delinquents: A Case Study in Effort and Result," *American Sociological Review*, XXI (June 1956), 312–30.

[51] Evelyn S. Guttmann, *Effects of Short-Term Psychiatric Treatment on Boys in Two California Youth Authority Institutions* (Sacramento: State of California, Department of the Youth Authority, 1963).

The results indicated that the Nelles psychiatrically treated boys had a lower violation rate than did the controls, while the wards treated at Preston did poorer on parole than the control youths. These different effects were probably the result of several factors. For one, the Preston boys were older than the Nelles subjects and they also differed in terms of certain psychological characteristics. In addition, the organizational climate in which psychiatric treatment was pursued differed in the two schools. In Nelles School, the psychiatric unit was new, it had high staff morale, and enjoyed other favorable conditions, while at Preston, the unit was older and was the focus of staff hostility from nonclinic personnel. Consequently, the psychiatrically treated boys at Preston may have received invidious handling from staff members which offset any gains from the special therapy.

One more case of psychiatric treatment in institutions was the PICO (Pilot Intensive Counseling Organization) project in California.[52] In that experiment, older California Youth Authority wards in Deuel Vocational Institution were divided into treatment and control groups. The treated offenders received intensive, individual therapy several times per week, along with some group therapy, while the control subjects were administered the regular Deuel program and little counseling. The subjects were also divided into "amenable" and "nonamenable" categories; the former were persons with anxiety levels that would make them responsive to therapy, while the nonamenables were subjects who were less anxious about themselves. The treatment agents were clinical psychologists and psychiatric social workers who gave intensive therapy to caseloads of about twenty-five subjects for an average period of nine months. The effects of the therapy were measured by a number of criteria, but a major one was parole violation. The results showed that the treated amenables had the lowest parole failure rate, followed by the control amenables, the treated nonamenables had the highest parole failure rate. The experiment apparently showed that psychiatric therapy is appropriate for some kinds of training school inmates but not for others. This is a conclusion with which many sociologists would agree, holding that the social relations and socially shared values, rather than the psyches, of many offenders need to be attacked and altered.[53]

---

[52] Stuart Adams, "The PICO Project," in Norman Johnston, Leonard Savitz, and Marvin E. Wolfgang, eds., *The Sociology of Punishment and Correction* (New York: John Wiley & Sons, Inc., 1962), pp. 213–24.

[53] See for example Donald R. Cressey, "Changing Criminals: The Application of the Theory of Differential Association," *American Journal of Sociology*, LXI (September 1955), 116–20.

Treatment Through Social Influences

Alteration of the social relations and attitudes of delinquents has been attempted in a number of ways, including street worker programs which try to get deviant groups to develop new social norms. In institutions this endeavor has often taken the form of group therapy, in which the treatment goal is to get group members to adopt new values and to put pressure upon each other to show allegiance to these new standards.[54] The problem with this sort of activity is that the group members are usually under counter pressures from other inmates in the training school to renounce the values being promulgated within therapy groups. In addition, the conditions of institutional life outlined in an earlier section of this chapter make it difficult to reward offenders in any meaningful way for any positive psychological or behavioral changes. The realization of these milieu obstacles to group treatment has led to the hypothesis that meaningful therapeutic intervention can best be conducted in the organization or institution structured so as to constitute a therapeutic milieu. In this kind of training school or other treatment site, all of the living experiences undergone by the subjects would be designed to pressure them toward allegiance to prosocial norms and behavior.

Probably the most famous effort to contrive a therapeutic milieu in an institution was the Highfields Project in New Jersey.[55] In that experiment, the delinquent subjects were placed in a small institution, formerly the mansion of Charles Lindbergh, which held about two dozen boys. The wards were given a treatment diet of "guided group interaction" (group therapy) in the evenings and, in addition, they were given opportunities to work for pay at a nearby mental institution. They were not compelled to work, as they might have been in a conventional training school, and they could be fired if they did not perform adequately. The architects of the program viewed the delinquent boys as normal youngsters with antisocial attitudes and self images. The boys tended to denigrate the importance of conventional work careers and regarded other conforming behavior patterns with scorn. This entire program of guided group interaction, along with the related work experiences and peer interaction, was directed toward pressuring the delinquents into new perspectives and improved work habits.

Several lines of evidence seem at first glance to confirm the value

[54] Group therapy is discussed at length in Gibbons, *Changing the Lawbreaker,* pp. 159–63.
[55] Lloyd W. McCorkle, Albert Elias, and F. Lovell Bixby, *The Highfields Story* (New York: Holt, Rinehart & Winston, Inc., 1958).

of the Highfields program. For one, as a part of the research program associated with that institution, a projective personality test was given to Highfields boys and to inmates of Annandale Reformatory, a conventional state institution, both at the time of admission and at a later point in their school stay. The test results indicated that the reformatory boys moved toward bleaker, darker outlooks on life during their stay there and may have become resigned to further deviation as a life career; the Highfields youths showed movement in an opposite direction.[56]

Lloyd McCorkle, Albert Elias, and F. Lovell Bixby also compared the parole success of Highfields boys with that of a group of Annandale inmates who had been incarcerated prior to the opening of Highfields but who were thought to be similar to the youngsters who were sent to the latter place. The reformatory inmates showed a failure rate of 33 percent in the first year upon release, compared to a figure of only 18 percent for Highfields releasees.[57] In a second evaluation of Highfields, H. Ashley Weeks compared a sample of Annandale parolees with released wards from Highfields.[58] He found that 47 percent of the former and 63 percent of the latter remained in the community and free from criminality for at least one year. Little difference was found in parole failure for white boys in the two places, but Negro boys from Highfields had a success rate of 60 percent, compared to 33 percent for Annandale Negro parolees.[59]

These parole statistics seem to show Highfields to be significantly more effective than the conventional reformatory. However, Lerman has recently reanalyzed Weeks' data, showing them to be less convincing as a demonstration of the effectiveness of Highfields.[60] Lerman indicates that 18 percent of the Highfields subjects did not complete treatment, having been returned to court as unsuitable for the program. Very few Annandale subjects failed to complete a stay there. When the Highfields boys who did not complete the program were included as program failures, the success rates for the two institutions turned out to be quite similar. Parenthetically, Lerman pointed out that the luxury of being able to reject potential wards for treatment is mainly enjoyed by private agencies, and that caution is in order therefore in evaluating claims they might advance about their rehabilitative efficacy.

[56] *Ibid.*, pp. 122–26.
[57] *Ibid.*, p. 143.
[58] H. Ashley Weeks, *Youthful Offenders at Highfields* (Ann Arbor: University of Michigan Press, 1963).
[59] *Ibid.*, p. 42.
[60] Lerman, "Evaluative Studies of Institutions for Delinquents," pp. 58–60.

The Fricot Ranch study was also an effort at milieu treatment.[61] The conventional, harmful training school milieu against which the experiment was directed is described in the following excerpt from the study report:

> When admitted to an institution for delinquents, boys bring with them delinquent values, a hostile attitude toward authority, and a rejection of conventional goals. The normal tendency of young boys in institutions is to cluster into informal groups, erect subtle barriers toward administrative efforts to reach them, and to maintain value systems at odds with the rehabilitative aims of the school. New boys coming into the school program participate in these natural groupings and are apt to undergo an experience which tends to reinforce their delinquent value system. While they may conform outwardly to the school program, no basic modification of delinquent attitudinal patterns takes place. When released, they once again seek associations and engage in behavior congenial to their delinquent character and values.[62]

In order to try to overcome this system which emphasizes control of boys and outward conformity on their part, a group of wards was placed in a twenty boy experimental lodge, in contrast to the regular fifty boy living units. The experimental subjects experienced intensified staff-ward contacts and other therapeutic experiences designed to pressure them toward prosocial values.

The results of this experiment initially seemed favorable to intensified milieu treatment. The parole violation rate for boys who had been released for one year was 32 percent for the experimentals and 48 percent for the controls. However, the violation rates for youths who had been released from the school for two years were nearly the same, while 80 percent of the wards in the treated and control groups who had been released three years earlier subsequently became reinvolved in lawbreaking. In short, the Fricot project seemed to retard the speed at which parolees become reinvolved in violations, but it did not significantly reduce the number who eventually get into further trouble. However, even this finding is suspect, for Lerman has observed that the control subjects were less frequently white youths and more often from poor homes than the experimental youths.[63]

Still another effort in this direction has been identified by Joachim Seckel, involving Paso Robles School and Youth Training School in California.[64] In Paso Robles where wards live in fifty boy living units,

61 Jesness, *The Fricot Ranch Study.*
62 *Ibid.,* p. 4.
63 Lerman, "Evaluative Studies of Institutions for Delinquency."
64 Joachim P. Seckel, *Experiments in Group Counseling at Two Youth Authority*

one dormitory was organized to provide small weekly group counseling, another had community meetings four times per week, and a third dormitory had both group treatment and community meetings. In the other institution, two of the four fifty boy units had small group counseling, while the other two received the conventional school program. The parole violation rates for different cottages varied for both schools, but in both, wards who had been exposed to group programs did no better on parole than did the controls.

The results of this study were paralleled in the Fremont experiment in California.[65] There, sixteen to nineteen year old males passing through the reception center were randomly assigned to the Fremont Program or to a regular Youth Authority institutional program. Those who were in the former received small group therapy, large group forums, half-day work assignments at the clinic, a school program, home visits, and field trips to various places of interest in the community. But the results were not encouraging, for the experimental and control group youths showed no statistically significant differences in recidivism after two years of follow-up exposure to parole. In addition, no differences were discovered in the seriousness of post-release offenses in which they engaged.

SUMMARY

After some observations about the flow of cases through the juvenile correctional machinery, we took up that brand of thinking in the area of deviant behavior which is usually identified as labeling theory —that perspective which maintains that when offenders are singled out by the police, courts, probation officers, institutions, and other labelers of deviance, they become stigmatized or subject to other social liabilities which markedly reduce their ability to withdraw from misconduct. We have attempted to marshal the available evidence on this view, but good data on the effects of the early stages of apprehension and disposition of offenders are lacking.

Much of this chapter centered about the training school, its social structure, and its effects upon wards who pass through it. Available data point to the benign impact of the institution, rather than to any

Institutions (Sacramento: State of California, Department of the Youth Authority, 1965).

[65] Joachim P. Seckel, *The Fremont Experiment: Assessment of Residential Treatment at a Youth Authority Reception Center* (Sacramento: State of California, Department of the Youth Authority, 1967).

directly harmful consequences upon delinquents. In short, the training school appears to be a satisfactory warehouse for the temporary storage of delinquents if the community demands that they be isolated for some time period, but it ought not to be supposed that the institution is a positive influence.

The following generalizations can be made from the information in this chapter:

1. The various segments of the correctional apparatus such as police bureaus, juvenile courts, probation agencies, and other organizations may have direct effects of one kind or another upon delinquent careers. However, virtually no research has been conducted concerning the impact of these structures upon delinquency, so that this subject represents one about which investigation is sorely needed.

2. Training schools in the United States vary somewhat in terms of size, institutional aims, and other conditions, but all appear to be principally structured around the goal of control of wards. Even in treatment-oriented training schools, the major focus of attention is upon conformity, prevention of escapes, and ends of that kind.

3. Training schools do not usually succeed in restraining wards from further lawbreaking, for parole violation rates from these places are quite high. Half to over three-fourths of first admissions to juvenile institutions apparently become reinvolved in delinquent conduct, although considerably fewer of them continue into adult criminality.

4. Training schools apparently have benign effects upon wards processed through them, so that although "reformation" does not usually occur, neither does the institution directly contribute to recidivism. Most training school wards emerge from these places with no more criminal skills or more serious antisocial attitudes than when they entered.

An unequivocal answer to the question of whether the training school can be converted into a therapeutic milieu is premature, but the studies considered here do not lend much encouragement to those who would remake the training school into a therapeutic clinic. Perhaps it is time to look for innovative alternatives to institutionalization, in which few if any offenders would be sent to training schools.

chapter eleven

FINAL
REMARKS

INTRODUCTION

The preceding ten chapters of this book dealt with a large quantity of descriptive material, delinquency theories, and research evidence on juvenile lawbreaking. But this text was designed to be more than simply a compendium of information on youthful deviance. Over forty propositions or generalizations were sprinkled throughout the preceding chapters, involving some major conclusions that can be inductively drawn out of the existing delinquency literature. Some of these generalizations are very broad, others are more specific, and all of them are stated in relatively imprecise terms. Similarly, some of these conclusions are supported by a large measure of empirical data, while the empirical accuracy of others is less clear. However, we would argue that these propositions are about as precise as is warranted by the delinquency data at hand. These broad conclusions can be taken as organizing hypotheses or contentions which might be subjected to more detailed study in delinquency investigations in the future.

These generalizations can be brought together in a single package, in the form of a propositional inventory about delinquency. The most general propositions have been listed first, and under them are arranged the more specific contentions which they summarize. The Roman numeral in parentheses following each generalization refers to

262

the chapter in which it originally appeared; the Arabic number designates the order in which it originally was presented.

PROPOSITIONAL INVENTORY
ON DELINQUENCY

The Extent of Delinquency

Behavior which violates delinquency statutes is commonplace, so that nearly all youngsters engage in at least some delinquent behavior during their juvenile careers. At the same time, marked variations occur among offenders in the extent and seriousness of their involvement in lawbreaking. Some juvenile delinquents engage in repetitive, serious forms of misconduct, while others are implicated only in relatively innocuous kinds of misbehavior. (IV-1)

> Less than 3 percent of the juveniles in this nation are referred to juvenile courts in any single year, although a larger portion of the youth population comes to court attention sometime during the adolescent years. Only about one-half of these referrals are regarded by court officials as serious enough to warrant the filing of a petition and a court hearing, the other half are dealt with informally. (II-1)

> Police agencies come into contact with almost twice the number of children known to the court. In general, they refer the serious cases they encounter to juvenile courts, while disposing of the less serious offenders informally, within the department, by admonitions and warnings. (II-2)

> A fairly large number of offenders is dealt with by public and private social agencies in the community, but many of the individuals they process are also known to the juvenile court. The majority of the cases known to agencies but which are unknown to the court are relatively petty ones. (II-3)

> A large number of youths at all social class levels and in all kinds of communities engage in acts of misconduct and lawbreaking which remain hidden or undetected. In this sense, nearly all juveniles are delinquent in some degree. However, many of the deviant acts of hidden delinquents are relatively minor ones, the kinds which would often be handled informally or ignored if reported to the juvenile court. (II-4)

> Not all of the hidden delinquency in the United States is petty and inconsequential. An indeterminate but important number of serious delinquencies is enacted by juveniles who manage to stay out of the hands of the police or courts. (II-5)

> Middle-class youngsters are relatively uncommon in the juvenile court compared to youths from lower income backgrounds. Police agencies are aware of a larger number of middle status delinquents, but most

of these children have been involved in relatively innocuous acts of lawbreaking. Middle-class delinquents known to the police tend not to be involved in repetitive, career patterns of misconduct. Many of the middle-class offenders who come to the attention of the police are "absorbed" back into the community, without referral to the juvenile court. (VI-1)

"Hidden" middle-class delinquency is widespread; nearly all middle income youths have committed at least a few acts which technically constitute delinquency. However, most hidden delinquency on the part of middle-class adolescents is relatively petty in form. (VI-2)

Middle-class youths do engage in some kinds of serious lawbreaking. These youths who are involved in serious delinquency have a relatively high likelihood of ending up in a juvenile court. Serious forms of middle-class delinquency include automobile theft—"joyriding"—and aggressive behavior. (VI-3)

Public stereotypes of middle-class youngsters which assert that many of them are caught up in serious vandalism, widespread use of alcohol, and sexual promiscuity, are not supported by much firm evidence. These kinds of behavior apparently are much less common than is often supposed by citizens. (VI-4)

Girls who have become the subject of attention by the police or juvenile courts tend to be involved in sexual delinquency or in activities which adults in the community suspect are indicators of budding sexual promiscuity on the part of the girls. Relatively few females are engaged in delinquency patterns similar to those of boys, although younger girls are most involved in theft behavior. (VII-1)

Some girls who are without official records as delinquents are nonetheless involved in hidden misbehavior. However, their deviant acts tend to be relatively petty ones, and, in addition, hidden female delinquents are generally less involved in misconduct than are hidden male offenders. (VII-3)

Police Handling of Delinquency

Those offenders who get into the hands of the police and processed through the juvenile justice system tend to be the more career-oriented delinquents who are involved in serious misconduct. However, the factors which enter into police apprehension, court referral, and other decisions are several, such that the offender's prospects of becoming identified as a "juvenile delinquent" are partially dependent upon characteristics of policemen, police departments, court personnel, and community influences. (IV-2)

Police officers deal with large numbers of juveniles, most of whom they handle informally without court referral. The decision to take a youngster to the court is often a legalistic one, at least in part. Those offenders who have been engaged in serious or repetitive acts of law-breaking are most likely to be turned over to the court. (III-1)

Police dispositions tend to be related to demographic characteristics of offenders, such that males, Negroes, lower-income youths, and older boys are most frequently dealt with formally by court referral. These demographic characteristics enter into dispositions in part because males, older boys, Negroes, and lower income youngsters appear to be disproportionately involved in serious, repetitive delinquencies. (III-2)

Police perspectives which hold that some groups, such as ghetto Negroes or other lower-class minorities, are particularly criminalistic probably lead to differential attention directed at them. Serious offenses by members of these groups then have a higher likelihood of being observed by the police and being acted upon. If so, the higher official crime and delinquency rates of these groups may be partially the product of police sentiments rather than a reflection solely of basic differentials in propensities toward crime. (III-3)

In those instances of less serious delinquency, police officers often base their disposition decisions upon the demeanor of the offender. Youths who affect particular clothing styles or who are defiant and hostile tend to be referred more often than polite and contrite youngsters are. It is probably also true that demeanor bears some relationship to seriousness of offense, such that those youths who have engaged in the most innocuous offenses also are most deferential toward policemen. This may explain why police dispositions show a general association with seriousness of misconduct. (III-4)

Police departments show variations in organizational structure over time. Differences in organizational makeup between police agencies also exist. Accordingly, police dispositions of offenders, including juveniles, are far from uniform throughout the country. (III-5)

Role-Types in Delinquency

Relatively stable patterns of delinquent roles, involving recurrent forms of deviant activity accompanied by uniform social-psychological role characteristics (self concept and attitude patterns) can be observed in the population of offenders. In these terms, it can be said that types of delinquency and delinquent role-careers exist. (IV-3)

Most juvenile offenders are relatively normal youths in terms of personality structure, in that they do not exhibit aberrant motives, deep-seated psychological tensions, or other marks of personality disturbance. Officially-processed delinquents often do show hostile attitudes, defiance of authority, and characteristics of that kind. However, these are not personality dimensions which are indicative of psycho-

logical maladjustment. In addition, some of these personality characteristics may be the product or result of correctional handling. At the
same time, there are some youthful lawbreakers who do show atypical
personality patterns to which their delinquency may be a response.
(IV-4)

Delinquency laws forbid a wide range of conduct, so that there are
a number of role patterns within the offender population. (Some delinquents restrict their activities to forms of predatory theft and allied
conduct, some are mainly involved in car thefts, still others are principally caught up in sexual misconduct, while still others exhibit aggressive behavior.) (IV-5)

The specific causal process that leads to one particular kind of delinquent role behavior involves a number of etiological variables and differs from that which produces another delinquent pattern. In this
sense, delinquent behavior is the product of multiple-causation. At the
same time, it is possible to identify the different etiological processes
which are involved in the various forms of delinquency. (IV-6)

Delinquent behavior is learned behavior, acquired in the processes
of socialization. Accordingly, the causes of juvenile misconduct are not
to be found in biological factors (even though biological variables may
play an indirect role in juvenile lawbreaking). (IV-7)

Delinquency Causation

The learning of delinquent roles is maximized in a criminalistic society, and the United States is such a society. Much delinquent behavior in the competitive, materialistic American society is societally
generated and takes the form of direct and indirect assaults upon
property. (IV-8)

Some delinquent roles are mainly the consequence of social class
variations in socialization and life experiences, along with other social-
structural variables. In particular, situations in which legitimate avenues to the attainment of common American goals and values are
blocked are importantly involved in certain forms of crime and delinquency. Those members of disadvantaged social groups and social
strata may be relatively commonly involved in deviant behavior which
is a response to their situation of social and economic deprivation.
Additionally, certain class-related influences in other social strata may
operate to produce juvenile offenders in those classes. For example,
problems of masculine identity may be more common in middle-class
groups than elsewhere, and may be importantly involved in middle-
class delinquency. (IV-9)

Although delinquents are found throughout neighborhoods and communities in American society, organized, group patterns of subcultural lawbreaking constituting a neighborhood tradition tends to be concentrated in urban, working-class neighborhoods. These neighborhoods share a number of ecological characteristics, such as physical deterioration and blight, the presence of vice, and kindred conditions. (V-1)

The most common form of subcultural misconduct is the "parent subculture" pattern of delinquency, characterized by behavioral versatility rather than specialization. Subcultural gang delinquency varies somewhat between communities of different size or other characteristics, so that in some, offender gangs are small and loosely structured, while in others, they are larger, more organized, and devoted to somewhat different kinds of lawbreaking. (V-2)

Working-class boys become involved in subcultural misbehavior out of a variety of circumstances, but most of the causal influences center about social or economic deprivation experienced by lower income citizens in metropolitan neighborhoods. While there is no single route to involvement in subcultural delinquency, a set of related circumstances stemming from the social class structure conjoin to generate this behavior. Some gang offenders are responding to problems of perceived lack of opportunity and economic deprivation, others are more concerned about immediate status threats, while still others are drawn into delinquency out of adjustment difficulties in school. (V-3)

Subcultural offenders tend to be the products of lower-class families in which criminalistic members are sometimes present, or families which exert relatively slight control over the behavior of the boys. Severe parent-child tension is not usually involved in these cases, but family factors of a less marked form do interact with social class influences in subcultural delinquency. (V-4)

Gang delinquents are not usually characterized by personality problems or emotional tensions, but they do exhibit antisocial attitudes, delinquent self images, and certain other social-psychological characteristics which develop out of their involvement in delinquent subcultures. (V-5)

A large number of theories of middle-class delinquency have been developed, centered about concepts such as youth culture, masculine identity problems, lack of commitment, status inconsistency, and other social-structural characteristics of middle-class strata. However, virtually no research has been conducted on these arguments, so that the causal processes in middle-class delinquency have not yet been clearly identified. (Not included in earlier chapters)

Although the United States apparently has the highest delinquency rates of nations of the world, juvenile misconduct has increased markedly in many other nations since World War II. The most pronounced increases in delinquency rates have been in European countries. Although the reasons for the upsurge of juvenile lawbreaking are numerous and complex, they center about recent industrialization, the growing complexity of societies and the breakdown of the old social order, and the increasing affluence of European countries. (IX-1)

In a number of ways, delinquency in England is similar to juvenile lawbreaking in the United States: boys are much more frequently involved in misconduct than are girls, juvenile lawbreaking occurs in loosely structured gangs, and it is most common in deteriorated, working-class neighborhoods similar to American "delinquency areas." Juvenile delinquency has apparently increased markedly in England since World War II. Juvenile offenders in that country are frequently drawn from the group of alienated, uncommitted working-class youths who are involved in the pursuit of short-run, hedonistic pleasures. Unlike American offenders, most of them do not show a marked sense of status frustration. (IX-2)

Some delinquent roles are produced by family and other socialization experiences which are not class-linked or class-specific. Among these are "parental rejection", "deviant sexual socialization," and others. These kinds of experiences occur at all social class levels. (IV-10)

"Under the roof" culture in the form of family tensions of one kind or another appears to be a major factor in female delinquency, although it is apparently also the case that various social class factors and social liabilities conjoin with parent-child relationships to push youngsters in the direction of delinquency involvement. (VII-4)

The screening processes of the police and courts operate so as to send the most serious female offenders into probation caseloads or to correctional institutions. Institutionalized female delinquents show the most pronounced backgrounds of social inadequacy. (VII-2)

Hypotheses about the existence of delinquency subcultures among girls are of undetermined accuracy, owing to the paucity of research on such questions. It may be that female delinquency subcultures exist in some neighborhoods in large urban communities, while they may be nonexistent in smaller communities. Then, too, claims about the function and meaning of delinquent acts to the participants in them (such as Grosser's contentions) must be subjected to research scrutiny, for the data now available do not bear directly upon such hypotheses. (VII-5)

Offenders who are engaged in bizarre forms of misconduct and/or who exhibit pathological patterns of personality structure are relatively uncommon among the total population of juvenile offenders and are even relatively infrequently encountered within the group of officially handled lawbreakers. "Behavior problem" kinds of delinquency include firesetting and deviant sex behavior, but the most common form of behavior problem lawbreaking is individualistic aggression. In turn, aggressive behavior comes in various gradations, so that unsocialized aggressive offenders are markedly deviant individuals, while other delinquents exhibit aggression and personality problems of a milder form. (VIII-1)

Overly aggressive offenders are the product of situations of parental rejection, with the most severe forms of aggression stemming from conditions of early and marked rejection and milder patterns from less marked instances of parental rejection. (VIII-2)

The Impact of Correctional
Experiences Upon Offenders

The "defining agencies" (police, probation services, courts, and so forth) play a part both in the definition of deviants and in the continuation of deviant roles. The result of apprehension and "treatment" may be quite contrary to the expected result. In other words, although one official function of correctional agencies and processes is the reformation of the offender, the actual outcome may often be the isolation of the person, reinforcement of the deviant role, and rejection of society by the offender, the final result being nonreformation. (IV-11)

The various segments of the correctional apparatus, such as police bureaus, juvenile courts, probation agencies, and other organizations, may have direct effects of one kind or another upon delinquent careers. However, virtually no research has been conducted concerning the impact of these structures upon delinquency, so that this subject represents one about which investigation is sorely needed. (X-1)

Training schools in the United States vary somewhat in terms of size, institutional aims, and other conditions, but all appear to be principally structured around the goal of control of wards. Even in treatment-oriented training schools, the major focus of attention is upon conformity, prevention of escapes, and ends of that kind. (X-2)

Training schools do not usually succeed in restraining wards from further lawbreaking, for parole violation rates from these places are quite high. Half to over three-fourths of first admissions to juvenile institutions apparently become reinvolved in delinquent conduct, although considerably fewer of them continue into adult criminality. (X-3)

Training schools apparently have benign effects upon wards processed through them, so that although "reformation" does not usually occur, neither does the institution directly contribute to recidivism. Most training school wards emerge from these places with no more criminal skills or more serious antisocial attitudes than when they entered. (X-4)

SUMMARY

These claims stand as a body of contentions which are supported by some empirical evidence, but which are in need of further research scrutiny. Hopefully, this explication of the major threads in the sociological perspective on delinquency will serve as a stimulus and guide to future work. Let us hope that books such as this will lead to greater concentration upon theoretically informed research and less upon the sort of mindless, eclectic "fact gathering" which has plagued the field of delinquency study in the past.

INDEX